LEE M. JOHNSON is Associate Professor of English at the University of British Columbia.

In his philosophic verse, Wordsworth identifies the history of poetry and geometrical thought as the two chief treasures of the mind and as main sources of his poetic inspiration. He assigns transcendental value to geometry and indicates that he attempted to apply its proportions to the laws of nature. In this book, Professor Johnson demonstrates how Wordsworth also employed geometrical patterns in the metrical construction of his verse and how the character of those patterns can be related to the poet's major philosophical values.

Johnson shows how Wordsworth, when writing about the nature and significance of geometrical thought in *The Prelude* and *The Excursion*, designs his verse paragraphs in accordance with simple geometrical proportions which are thereby associated with the metaphysical value he attributes to geometry. Wordsworth finds geometrical forms to be hidden in the natural landscape and inherent in the structure of perception itself.

This book is the first to make a sustained description of Wordsworth's symbolic patterns and metrical forms in his philosophic verse, with major examples drawn from *Tintern Abbey, The Prelude, The Excursion*, and the *Immortality Ode*. Although it presents an approach which differs radically from any in the established criticism of the poet, it is basically at one with the large body of work that concerns the nature of Wordsworth's imagination.

LEE M. JOHNSON

Wordsworth's Metaphysical Verse

Geometry, Nature, and Form

UNIVERSITY OF TORONTO PRESS
Toronto Buffalo London

© University of Toronto Press 1982
Toronto Buffalo London
Printed in Canada

ISBN 0-8020-5582-6

Canadian Cataloguing in Publication Data

Johnson, Lee M.
   Wordsworth's metaphysical verse

   Includes index.
   ISBN 0-8020-5582-6

   1. Wordsworth, William, 1770-1850 – Criticism and interpretation. 2. Wordsworth, William, 1770-1850 – Knowledge – Mathematics. I. Title.

   PR5881.J64   821'.7   C82-094015-1

To B.E.J., M.P.J., and J.S.B.

Wordsworth was a profound admirer of the sublimer mathematics; at least of the higher geometry. The secret of this admiration for geometry lay in the antagonism between this world of bodiless abstraction and the world of passion. And here I may mention appropriately, and I hope without any breach of confidence, that, in a great philosophic poem of Wordsworth's, which is still in MS., and will remain in MS. until after his death, there is, at the opening of one of the books, a dream, which reaches the very *ne plus ultra* of sublimity in my opinion, expressly framed to illustrate the eternity and the independence of all social modes or fashions of existence, conceded to these two hemispheres, as it were, that compose the total world of human power – mathematics on the one hand, poetry on the other.

Thomas De Quincey

Preface

By expressing his sense of Wordsworth's profound admiration for geometry, Thomas De Quincey, who was well acquainted with both the manuscript of *The Prelude* and its poet, supplies the epigraph for this book, which examines the relationship between Wordsworth's geometrical thought and his metrical practices. In a sense, then, this book considers Wordsworth's philosophical verse afresh by turning the clock back the better part of two centuries to the poet and his contemporaries, some of whom, such as De Quincey and Coleridge, knew, as we do not, that mathematical and metrical principles have a great deal to do with one another. Even though it is so clearly derived from Wordsworth's own appraisal of geometry and from elementary features of the metrical tradition, the mode of analysis employed in this book will probably come as a shock to Wordsworth specialists, who are familiar mainly with psychological criticism. Interest in psychology, states of consciousness, and even psychoanalysis has led to a deeper exploration of epiphanic moments in Wordsworth's poetry and to a keener sense of the ways in which his works prefigure a characteristic psychological mode of much modern literature written, say, by Joyce, Proust, Chekhov, and others. To approach Wordsworth from a modern point of view is often, of course, to see him as a forerunner of that view. To establish his contributions to the metrical tradition, as is done here, is to show his consolidation of the best work that preceded his own. At first glance, then, it might appear that another dispute between ancients and moderns is at hand. It would nevertheless be a mistake to conclude that this book merely opposes, rather than supplements, modern critical attitudes; for it joins most modern criticism in assuming that Wordsworth's accounts of his own psychology and states of consciousness are central issues. The difference is that intense psychological activity and epiphanic moments in the poems are examined here, not as ends in themselves, but as means to the expression of a rational idealism which is artistically demonstrable in the primary texts.

Those who have related the poet's educational background – which does not presuppose a separation of the humanities from the sciences – to his principal artistic and intellectual concerns are the Wordsworthians to whom I am most deeply indebted: John Jones, B.R. Schneider, Jr, Flemming Olsen, and G.H. Durrant. My debt to my colleague and friend G.H. Durrant cannot be measured. His books on Wordsworth, his mastery of metrical analysis, and his understanding of the poet's intellectual backgrounds – especially those which draw upon classical literature and the history of science – have been of signal importance to the formulation of my own views. The occasional merits of the book reflect his role as the immediate audience for whom the writing was undertaken. I am also indebted to H.G. Edinger, who, as a classicist familiar with and practised in the mode of analysis I have used, has greatly contributed to its precision and propriety. For his careful readings of the complete manuscript and assessments of its methods in relation to modern critical theory, Bogdan Czaykowski also receives my heartiest thanks.

For the material benefits of time and money which have aided this investigation of poetic idealism, I am indeed grateful to the University of British Columbia and to the Canada Council. For permitting access to the manuscripts of all the poems discussed in this book, the trustees and librarian of Dove Cottage, Grasmere, receive similar thanks. Overriding all other acknowledgments is the appreciation I have for my family – Sharon and our four children – who have helped me retain a sense of humour about a sense of proportion.

This book has been published with the help of a grant from the Canadian Federation for the Humanities, using funds provided by the Social Sciences and Humanities Research Council of Canada, and a grant from the Andrew W. Mellon Foundation to the University of Toronto Press.

Contents

PREFACE / vii

Introduction / 3

1 The Geometrical Idea of Wordsworth's Poetry / 23

2 The Topologic Self of *The Prelude* / 67

3 The Geometrical Imperative of *The Excursion* / 123

4 The Art of Conceptual Form / 175

APPENDIX
Form and Value in Music: Geometry and the Fugue / 219

NOTES / 229

INDEX / 239

Wordsworth's Metaphysical Verse
Geometry, Nature, and Form

Introduction

Consider the following hypothetical situation: a poet names the history of poetry and geometry as the two main sources of his inspiration. His greatest ambition is to write poetry based on transcendental values, and he thus expresses a preference for poets whose works depend on timeless spiritual patterns. Relying on a long tradition of rational idealism, he also finds transcendental value in geometry and proceeds to exemplify that value whenever he writes of geometry by designing his thoughts in accordance with simple, yet philosophically sophisticated, proportions. The geometrical design of his poetry is not, however, limited to discussions of geometry itself but occurs, as well, at other infrequent but highly significant moments when he consolidates his most ambitious thoughts and attempts to express a relationship between temporal and timeless conditions. For example, symbolic geometrical patterns in the forms of his verse accompany his discussions of early childhood, a state which concerns spiritual origins and which, in keeping with the Platonic notion of recollecting ideas from a prior existence, helps to account for a source of geometrical thought, for this poet's attribution of the highest value to it, and for his use of it as the rational keystone of a belief in a principle of immortality. The charm of ideas such as pre-existence and immortality – being lost on modern culture, which is apt to find them unusual, if not distressing – shows this poet to be, of course, almost as outdated as Plato himself.

Because all artists must rely – whether consciously or not – on concepts of symmetry and proportion so that their works may take on characteristic and often coherent shapes, one may well ask what distinguishes this poet from others. First, we know that this particular poet has a thorough educational background in the study of geometry, that he explicitly acknowledges his indebtedness to geometrical thought, and that his use of geometrical design does not occur randomly but only in climactic passages which posit the existence of a transcendental order beyond the bounds of time and space. So striking is this conjunction of transcendental thought and its particular geometrical design that one can successfully predict where such passages will occur. In other words, our poet does not randomly or unconsciously fall into characteristic formal patterns but is demonstrably selective in his use of them for particular purposes. Second, our poet, who is one of those old-fashioned masters of metrical composition, writes works which show how the metrical principle – or the regulation of actual words and rhythms by abstract form – is extended consistently throughout his works from the small to the large: from the metrical foot and the rhythms of syllables which occupy that foot to the metrical line-length and the actual phrases in that line to the abstract geometrical form of a passage in relation to its syntactical and thematic divisions. In short, all aspects of abstract metrical form – from the metrical foot to the geometrical design – are lucidly co-ordinated to the same purpose of showing how the merely verbal content of a passage, which is perceived by the senses only, is governed by abstract ideas and forms that are not sensuously perceived but are known in contemplation by the rational intellect. The distinguishing features of this poet's works, then, come down to the sense in which those works are products, not of chance and arbitrary unconscious activity, but of a precise and deliberate mind whose rational methods of composition constitute a welcome aid to interpretation. Recognition of those methods, however, would simply recover, for many readers, some of the practices of the metrical tradition, which is now largely defunct and forgotten but within which any accomplished poet produced metrically expressive and structurally lucid verse.

What this book invites the reader to do is to consider the degree to which the preceding description is merely hypothetical when applied to the poems of William Wordsworth. That description was written, after all, to coincide with verifiable aspects of his life and works. His study of geometry, as is well known, began at

Hawkshead school, continued at Cambridge, and, most important, occupied him for an entire year in his mid-twenties, during which he supplemented the composition of poetry by working again through all of Euclid's *Elements*. Having satisfied himself that the nature of mind was not exclusively determined by the limits of materialism, he returned fully to the composition of poetry and was launched on a career as a major poet. At various places throughout *The Prelude* and *The Excursion*, Wordsworth tells us that geometry is one of the main sources of his inspiration. His ability to exemplify his philosophical indebtedness to mathematics by means of a complementary artistic indebtedness in the existence of specific geometrical forms that lie behind the textures of his verse constitutes, of course, a principal concern of this book. Although less sympathetic readers may wish to treat the material on the discovery of symbolic geometrical design in Wordsworth's greatest utterances as an hypothesis only, let it be remembered that a good hypothesis is capable of being tested and verified. There is nothing in this book which is not rationally demonstrable and capable of verification by anyone who takes the trouble to read texts carefully. What emerges is a body of literary facts – descriptions of the forms in this poet's philosophical verse – which need simply to be refuted, qualified, or accepted. Allied to this is an inevitably more subjective interpretation of those facts but one which closely follows Wordsworth's own statements on the value of studying geometrical thought. Other, more sympathetic readers, who have not neglected this poet's interest in geometry, astronomy, and strict correspondences between the forms of mind and nature, might appreciate the following observations: when Wordsworth says in Book VI of *The Prelude* that he studied geometrical ratios and proportions and then attempted to apply them to a description of natural laws, it seems clear that the reader is entitled to accept this information as a serious insight into the poet's mind and verse. Having received important information, the reader should perhaps even employ it in his further understanding of the poet's work. To recognize that Wordsworth does indeed describe nature geometrically and that he even had particular ratios and proportions in mind is simply to take seriously what he plainly tells us and to follow its implications in a judicious manner. The identification of particular ratios and proportions is facilitated by taking the poet's educational background seriously and by assuming that his long exposure to Euclid's *Elements* – the work explicitly celebrated in Book V of *The Prelude* – is his chief source of mathematical information. At this point, with the *Elements* in one hand and the poems in the other, the reader measures his further progress by testing his critical sensitivity and mathematical knowledge.

The advantages and limitations of the mode of analysis used throughout this book may now be illustrated with reference to a short and self-contained poem, 'St. Paul's,' which ultimately suggests that the architecture of the cathedral and of the poem itself has a power of abstract thought that provides a spiritual emblem of strength and hope:

> PRESS'D with conflicting thoughts of love and fear
> I parted from thee, Friend, and took my way
> Through the great City, pacing with an eye
> Downcast, ear sleeping, and feet masterless
> That were sufficient guide unto themselves,   5
> And step by step went pensively. Now, mark!
> Not how my trouble was entirely hush'd,
> (That might not be) but how, by sudden gift,
> Gift of Imagination's holy power,
> My Soul in her uneasiness received   10
> An anchor of stability. – It chanced
> That while I thus was pacing, I raised up
> My heavy eyes and instantly beheld,
> Saw at a glance in that familiar spot
> A visionary scene – a length of street   15
> Laid open in its morning quietness,
> Deep, hollow, unobstructed, vacant, smooth,
> And white with winter's purest white, as fair,
> As fresh and spotless as he ever sheds
> On field or mountain. Moving Form was none   20
> Save here and there a shadowy Passenger
> Slow, shadowy, silent, dusky, and beyond
> And high above this winding length of street,
> This moveless and unpeopled avenue,
> Pure, silent, solemn, beautiful, was seen   25
> The huge majestic Temple of St. Paul

INTRODUCTION

> In awful sequestration, through a veil,
> Through its own sacred veil of falling snow.
> (*PW*, IV, 374-5)[1]

Before taking into account the superimposed solid and dotted lines, which refer to the poem's form as established by its four sentences, one may note that, to some readers, the merely verbal meaning of this text may not be convincing; for the claims of hope – 'An anchor of stability' – may not seem justified by a 'visionary scene' which is presented so perfunctorily. Indeed, 'St. Paul's' does not complete the pattern of a typical Wordsworthian utterance, which not only, like the present lines, commences with the speaker in a pensive or even in a depressed mood and then proceeds to an external image conducive to joy or restoration but which also goes on to a further development, often of great complexity, and the speaker's analysis of how his own thoughts and feelings have been altered. So strong is this pattern, whether in the deceptively simple lyric 'I wandered lonely as a cloud,' or in the extended and difficult ruminations of *The Prelude*, that the absence of a return to the speaker's sensibility and self-analysis in 'St. Paul's' may alone constitute a sufficient ground for disappointment. Any defence of the poem along the lines of customary modern critical approaches is perhaps not strong enough to overcome the sense of its ultimate deficiency, although devotees of archetypal criticism might be quick to point out that the juxtaposition of 'this winding length of street' and the 'majestic Temple of St. Paul' is as clear and forceful an illustration of the prophetic complex of labyrinth and temple as one could ever wish to find.

What the poem offers, then, without further comment and analysis by the speaker, is an ascending scale of perceptions that range from an undirected and passive state, in which even the physical senses are barely functioning, to ordinary consciousness and from that to a super-conscious and visionary mode of apprehension. More specifically, the gradual elevation of the speaker's soul is outlined by a contrast within each of the two pairs of the poem's sentences. The first contrast in the opening pair of sentences (1-11) sets his troubled mind and dormant senses – 'eye/ Downcast, ear sleeping, and feet masterless' – against the unexpected 'gift' of hope and the stirring of imagination. The second pair of sentences (11-28) establishes another contrast: between his restored consciousness – 'I raised up/My heavy eyes' – and the vision of the cathedral, which 'was seen' in the passive voice apparently because the speaker is now caught up in a mode of perception that takes him beyond his ordinary, active consciousness to a larger and more indefinite perspective in which any observer, however omniscient, may be a participant. The exalted calm in which the speaker is finally engaged is, of course, the inverse of the troubled passivity with which the poem began.

A careful movement from downward to increasingly upward planes of perception and from concrete to abstract diction reveals how the ascending mode of apprehension is accomplished. In lines 1-11, the speaker's gaze is directed earthward and even focuses on his 'masterless' feet. Ordinary consciousness returns in lines 11-20 with the establishment of a horizontal plane of perception that follows a 'length of street/Laid open in its morning quietness.' The only deviation from this horizontal plane occurs with the introduction of a simile – 'As fresh and spotless as he ever sheds/On field or mountain' – natural images which not only signal returning health but, by means of the mountain, introduce into the poem for the first time the possibility of a vertical plane. As if pursuing a momentary inspiration, Wordsworth focuses the final part of the poem (20-8) on an urban mountain, the cathedral itself, which, standing 'high above this winding length of street,' becomes the chief agent in directing perceptions vertically to the source of the pure, fresh, morning snow, a 'sacred veil' of heavenly protection and presence. At the same time, the progress of the poem shows a shift in diction from concrete to abstract terms. Nowhere is this contrast more apparent than in the poem's second pair of sentences (11-28), for images at first presented in customary and definite contexts of space and time – 'familiar spot,' 'morning,' 'winter's purest white,' 'field and mountain' – reappear in abstract and indefinite contexts: 'Moving Form,' 'shadowy Passenger,' 'dusky,' 'In awful sequestration, through a veil.' Clearly, the definite forms of images which are perceived by the senses and by ordinary consciousness give way to those which are appropriate to the abstract intellect and to the spiritual essence represented by the cathedral and its 'sacred veil of falling snow.'

The influence of abstract thought, which becomes conspicuous in the diction and imagery as the text progresses to the vast tranquillity of its conclusion, is also apparent more minutely in the increasingly strong influence of its abstract metrical form and in the developing massiveness of its language, both of which build up impressively over the course of the poem to surround its architectural subject in phrases of almost static and monumental character. Although it is generally the case that any poem with a highly symmetrical and repetitive structure tends to elicit parallelisms in phrasing and other repeated grammatical sequences, most of the parallel phrases in this poem are concentrated in the final pair of sentences (11-28) which describe the speaker's emergence from his depression. Especially prominent examples are the repeated phrase 'length of street' (15, 23) and the weighty lists of adjectives (17, 22, and 25). The string of adjectives in line 17, for example, displays a highly formal and organized pattern of versification – 'Deep, hollow, unobstructed, vacant, smooth' – in which the number of syllables in each word establishes a chiastic sequence of one, two, four, two, and one, respectively – an ordered series that is appropriate to the restoration of full consciousness signalled by the appearance of the 'length of street.' The corresponding grammatical and rhythmic patterns in lines 22 and 25 – 'Slow, shadowy, silent, dusky' and 'Pure, silent, solemn, beautiful' – also add to the parallelisms of the poem's conclusion. In this way, all three lines contain large numbers of stressed syllables and in their similar rhythms and phrasing refer back and forth to one another, retarding the movement of the poem and increasing its density and resonance. Needless to say, such deliberately organized and artistically elaborate lines suit an evolving consciousness and are not found in the poem's opening pair of sentences, in which a less formal style attends the speaker's initially disoriented state.

The poem's developing power of abstract thought may also be perceived in the difference between phrases which are enjambed and those which conform regularly to the given metrical linelength. The conceptual basis of Wordsworth's attitude towards metre in his blank verse is fairly complex and receives further treatment in the final chapter. For the present, it may be sufficient to note that Wordsworth treats metre as a fixed and given principle which is binding on both poet and reader. That is to say, one does not, when reading, hear the abstract patterns of a given metre but hears, instead, the rhythms and sounds of actual words as they move in varying relationships to an ideal metrical norm. The principle is the same whether one considers the relationship of syllables to a metrical foot or of grammatical units and phrases to metrical line-length. In 'St. Paul's,' for example, enjambed phrases nearly aways accompany expressions of distress, but phrases contained by the metrical line-length are attended by repose. Thus, in the poem's opening two sentences (1–11), a preponderance of enjambed phrases complements the speaker's despondency – the principal exception being the counterbalancing phrase 'Gift of Imagination's holy power.' Not surprisingly, the regularity of phrasing becomes more pronounced in the final pair of sentences (11–28) as metrical boundaries are observed with greater care: for example, 'Deep, hollow, unobstructed, vacant, smooth'; 'This moveless and unpeopled avenue'; 'Through its own sacred veil of falling snow.' In other words, the degree to which abstract metrical form regulates actual language is greatest in lines that contain positive sentiments and images and is most successfully attained and conspicuous in direct relation to the introduction of abstract verbal content.

To move from abstract metrical to abstract geometrical form is merely to extend the metrical principle to its largest dimensions. Just as one should distinguish between the rhythms of actual syllables and the metrical feet they occupy, so one may distinguish between the overall physical structure of the poem and its metaphysical form. In this case, the physical structure consists of four sentences arranged in pairs and is apprehended as such by the senses. Its metaphysical form is an abstract geometrical proportion known only in intellectual reflection but in accordance with which everything in the merely physical structure of the poem nevertheless moves. The dotted lines superimposed on 'St. Paul's' merely call attention to what one readily perceives: the first two sentences in lines 1–11 are paired as a result of having similar lengths – approximately five lines each – and a common subject – a description of the speaker's despondency; the final two sentences are longer but are also paired thematically in their treatment of the speaker's restoration and by virtue of having, again, similar lengths of roughly nine lines each. The simple balanced symmetries of equivalence within the paired sentences reveal a problem, however, that is not so readily perceived and is best left to reflection: the main division of the verse paragraph – as is indicated by the solid line – is between the two pairs of sentences, and this is not a balanced equivalence but an asymmetrical relationship between a section of verse which covers nearly eleven lines and another which goes on for slightly more than seventeen lines. Since – as we know from the paired sentences – Wordsworth was perfectly capable of sustaining simple symmetrical balances in his writing, why did he disturb them by making the main division of the poem asymmetrical? Merely for the sake of variety? Perhaps – were it not apparently at the expense of aesthetic order, clarity, and beauty. The answer – however unexpected or inappropriate with regard to most other English poets – is perfectly appropriate with regard to Wordsworth, who had an excellent knowledge of elementary geometry: the asymmetrical division of the poem exists to promote the achievement of an even higher and more sophisticated kind of symmetry. The higher and purely abstract geometrical symmetry of the poem is also, in one sense, extremely simple and involves, as do the lengths of the paired sentences, a relationship between two parts only. In short, the relationship shows that the length of the first part (1–11) in relation to the length of the second (11–28) should be the same as the length of the second part in relation to the entire poem. In other words, the smaller part (a) is to the larger (b) as the larger (b) is to the whole (a + b) – $a:b::b:a+b$. It is that simple. An empirical test would confirm that the first 10.8 lines are approximately 0.62 as long as the final 17.2 lines, and that the last 17.2 lines are approximately 0.62 as long as the 28 lines of the whole poem. That is to say, the ratio of smaller to larger parts is constant – a continuous geometrical proportion, known also in Wordsworth's day as continuous division and nowadays as the golden section.

Why should Wordsworth wish to compose poetry in this geometrical manner? Because some, although not all, artists have need of symbolic forms, they attribute thematic and philosophic value to certain artistic configurations so that their non-verbal artistry may complement, heighten, or make up for deficiencies in their merely verbal content. It just so happens that one of Wordsworth's most significant symbolic forms has a purely geometrical character. The reasons for his choice of such a form are straightforward and involve his conviction that geometry may serve as a rational foundation for his philosophical idealism. He tells us in *The Prelude*, for example, that geometrical thought is an image or manifestation of a being that 'is, / And hath the name of, God,' is thereby a transcendental emblem which is superior to 'the boundaries of space and time,' is an abstraction 'incapable of change,' and is an immaterial agent which exalts the mind to a region into which 'the disturbances of space and time . . . find no admission.'[2] But what may one say of this in regard to Wordsworth's stated interest in 'simple, pure / Proportions and relations'? (*Prelude*, 1805, VI, 144-5). The continuous geometrical proportion which gives 'St. Paul's' its form is certainly simple – one of the simplest of all ratios. Yet, however simple as a purely geometrical concept, it is also an infinitely non-repeating decimal fraction and is therefore incapable of complete definition in arithmetical terms and incapable of exact existence in the material universe. That is why one has to use the word 'approximately' when using numbers to describe the geometrical form of 'St. Paul's.' The exact form of 'St. Paul's' exists only in the mind as a purely geometrical abstraction, a simple proportion which has, moreover, been an item of mathematical contemplation at least since classical antiquity. Wordsworth's use of continuous proportion as a symbolic form in his poetry calls attention to its simplicity as an aid to poetic composition, the ease with which it may be thought of as a transcendental concept, and its propriety in representing, in as brief a compass as possible, the philosophical idealism he finds in geometrical thought.

Returning now to 'St. Paul's,' we may be in a better position to understand why the ascending scale of perceptions in the poem concludes with a view of the cathedral, an increasing presence of abstract diction and imagery, and a more rigorous influence of abstract metrical patterns on actual language. Although images along horizontal and vertical planes established by the length of street and the cathedral are the only verbal ways in which Wordsworth can construct a geometrical 'frame' for ordering common empirical experience, the poem has also established at its conclusion a precise approximation to an exact geometrical abstraction and an immaterial symbolic form that is ideally suited to the cathedral's role in providing 'an anchor of stability.' Christopher Wren's greatest work, which is itself a miracle of geometrical design, the religious purpose of the cathedral, which is touched on by the 'sacred veil of falling snow,' and the geometrical form of Wordsworth's poem all coincide and are realized in the final line as a reminder that behind physical appearances is an immaterial order that calls on the power of abstract thought. In 'St. Paul's,' the 'Imagination's holy power' is, in the words of *The Prelude*, 'but another name' for 'Reason in her most exalted mood' and stands at the heart of Wordsworth's idealist aesthetic, which is 'in sense conducting to ideal form,' an ascending scale of perceptions that may, in one of its manifestations, conclude, of course, in rational geometrical form (*Prelude*, 1850, XIV, 76, 190, 192).

A distinguishing quality of the preceding analysis is that it offers a way of interpreting some of Wordsworth's poems on the basis of an internal and textual standard which is demonstrably appropriate to what he wrote. As such, this type of analysis may strike some as a refreshing and desirable alternative to those interpretations of Wordsworth's poetry which rely heavily on non-literary systems of value – usually drawn from modern psychology and philosophy – and which have no parallels in, and are even contradicted by, the texts themselves. The chief limitation of a mode of analysis which involves an understanding of elementary geometry is, of course, its rarity: however easily its methods lend themselves to verification, an initial and understandable resistance to something which is apparently unfamiliar may arise and not begin to abate until one realizes that geometrical analysis is really nothing more than old-fashioned metrical analysis writ large.

Were familiarity with small-scale metrical and large-scale geometrical analysis something one could assume, one might, at this point, simply append a long footnote which would list all the other occurrences of symbolic geometrical design in Wordsworth's poems. A more extended description would appear to be necessary, however, so that the unfamiliar may become familiar by means of the cumulative weight of evidence and analysis which would not only demonstrate the absolute propriety of this approach to Wordsworth's poems but would also anticipate some misinterpretations of its literary application and value. One might wonder, for example, whether the geometrical form of 'St. Paul's' is unique in Wordsworth's poetry and constitutes a singular coincidence which arose because, when writing a poem on an architectural subject, the poet either consciously or unconsciously was in an architectural frame of mind that led, perhaps only on this one occasion, to an architectural result. What can be demonstrated, however, is that the symbolic geometrical form of 'St. Paul's' also occurs elsewhere with a similar achievement of literary decorum and integrity. To cite a few instances: continuous geometrical proportion organizes the dream-vision in Book V of *The Prelude* and thereby emphasizes the poet's view that geometry and poetry have a transcendental character. The ascending scale of perceptions in the climbing of Snowdon is presented in the same geometrical form as that of 'St. Paul's' with the same thematic implications. *Tintern Abbey* also employs the same symbolic form and thus shows that what Wordsworth calls the 'forms of nature' exist not only empirically but in accordance with abstract design. The architecture of nature and the architecture of a cathedral both reveal the physical and metaphysical properties of subject and object. As a symbol of transcendental order, geometrical form of the kind found in 'St. Paul's' is equally appropriate to the *Immortality Ode* and its discussion of the human spirit's metaphysical origins in relation to growth and development.

One might now wonder whether geometrical design – far from being peculiar to 'St. Paul's' – is capable of being discovered anywhere – and not only in Wordsworth's poetry. In Wordsworth's case, at least, perhaps one might surmise that his thorough education in geometrical thought simply produced a cast of mind which habitually fell into geometrical patterns, whether he was aware of them or not. Again, what can be demonstrated is that the particular geometrical form of 'St. Paul's' occurs only in Wordsworth's major poetry and, within the major poems, only at rare but special moments. The vast majority of Wordsworth's blank verse, for example, is not geometrically designed in highly charged, symbolic forms: it is simply not credible to think that their restriction to passages of metaphysical consolidation is a result of accident or mere probability. We shall therefore be concerned with only a few passages in his major poetry. They happen to have, however, the thematically ambitious status and functions of those just cited and are therefore crucial to an evaluation of Wordsworth's poetic powers at their apogee.

With regard to the possibility that symbolic geometrical design is, in any sense, characteristic of the verse of other poets, one may say that classicists have so argued with regard to some ancient writers and that these findings are discussed in the final chapter of this book. With regard to English poets – and here, for reasons of space and sanity, is the one aspect of this book which is insufficiently documented – I have been unable to find any instance of Wordsworth's kind of symbolic geometrical forms in any of the poems of Tennyson, Keats, Shelley, Coleridge, and Milton. The absence of continuous proportion in the works of other major English poets is not surprising, for the ratio seems to require a more than casual acquaintance with elementary geometry. Only Wordsworth, moreover, has ever written verse which acknowledges his love of specifically geometrical thought – although some, like Blake, have expressed their contempt for it – or has stated how significant that thought has been to him. It is, of course, possible to impose geometrical forms – such as the golden section – randomly and mindlessly on any verse, breaking up sentences and themes in mid-line and blithely ignoring the literary purpose and verbal content of the text, but the only thing verifiable about such an exercise is that it is a waste of time. It is worth noting, however, that symbolic forms can have other than geometrical definitions: for example, Milton's occasional employment of symbolic forms in his blank verse – which were, incidentally, known to Wordsworth – is touched on in the first chapter during a discussion of symbolic patterns in general. What distinguishes any symbolic forms – whether or not they are geometrical – from those of no deliberate thematic significance is that the symbolic patterns have an identifiable relationship to verbal content and a literary purpose which is not incidental but central to a consideration of poetics. In sum, the entire point of symbolic forms is that they are full aids to interpretation which can be recognized and shared as such by most readers.

One might still be concerned that the identification of continuous proportion could be more problematical than that of other, more widely used symbolic patterns such as the circle or ring-structure, which would yield manifestly close verbal and formal links at the exact centres or between beginnings and ends of stanzas or paragraphs. After all, a golden section may appear at either of two points in a passage – the ratio being calculable from either end – and any passage which has a unity of some kind might accommodate a division somewhere in the vicinity of one of those two points. What is to prevent a reader from manipulating evidence – especially in long, complex verse paragraphs, in which numerous possible divisions could lend themselves to cheating – or from simply blundering into spurious geometrical divisions in Wordsworth's poems? As was demonstrated by 'St. Paul's,' the checks against wilful or innocent misconstructions are both formal and thematic. In strictly formal terms, the internal design of Wordsworth's blank verse paragraphs is built upon simple symmetrical equivalences; those of similar size are grouped together and differentiated from those of other sizes. Thus, the first two sentences of 'St. Paul's' – which are each about five lines long – are paired and separated from the final two sentences of approximately nine lines each. The golden section exists between the two pairs of sentences – a division which Wordsworth's use of a dash intensifies – and is at the first of two points of geometrical interest in the entire paragraph. The second of those two points is in the middle of a simile – 'As fresh and spotless' – in the middle of a larger phrase and obviously bears no relation to any of the poem's divisions by sense, syntax, or structure. Here, as in all the passages cited in this book, the affinities or distinctions between simple binary equivalences establish parallels, contrasts, and internal balances that would, even in a purely mechanical way, indicate where a larger and governing geometrical division exists. These internal balances are not, of course, simply mechanical but are inseparable from the sense or verbal content. Thematically, simple symmetrical equivalences link similar contexts together; the asymmetrical form of continuous proportion juxtaposes different contexts, usually involving – as Wordsworth's attributions of value to geometry suggest – a relationship between temporal and transcendental conditions. In 'St. Paul's,' the geometrical division of the paragraph marks a shift in language from material to immaterial signification; to define a point of golden section at the other end of the poem would require a violation of both its thematic and structural characteristics and would consequently have no textual support. Because the principles of composition in 'St. Paul's' are the same as those in the rest of Wordsworth's blank verse, one can ascertain the design of a passage on the basis of clearly demonstrable patterns of theme and structure that do not admit ambiguity. Even the largest and most complex verse paragraphs are no more obscure in their use of forms than is 'St. Paul's,' and the simple binary subdivisions in a longer passage will therefore, throughout this book, normally be identified in the course of describing symbolic geometrical patterns.

Although it is not difficult to describe a method of identifying the clear and unequivocal formal qualities of Wordsworth's verse, such a description may still seem disturbing; for most readers are not accustomed to look at poetry in this way, any more than they were in Wordsworth's time. The absence of metrical, geometrical, and other strictly formal analyses in Wordsworth's prose and correspondence is in consideration of his audience and shows him, moreover, to be no different from any other poet before him. The few analyses he provided therein are typical in that they are more from the reader's than from the poet's point of view and are restricted to specific matters – nearly always of diction and imagery – which are suited to the literary competence of the general reader or address a specific problem raised by a particular correspondent. As a consequence, it is the merely verbal surface of a poem rather than its form which usually occupies the prose. For example, in his comments to Lady Beaumont on 'With Ships the sea was sprinkled,' Wordsworth nowhere calls attention to octave-sestet relationships or to metrical effects in this artistically sophisticated sonnet. His remarks on *Resolution and Independence* in the Preface of 1815 do not – despite the great care he took to master an exceptionally large range of verse-forms – discuss the importance to the poem of its rhyme royal stanzas or concluding Alexandrines. He does not even bother to say that a poem is in blank verse or that, although he discovered the existence of a symbolic form in Milton's blank verse, he also used this form for the expression of climactic moments in his own long poems. To assume that Wordsworth never did anything without its having been duly recorded in prose by himself or by his sister, friends, or other members of the 'Wordsworth circle' is to be placed in the intolerable position of denying the existence of all the poet's artistic resources – his employment of rhetorical figures, tropes, and schemes, his choices of metres and stanzas, or his use of conventions and traditions. Conversely, it would be just as absurd to argue that if a theme or concept of artistry mentioned in prose is not corroborated by a poetical discussion or demonstration, then the theme or concept must not exist. In defending the need for a metrical analysis of metrical poetry, one is not, in any event, driven to uphold a patient hope that, with regard to Wordsworth's life or artistry, the truth, like Annette Vallon, will eventually come out: the published textual evidence contains an abundance of explicit information which accounts for Wordsworth's symbolic forms and clearly justifies the investigation of them. They have been neglected through no fault of the poet but only because readers have not been trained to look for them.

The fundamental assumption of this study, then, is that metrical compositions are likely to be illuminated by metrical analysis and its geometrical extension. The infrequency of metrical analysis in literary criticism and its abandonment to a veritably antiquarian interest are difficult to justify in view of the nature of metrical poetry. Nearly all criticism of Wordsworth's poems – and of all other older poetry, for that matter – would not be markedly different if it turned out that the primary texts were actually written as prose. The narrowing of interest to only the verbal surface of metrical poetry has promoted 'sensationalist' and physicalist aesthetics, or a response to poems which is limited to what the senses perceive and which cannot therefore deal competently with abstract metrical and geometrical patterns. At the same time, it is desirable to avoid the most common shortcoming of metrical analysis, which is all too often content to provide little more than an unhelpful catalogue of statistics and is thereby able to shed but a faint light on the verbal content of a text. This study therefore attempts to link the strictly textual concerns of metrical analysis to the thematic concerns of literary history and biography. The resulting interpretations sometimes suggest alternatives to readings that are based on attention solely to verbal content in relation to psychoanalytical, modern philosophical, and other non-literary frames of reference.

Some of the differences between a metrical analysis and more familiar modern approaches are touched on in the following summary of this book's four chapters, each of which concentrates on one of Wordsworth's principal works. The first chapter ends with a discussion of *Tintern Abbey*, the second concerns *The Prelude*, the third *The Excursion*, and the last concludes with some thoughts on the *Immortality Ode*. The first chapter, 'The Geometrical Idea of Wordsworth's Poetry,' makes it clear that, to Wordsworth, geometrical form is not an end in itself but part of his range of symbolic forms that have a distinct and highly defined literary purpose. A distinction between ornamental and symbolic patterns – between those which are chiefly aids to composition and those which are also full aids to interpretation and possess a thematic significance – leads to a discussion of several two-part forms that have either ornamental or symbolic properties. The ornamental pattern which is characteristic of nearly all of Wordsworth's blank verse is illustrated and then contrasted with the use of the blank verse sonnet as a symbolic form in the poems of both Wordsworth and Milton. A geometrically designed blank verse sonnet from *The Excursion* is then analysed to show the nature of symbolic poetic form and the relationship of blank verse sonnets to geometrical form. The symbolic value of geometrical patterning first receives careful treatment for its mathematical properties before its literary functions are demonstrated in 'Yew-Trees' and *Tintern Abbey* – chosen to illustrate Wordsworth's philosophical idealism in the consideration of the forms of nature and the nature of mind. The clearly demonstrable symbolic geometrical form of *Tintern Abbey* establishes an alternative to empirical and pantheistic interpretations of the poem and to overviews of Wordsworth's career which suggest that he was not an idealist in the late 1790s.

The form of *Tintern Abbey* – a blank verse Pindaric ode designed as a double golden section – foreshadows the greatest passages in his major work, which becomes the subject of chapter two, 'The Topologic Self of *The Prelude*.' The main argument of the chapter is that the forms of external nature experienced by the poet in his childhood and early youth condition his sensibility and eventually become one with the innate mathematical forms of mind which are recognized by the mature poet and applied to his perception of the material universe. Geometrical form thereby appears to be hidden in natural forms, just as it is in poetic form itself so that art may also achieve 'A power like one of Nature's' (1850, XIII, 312). The process by which the transcendental kingdom of mathematics and the mutable world of external nature merge reaches its triumphant culmination in the ascent of Snowdon, the description of which convincingly reveals the poet's progress from psychological to geometrical patterns of perception. His attempt to incarnate the immaterial abstractions of geometry in the perception of actuality itself is reflected in the title of this book, which might simply have been named 'Wordsworth and Geometry' or 'Wordsworth and the Rational Imagination' except that these titles would have missed the point of it all: namely, that geometry is of no serious interest to the poet unless it is of use in the consideration of the forms of nature and in the daily life of this world. The book's title therefore alludes to the second and more important stage of Wordsworth's relationship to geometrical thought – its utility in providing a 'sensuous incarnation' of 'ethereal and transcendent' truth. As a result, the chapter suggests the limitations of those readings of the poem which deal merely with psychological aspects of the poet's experience and not with the ways they are transcended in the achievement of laws of perception regulated by mathematical principles. Not only the forms of the most significant blank verse paragraphs, but also their language and prosody, correspond to geometrical modes of apprehension and demonstrate with the utmost clarity what nearly all readers, for other reasons, have always known – that the Snowdon episode is the finest consolidation of all that is most characteristic and best of Wordsworth's purposes in *The Prelude*.

The demonstration of mathematical methods and themes continues in the third chapter, 'The Geometrical Imperative of *The Excursion*,' and adds further examples to the cumulative weight of the book's principal arguments. There is, however, this essential difference: whereas the chapter on *The Prelude* concentrates on epistemological questions, that on *The Excursion* emphasizes the moral dimension in Wordsworth's employment of geometry. Nowhere is the ethical component of his thought seen more clearly than in the geometrical exposition of the scale of being, which, if apprehended properly, exercises the synthetic powers of reason and promotes conduct that presupposes care for all the gradations on the scale. In this regard, although all the poem's main characters have a relationship to geometrical thought, the analytically fragmented and broken geometry of the Solitary's major utterances reveals that his excessive attachment to isolated parts of the scale of being is accomplished at the expense of the whole and corresponds to his moral impairment. The Wanderer, by contrast, enunciates a geometrically transcendental vision of the scale of being so that he may impart value to all forms of life and simultaneously assign a constructive role to individual and cosmic death as the logically necessary means by which the existence of eternity is affirmed as an ontological principle. The ways in which both Wanderer and Pastor extend their respective forms of transcendentalism to the scales of social life and moral behaviour occupy the latter stages of the chapter, which concludes with some speculations on what major poems Wordsworth could have attempted after completing the comprehensive achievements of *The Prelude* and *The Excursion*.

As a counter to any misleading impression that Wordsworth is peculiar in his reliance on geometrical principles and symbolic forms, the final chapter, 'The Art of Conceptual Form,' takes a synoptic look at the use of abstract metrical patterns in the history of poetry. The chapter opens with a review of the golden section as it has been discerned in classical verse and then moves on to its principal business, which is to develop an elemental, if perhaps elementary, discussion of English prosody into a philosophical treatment of poetic form: the relationship of conceptual to actual forms of expression as they occur on the larger scale between immutable geometrical design and mutable language and on the smaller scale between the fixed principles of metre and the variable natures of rhythm and diction. After the association of Wordsworth's prosody with that of other English poets who also demonstrate a mastery of conceptual form, a passage from 'Home at Grasmere' serves as a representative example of how all aspects of form in Wordsworth's verse – from the metrical foot to the geometrical scheme – are regulated in accordance with one common principle. In an attempt to consolidate observations on prosody with the main arguments of the entire book, the chapter concludes with a discussion of the conceptual form and geometrical design of the *Immortality Ode* in relation to Wordsworth's belief in what he calls the 'principle of immortality' (*PW,* V, 445).

CHAPTER ONE

The Geometrical Idea of Wordsworth's Poetry

The analysis and interpretation of metrical poetry cannot be considered complete until its metrical nature has been taken into account. Now, by definition, metrical verse is patterned. The organization of language in accordance with metrical form not only refers to the regulation of syllables by the metrical foot but also reflects the general functions of the metrical principle: its larger patterns of balance and symmetry against which the poet may measure the rhetorical and thematic divisions of a text. It is with those larger patterns of symmetry in Wordsworth's poems that this book is principally concerned.

As is true of all critical approaches, the examination of the metrical principle in a text may be sensitive or silly. A sensitive analysis of metrical patterns has a more thorough textual basis than other approaches, yields results that are at once more objective because of their demonstrable and verifiable character, and leads directly into considerations of a writer's poetics. As such, attention to patterns of metre and symmetry promotes a precision of interpretation which is not equalled by customary thematic approaches and their restriction to matters of diction, imagery, and rhetorical figures alone. Metrical analysis is its own worst enemy, though, when it produces statistics that have no discernible thematic significance or when it arrives at the discovery of a pattern that is then seen everywhere without, again, any thematic justification – as if the pattern had been pasted onto the beholder's eye so that he was no longer capable of seeing anything else. In addition, metrical forms and symmetry do not always mean the same things to all poets: for example, to some poets, metre is an abstract pattern; to others, a physically measurable unit of time which is based on actual rhythms. Furthermore, some poets practise a more highly developed metrical art than others. To Wordsworth, for example, metrical considerations were always of paramount importance and even occupied a central position in his first major prose essay, the Preface to *Lyrical Ballads*. On the other hand, there are even a few poets who have had no good reason whatsoever for writing metrically, except that they think this is how proper and pretty verse should sound. All these matters are taken up more fully in the final chapter. What needs to be stated here is that metrical forms and symmetry do exist – and quietly await our recognition of them – but that the art of metrical analysis consists of knowing when discussions of them are useful and appropriate.

The propriety required of metrical analysis may be illustrated by a brief look at Wordsworth's 'Prelude, Prefixed to the Volume Entitled "Poems Chiefly of Early and Late Years"' – a graceful and elegant work in blank verse which was published in 1842. In contrast to rhymed verse, whose jingling sound of like endings helps to establish larger structural patterns, blank verse has no inherent properties to carry the design of a poem beyond the limit of one line. The need for larger patterns is therefore, in the case of blank verse, especially acute. It happens that Wordsworth's 1842 'Prelude' is composed as a single blank verse paragraph of fifty-four lines which subdivides into four parts of roughly fourteen lines each. The poem is thus made up of symmetrical balances among four metrically equivalent sections. What significance does this pattern hold for the poem? I can do no better here than to quote Otto Skutsch, who, in a major essay on significant and meaningless patterns in Vergil's *Eclogues*, has this to say of a similar problem raised by patterns of numerical symmetry in one of Vergil's poems:

> Now what can this possibly signify in terms of a meaning intended by the poet? Nothing whatsoever! It is just a pretty pattern, and perhaps the poet would not even have been greatly distressed if his hearers or readers had not noticed it. It was just an order which he created for himself, and to which he worked. And yet, although it does not

mean anything as far as the poetic intention is concerned, that order may mean something for the critic. It may enable him to discern with greater clarity the progress of thought and the delimitation of sense groups; in short, it may be an aid to interpretation.[3]

By the same token, the symmetrical internal design of Wordsworth's 1842 'Prelude' is 'just another pretty pattern' which probably helped the poet to fashion a coherent verse paragraph but which has no necessary link to the verbal content of the poem. The reader's awareness of the pattern, however, would help him to follow the poet's units of thought precisely and to make relationships and associations which would be less liable to distort the sense of the entire text for the sake of one of its parts that, for merely subjective reasons, happened to have an especial appeal.

What we may do, then, at the outset is to distinguish between ornamental and symbolic patterns. Among these larger metrical patterns, let us use the word 'ornamental' to describe those which are merely 'pretty': that is, patterns which are aids to composition, may have a limited use as aids to interpretation, and have no direct implications for the particular verbal content of a text. In contrast, let us call those patterns 'symbolic' which have a verifiable thematic significance, a conspicuous influence on the particular language chosen for a passage, and a status not only as aids to composition but as full and critical aids to interpretation that may be ignored only in indifference towards the fact that metrical poetry rather than free verse or prose is being read. The only complicating factor to be noted is that, although an ornamental pattern may not be considered symbolic, a symbolic pattern may be built upon ornamental units. It is simply a question of recognizing a hierarchy of formal organization. Thus, one may come across a poem in which the larger metrical divisions consist of two four-line passages followed by two three-line passages. The symmetrical balances among the pairs of four-line and three-line passages constitute an ornamental pattern that may be recognized as a source of pleasure in itself while having no significance for the basic sense of what one is reading. Should the same ornamental pattern of two four-line and two three-line units serve as the underpinning for a

Petrarchan sonnet, however, and should the resulting octave and sestet be fulfilling their traditional functions of placing in contrast profane and sacred aspects of a single subject, one then may consider the intellectual pleasure which attends the recognition of symbolic form. That is to say, ornamental patterns, although of no symbolic interest in themselves, may sometimes be found in other patterns which are at the top of a hierarchy of forms.

In this book, the descriptions and interpretations of ornamental and symbolic patterns in the poems of Wordsworth are chiefly concerned with his blank verse and concentrate on examples of symmetry between two parts. The chief ornamental pattern to be discussed is the symmetrical equivalence or simple binary between two metrical sections of equal size. Simple binaries are the staple pattern of Wordsworth's blank verse technique, and they work in tandem with the numerous parallels, contrasts, and doublings of content that characterize his orderly and balanced style of writing – although the resulting richness of syntactical texture prompts some less charitable readers to note the verbosity of his style. The main symbolic patterns to be considered are both asymmetrical binary forms. The first is the blank verse sonnet with its four-to-three ratio of octave to sestet. The second is continuous geometrical proportion, an extremely simple but sophisticated two-part ratio in which the magnitude of the smaller section is to the larger as the larger is to the whole. The symbolic value of these two forms is established by Wordsworth's attributions of significance to sonnet-form and to geometrical thought. Unlike the simple binary, these asymmetrical symbolic patterns occur infrequently but always to great imaginative purpose and sweep by presenting, in their most characteristic appearances, a sustained perception of one subject in two different contexts which depends on a relationship between temporal and transcendental conditions. As such, these asymmetrical symbolic patterns exist in the climactic moments of *The Prelude* and *The Excursion* and carry the burden of Wordsworth's most ambitious thought.

Let us now proceed to a geometrically inclined *gradus ad Parnassum*, beginning with the ornamental pattern of the simple binary and concluding with the symbolic form of continuous geometrical proportion. The simple binary, as has been noted, merely indicates a symmetrical agreement of magnitudes. This basic and ornamental pattern is nearly ubiquitous in Wordsworth's blank verse and is also of importance in building up the much more significant patterns of symbolic value. Although it is his standard means of imparting metrical order to his works, it is by no means restricted to the poems of Wordsworth alone. A poet needs no special training in order to compose verse paragraphs which show simple binary structure: he has only to pay some attention to the balancing of parts that have similar dimensions or magnitudes. If a stanza or verse paragraph has, say, twenty lines, it will, as a simple binary, divide approximately or precisely in half; and each half may, in turn, resolve into another binary division. The resulting ornamental pattern, however aesthetically pleasing, has no particular significance by itself but can be immensely useful in the creation of a balanced style. Perhaps the chief value of simple binary divisions is their efficacy in establishing metrical boundaries for parallelisms of similarity or contrast in the distribution of thoughts and images within paragraphs, thereby promoting the appearance of orderly relationships. Poets as diverse as Horace, Milton, Pope, Thomson, and Young – to name a few of especial interest to Wordsworth – have all embraced the simple binary as a normal instrument of metrical composition. Simple binary form is built into Pope's couplets, of course, and his frequent extension of the principle to a paragraph of couplets seems especially appropriate. Yet this ornamental pattern is just as clear and effective in the blank verse paragraphs of Thomson's *Seasons*, in which symmetrical balances, such as those found in the section on 'the Passion of the Groves,' enhance Thomson's vision of nature's harmony and order. And – perhaps most important to the creation of Wordsworth's blank verse style – the normal run of Milton's paragraphs in *Paradise Lost* and *Paradise Regained* shows simple binary, as well as simple ternary, forms. Milton's ornamental patterns are so evident that the poet at times even reveals his self-conscious use of them, as in the invocation to Book VII, in which the phrase 'half yet remains unsung' indicates the binary division of the paragraph as well as that of the entire epic. But whatever the individual case, simple binary patterns may be as useful in the co-ordination of rhymed stanzas as they are in the organization of blank verse paragraphs, which have no other obvious architectural aids such as a fixed stanza-length or a rhyming pattern.

The distinguishing features of Wordsworth's simple binaries are that they offset the given structural deficiency of blank verse, promote his achievement of a balanced style, and serve as a reminder that his verse paragraphs are built up and constructed as if they were architectural propositions. His habitual reliance on simple binary patterns in his blank verse is noticeable throughout his career: from *Tintern Abbey*, which will be discussed later because it also reveals symbolic patterns, to the 1842 'Prelude, Prefixed to the Volume Entitled "Poems Chiefly of Early and Late Years",' which has already been touched on at the beginning of this chapter. To use an architectural metaphor in describing the formal patterns of Wordsworth's poems is apt, for, on the most general level, he thought of the interrelationships among his poems architecturally, comparing his works, as is well known, to a 'gothic church.' More specifically, he could call his individual poems objects or 'things' with distinct boundaries which are simultaneously physical and metaphysical (for example, *PW*, III, 21). Furthermore, the clear sense of spatial and temporal extensions and patterns that comprise the completed object, the poem, derives from words, which not only signify, but are themselves – as he noted – things (*PW*, II, 513). In summarizing the relationships of perceptions to words and of words to the completed structure of the poem, it is appropriate to employ his characteristic metaphors drawn from architecture and the nature of light: the world constitutes a home for natural powers, forms, and things, all of which are unilluminated in wordless perception but which, when named, also dwell in the more isolated and enlightening structures of words; but words themselves are things which inhabit even more elaborate structures, attaining their greatest imaginative luminosity in the most formal linguistic patterns, such as those found in the best poetry. Wordsworth's notions of poetic language involve stages of interaction between the patterns of perception and those of artistic execution and usually depend upon the simple binary as a means of clarifying how those stages are constructed, even though they may superficially appear to be buried in smaller, more complicated syntactical structures.

A representative illustration of how Wordsworth's patterns of perception work with the ornamental pattern of simple binary form occurs at the end of Book V of *The Prelude* in which he celebrates the ability of 'glittering verse' in the poems 'Of mighty Poets' to establish well-defined contexts or homes for perceptions and words:

> Here must we pause: this only let me add,
> From heart-experience, and in humblest sense
> Of modesty, that he, who in his youth
> A daily wanderer among woods and fields
> With living Nature hath been intimate,   5
> Not only in that raw unpractised time
> Is stirred to ecstasy, as others are,
> By glittering verse; but further, doth receive,
> In measure only dealt out to himself,
> Knowledge and increase of enduring joy   10
> From the great Nature that exists in works
> Of mighty Poets. Visionary power
> Attends the motions of the viewless winds,
> Embodied in the mystery of words:
> There, darkness makes abode, and all the host   15
> Of shadowy things work endless changes there,
> As in a mansion like their proper home.
> Even forms and substances are circumfused
> By that transparent veil with light divine,
> And, through the turnings intricate of verse,   20
> Present themselves as objects recognized,
> In flashes, and with glory not their own.
> (1850, V, 584–605)

The paragraph shows how binary perceptions and binary ornamental patterns can complement one another. Its twenty-two lines divide approximately in half, and each half contains two principal subjects. In the first half, the 'living Nature' of the external universe and the 'great Nature' of poetry itself are the main concerns, and Wordsworth seems to rely on his frequent claim that the mind's sense of an order behind the details of external nature is similar to its sense – as the phrase 'In measure' hints – of patterns underlying the initial attractions of 'glittering verse.' The general comments on nature and poetry in this first section are specified in the concluding half of the entire passage by remarks on the more technical and internal workings of language itself. Here the principal relationships are those of the objects of perception to words and of words themselves to the fully developed and organized language of poetry. That is to say, even the shadowy 'forms and substances' are enlightened and flash with a 'glory not their own' not only because they are lodged in words but also because the words that signify them are themselves lodged in 'the turnings intricate of verse.' And those larger structures of verse are – to continue Wordsworth's analogy in accordance with the parallelisms in this passage – the bright mansions of specific poetic forms created directly by the mind as its relatively dark and 'visionary power' of sensibility evolves into the full intelligence of imagination, the force which, to Wordsworth, sheds the light of rational order on the world. Now, if we stand back from the parts and take in the entire paragraph, we can observe how simple binary form calls attention to overarching parallels in content. Each half of the passage moves from the subject of nature to that of poetry, and the 'glittering verse' near the end of the first half is balanced by the 'flashes' of verse at the end of the second. Similarly, the phrase 'In measure only dealt out to himself' – a phrase which in isolation is not particularly suggestive – is preparatory to 'the turnings intricate of verse,' and both the measures and turnings of metrical poetry evoke a common term, that of dancing. In large part, then, to understand the 'great Nature' in the works of 'mighty Poets' is to lodge their rhythms, measures, and prosody in the mind and heart and to let those elements of form and language dance therein, a process anticipated by the relationship of the Wordsworthian sensibility to the language of the sense: to the 'Woods and fields' and to 'the motions of the viewless winds.'

Although the ornamental pattern of simple symmetrical equivalence has no symbolic value, recognition of its nearly universal occurrence in Wordsworth's blank verse may help to sort out syntactical relationships which are, as here, indeed worthy of 'turnings intricate.' The counterbalance to his complicated syntax is, in short, to be found in the simple metrical divisions of his verse paragraphs. The meanings of words and syntactical relationships are often uncertain by themselves and thus benefit from their governing contexts of fixed structural patterns such as the binary equivalences under discussion. These patterns – after the reader has become familiar with their respective functions – indicate how the clarity of the whole irradiates all the parts and how, in an entire passage, many linguistic parallels and contrasts are to be expected, taken as certain, and used to overcome local semantic difficulties. Much of Wordsworth's poetry, in other words, can be read deductively in the light of balanced metrical patterns, which are of such simplicity as to be accessible to almost anyone's comprehension and which bring welcome relief to the necessity of groping through passages word by word and phrase by phrase.

Awareness of the simple binary not only identifies the most common pattern in Wordsworth's blank verse but also calls attention to his characteristic mode of perception, which, as we have just seen, involves the interlinking of polarities: the low with the high, the humble with the sublime, the near with the far, the natural with the human, the human with the divine, the private with the public, the past with the present, things temporal with things eternal . . . It is his habit to present his thoughts and images in such pairings, and his ability to forge convincing bonds between greatly disparate elements in a pair is a measure of his imaginative power. In general, the ornamental pattern of the simple binary complements the imagination's polarities and tends to comprise logical and straightforward divisions of a subject in a manner resembling that of the preceding lines from *The Prelude* in which the power of nature and of the language of the sense invites comparisons with the power of poetic language. As that example suggests, polarities of perception lend themselves to presentation in simple binary form when they call upon a discursive and analytical mode of language and upon the principles of similitude which are compatible with the normal workings of common sense. Most of Wordsworth's blank verse is composed of simple polarities in simple binary form, and the results, if not always of the highest poetic interest, are nevertheless reasonably ordered and well grounded in the operations of the common mind, no matter how much his language may dignify them.

When, however, his polarities of perception involve a less discursive and more intuitively difficult and synthetic imaginative insight, such as the relationship between human and divine forces – when, in short, his mind is fully engaged in expressing the presence of transcendental patterns – he is much more apt to embody his thoughts in symbolic patterns based on the asymmetrical binary forms of the blank verse sonnet and continuous geometrical proportion. Despite their technical differences, these two symbolic forms benefit from being discussed together in the same context. They share similar literary functions in containing highly ambitious modes of imaginative activity, and their infrequent appearances in a long poem indicate the places at which the poet sums up his argument and therefore at which major points of reference are established for the determination of the poem's larger aspects of movement and design. Because both symbolic forms serve similar literary purposes, a brief discussion of Wordsworth's blank verse sonnets may stand as an introduction to the less familiar properties of continuous geometrical proportion.

A preliminary remark which bears on Wordsworth's adaptation of the sonnet as a symbolic form in blank verse paragraphing is that he was not the first to do so. The concept of unrhymed sonnets is unfamiliar to readers today, but it certainly existed in Wordsworth's mind: so much so, that he identified their occurrence in poetry other than his own. In his letters and critical prose, he rarely revealed the secrets of his own artistry, although he once told a friend about 'a perfect sonnet without rhyme' in *Paradise Lost*.[4] In his attitude towards rhymed and unrhymed sonnets, as in so much else, he is clearly indebted to Milton, whose blank verse sonnets I have elsewhere discussed as well as having touched briefly on a few examples by Wordsworth himself.[5] Ever since that afternoon on 21 May 1802, when Wordsworth 'took fire' after a reading of Milton's sonnets and began composing his own with a new vision of the form, he associated sonnet-form with Milton and therein perceived a relationship between a special kind of imagination and a particular artistic mode that also held a personal significance for himself. To Wordsworth, after all, Milton symbolized the transcendental poet, the foremost example of the 'meditative Imagination, of poetical, as contradistinguished from human or dramatic Imagination' typified by Shakespeare (*PW*, II, 439). In saying of Milton that 'all things tended in him towards the sublime' so that he could best 'see and tell / Of things invisible to mortal sight,' Wordsworth is suggesting that, whereas both meditative and dramatic imaginations probe the intricacies of human nature, the meditative strain is also concerned to locate the human context within a larger dimension of timeless spiritual pattern (*PW*, II, 440; *PW*, III, 386 - a sonnet which concludes with Milton's lines in a tribute to the transcendental imagination). With Milton, sonnet-form, and the work of the meditative imagination so firmly interlinked in Wordsworth's mind, it comes as no surprise to learn that blank verse sonnets are symbolic patterns that accompany the presentation of subjects in transcendental contexts.

The chief technical feature of Wordsworth's blank verse sonnets is his decided preference for the Petrarchan form - a preference which upholds the Miltonic origins, form, and imperatives of his own examples and which also reveals his tastes in proportion and symmetry. He disliked the varied segments, concluding couplet, and imbalanced design of the Shakespearean form, only two minor instances of which exist among the hundreds of sonnets he wrote.[6] The Petrarchan form - which, incidentally, has historically held a greater attraction for poets of an idealist's temperament - is clearly built upon a simple binary equivalence between the enclosed quatrains of the octave and another equivalence between the tercets of the sestet. The similarities and contrasts of thought shaped within the binary forms of the octave and sestet suggest further that the two main sections of the Petrarchan sonnet should be paired with each other in an overarching binary relationship. But of course the proportion of octave to sestet is not a simple binary relationship but an asymmetrical, harmonic ratio of four-to-three. As a harmonic binary, the Petrarchan sonnet has been employed not merely to establish simple parallelisms in the manner suited to the one-to-one division of a binary equivalence but to facilitate major shifts of perspective between the contrasting proportions of octave and sestet. The shift often appears to be so prominent that it has given rise to the notion of a *volta* or 'turn,' but this is somewhat misleading if it presupposes an element of discontinuity or even dramatic conflict which is, I think, foreign to the character of the Petrarchan sonnet.[7] It is more common for a Petrarchan sonneteer to treat a subject continuously but in contrasting perspectives: thus, for example, the sonneteer may in the octave present a subject in an earthly context and then in the sestet consider it from a celestial perspective. This is often the practice of Petrarch, Dante, and Milton. It is also that of Wordsworth, who frequently juxtaposes two scales of time in his poems - a technique especially well suited to the contrasting internal proportions of his sonnets, whether rhymed or in blank verse. Even in 'The world is too much with us,' which is probably his most dramatically powerful sonnet, the principal image, the sea, maintains its nature in two different contexts, one temporal and the other timeless. In the octave, its temporal setting, its grandeur is actual though unfulfilled because, as the speaker asserts, the modern mind is too distracted and preoccupied to understand the sea's promptings. In the sestet, the seascape is fulfilled by its gods, Proteus and Triton, in the timeless realm of mythology where the mind, freed from the world's distractions, may properly contemplate the sea or any other aspect of nature. The similar characteristics of Wordsworth's blank verse sonnets show that it is the presence not of rhyme but of a form's metrical proportions and thematic functions that constitutes its essential properties.

 Notable chiefly for the clarity and simplicity of its didactic style, a blank verse sonnet from the final book of *The Excursion* provides a representative illustration and summary of the thematic and structural characteristics of symbolic form that have been outlined here. This particular passage occurs at a crucial point in Book IX: the entire poem, as well as the book, has reached its concluding section, just after all the poem's characters have made their last excursion together and have witnessed a magnificent sunset. It is given to the Pastor to sum up their feelings, and he begins by providing a lofty, markedly Miltonic evaluation of what they have experienced:

   Eternal Spirit! universal God!
   Power inaccessible to human thought,
   Save by degrees and steps which thou hast deigned
   To furnish; for this effluence of thyself,
   To the infirmity of mortal sense   5
   Vouchsafed; this local transitory type
   Of thy paternal splendours, and the pomp
   Of those who fill thy courts in highest heaven,
   The radiant Cherubim; – accept the thanks
   Which we, thy humble Creatures, here convened,   10
   Presume to offer; we, who – from the breast
   Of the frail earth, permitted to behold

The faint reflections only of thy face –
Are yet exalted, and in soul adore!
(*Excursion*, IX, 614–27)

The tone of exaltation and the transcendental content, which are common to many of Wordsworth's blank verse sonnets and which almost invariably accompany passages designed in continuous geometrical proportion, depend in this case on several adaptations of Miltonic themes and techniques. Much of the diction – the phrase 'this effluence of thyself, / To the infirmity of mortal sense / Vouchsafed' – is, of course, almost pure Milton. The religious terms in which the scale of creation ranges from 'mortal sense' to 'radiant Cherubim' and the structural features by which the fourteen-line sentence becomes an enjambed octave and sestet disclose a Miltonic letter and spirit, emphasizing the symbolic values Wordsworth associated with the meditative imagination and sonnet-form. The divisions superimposed on the text show the quatrains and tercets, as well as the octave and sestet themselves, to be heavily enjambed in a manner resembling that of many of Milton's and Wordsworth's rhymed sonnets. The enjambement does not exist merely to increase a rhetorical effect, however, but is entirely based – as will be discussed shortly – on metrical divisions which are geometrically determined. For the present, it is sufficient to note that the disposition of the content follows simple and straightforward relationships between God and man through the intervention of nature. Nature – the term common to both celestial and human powers – reveals them to be inversions of each other. The octave is itself a highly condensed summary of the scale of being. Both syntactically and thematically, appellations of celestial power surround the human and natural realms, which are named in the central portion (5–6). In the sestet, the human realm surrounds the natural, and, working backwards, we can see that the pattern of the entire blank verse sonnet is now complete: the internal soul of the mind is to external nature as nature and the mind are to transcendent spirit.

The symbolic form of this utterance, carrying as it does the weight of a peroration, obviously becomes a focal point for the various contexts in which it participates. Within its own larger verse paragraph, the blank verse sonnet's movement from divine to human concerns constitutes something of a thesis which is then repeated and developed over the course of the ensuing thirty lines as they commence by celebrating those who attain spiritual power and conclude by exhorting those who hold to worldly values to recall their loftier traditions. The movement from an idea of the divine realm to verification of its presence in actual human affairs is characteristic not only of the blank verse sonnet and of its verse paragraph but also of *The Excursion* as a whole. On the largest scale, this characteristic pattern exists in the general transition from the more metaphysical cast of the first four books to the more human and ethical narrations of the next four. On a smaller scale, the same pattern is found within individual books, occurring at the outset as the intellectual and personal background of the Wanderer gives way to his elegiac tale of Margaret. Even in Book IV, which is the most purely philosophical section of the poem, the opening prayer to the Deity and thoughts on the structure of the mind eventually yield to the practical concern of how personal, social, and scientific developments are thereby illuminated. More specific yet are the ways in which the Pastor's blank verse sonnet in Book IX compares with blank verse sonnets elsewhere in the poem and completes the character of the Pastor himself. In later chapters, we shall examine several blank verse sonnets about and by the Wanderer. Each of these passages, although more descriptive and less exclusively didactic than the Pastor's lines from Book IX, reveals the same ambitious strain and symbolic form which derive from and elaborate on the Miltonic heritage. It is in parallel with such passages that the Pastor's blank verse sonnet stands, helping to augment and strengthen the conclusion of the poem as well as showing that the source of his humility and charity, which were so amply demonstrated in the narratives of the dead, resides, as does the Wanderer's, in a Miltonic and Wordsworthian complex of grandeur and transcendence.

Perhaps the best way of indicating the function and importance of the Pastor's blank verse sonnet is to waive, at this point, a detailed substantiation of the preceding claims – an attempt which would not be difficult but would be unnecessarily lengthy – in favour of a closer examination of why the passage is enjambed so heavily. It was intimated earlier that the enjambement is not a matter of accident but of geometrical design. The passage is

divided and subdivided in such a way that the lines on God, those on nature, and those on the human mind approximate a constant ratio with respect to one another. Because all these divisions derive from an abstract geometrical concept, they are based on the number of abstract metrical feet allotted to each subject. The forty-three metrical feet of the octave (1-9), for example, divide into two heavily enjambed quatrains, the first of which (1-4), with sixteen and a half metrical feet, concerns the divine aspect of God, and the second of which (4-9) has twenty-six and a half metrical feet directed to His material manifestations. In the octave, then, God's transcendental nature (the first sixteen and a half feet) is to His immanent nature (the remaining twenty-six and a half feet) as His immanent nature is to the totality of His being (forty-three feet): that is, in numerical approximations, 16.5:26.5:
:26.5:43 – a ratio in which each term is roughly 0.62 of that which follows it. The arithmetical approximations are imprecise, incidentally, because, as our subsequent examination of the ratio's properties will show, it is purely abstract geometrical construction which cannot be fixed exactly by any numbers. In practice, any numerical combination, such as 0.62, which is larger than three-fifths and smaller than two-thirds, may serve the purpose of representing the ratio without confusion. The octave itself observes the same proportion in relation to the entire sonnet, the seventy metrical feet of which, when multiplied by the ratio, yield the forty-three feet of the octave and the twenty-seven feet of the sestet – 27:43::43:70. What is established in this case is a mathematically constant relationship of the finite creation represented in the sestet to the infinite Creator depicted in the octave and of the Creator to the whole of eternity and time. Finally, the enjambed tercets of the sestet's twenty-seven metrical feet reveal that the thanksgiving of the poem's characters (9-11) and the exaltation they experience (11-14) are in the same ratio that governs all other parts of the sonnet. In sum, every section of the passage relates to every other section in fulfilment of an objective pattern: God, man, and nature are linked together along a mathematically constant continuum which, in the order of the poem, issues from its divine source.

Wordsworth's procedure in designing the Pastor's blank verse sonnet is, of course, an instance of continuous geometrical proportion. The conjunction of two symbolic forms in this one passage – the blank verse sonnet and continuous proportion – is, so far as I know, unique in Wordsworth's poetry. Other sonnets and poems which are rhymed have, with only a few extraordinary exceptions, no need of geometry's architectural assistance and are therefore devoid of the geometrical pattern that is found here. Continuous proportion is, in other words, restricted almost exclusively to blank verse, a medium which is structurally deficient. In the poetics of *The Excursion*, the doubly symbolic patterns of the Pastor's blank verse sonnet may be excused, however: their singular conjunction in the Pastor's most significant utterance links his sensibility to that of the Wanderer, whose greatest speeches are geometrically designed, and provides the poem with a matter and manner appropriate to its closing pages and resolution of arguments. The combination of symbolic patterns also underscores the point that the thematic functions of the blank verse sonnet and continuous proportion are equivalent.

It is not necessary to be a prosodist, classicist, specialist in Renaissance poetics, or other scholar who is trained to comprehend the need and have the capacity for the metrical analysis of metrical poetry in order to perceive that the geometrical design of the Pastor's blank verse sonnet is a demonstrable and verifiable literary fact, a symbolic pattern in a highly developed metrical art. Why Wordsworth used such a pattern and how one should interpret it are, however, questions that require further attention. One may begin by pointing out that Wordsworth was not the first poet to have employed mathematical patterns and continuous geometrical proportion in particular, any more than he was the first poet to have incorporated sonnet-form into his blank verse paragraphing: there are classicists, for whom metrical analysis is an almost daily activity, who have argued that continuous proportion is a structural characteristic in the poetry of Vergil, Horace, and other ancients. My indebtedness to and qualifications of some of their findings are in the final chapter of this book. We must allow, though, that Wordsworth's knowledge of continuous proportion is not dependent on earlier poets but is something he acquired during his study of mathematics. The advantage Wordsworth presents over other poets, in this respect, is that in his verse he tells us explicitly and in considerable detail the intellectual value such studies had for him. It is then simply a question of following his own acknowledged sources of intellectual value to the symbolic patterns based on them. What all this means, in short, is that, whereas a full consideration of metrical patterns is always justified in principle and appropriate to the analysis of metrical verse, such a consideration of Wordsworth's poetry – in view of his stated interests in metrical composition and geometrical thought – is so obviously necessary that the refusal to examine the full range of metrical patterns in his verse cannot be defended.

By taking seriously Wordsworth's statements on the sources of his convictions and by following them through to their artistic presentation in his verse, we arrive at one of the main concerns of this book. It is evident that, to Wordsworth, the two chief treasures of the human mind are poetry and geometry, or, as he puts it in *The Prelude*, 'poetry and geometric truth, / And their high privilege of lasting life' (1850, V, 65-6). The assumption that poetry and geometry are the two foundations of the meditative imagination and that they both possess an imperishable nature is repeated in *The Excursion*, in which the Wanderer, whom Wordsworth acknowledged to be his alter ego, is said to have ranged among things that 'breathed immortality' and thereby, in his reading, to have found a kindred value in the poems of 'that mighty orb of song, / The divine Milton' and in 'books that explain / The purer elements of truth involved / In lines and numbers' (*Excursion*, I, 249-50, 252-4). The significance of poetry – Milton's, in particular – to the transcendental properties which Wordsworth believed to belong to the mind has long been appreciated; but the equivalent importance of geometrical thought needs to be stated more fully. In both *The Prelude* and *The Excursion*, Wordsworth tells us that geometry is a metaphysical study which relates the immaterial mind directly to the nature of a transcendental God: that it leads beyond 'the boundaries of space and time' to 'an abstract intelligence' that exists 'where time and space are not' and that 'is, / And hath the name of, God' (*Prelude*, 1850, VI, 135, 139; *Excursion*, IV, 75-6). In addition to the evidence it provides for Wordsworth's philosophical idealism and beliefs in immortality and the existence of a transcendental order, geometrical thought is singularly useful for the comprehension of the material universe. Asserting that geometrical forms clarify the forms of nature and of the external universe, he tells us that he meditated 'Upon the alliance of those simple, pure/Proportions and relations with the frame/And laws of Nature' (*Prelude*, 1805, VI, 144-6). Now, just as he demonstrated and exemplified his indebtedness to transcendental poetry by employing, at times, the Miltonic blank verse sonnet as a symbolic form, so he demonstrated and exemplified his indebtedness to geometrical thought by designing some of his utterances in accordance with 'simple, pure/Proportions and relations.' In the earliest blank verse passages which were later to be incorporated into *The Prelude*, we find him doing 'sums' in the margins and adding up lines – a working habit to be expected from a poet who was so conscious of symmetry and proportion in his blank verse paragraphs.[8] All one needs to recognize is that Wordsworth's attempts to apply specific geometrical proportions to the workings of nature are consistent with the attempt to find out how his 'sums' apply to the workings of his poetry: specifically, what one needs to do is to identify the demonstrable kinds of symmetry and proportion that exist in those passages which discuss geometrical thought. As it turns out, and as this study subsequently demonstrates, whenever he discusses geometry and its symbolic value to his transcendental outlook, he presents his views in the form of continuous geometrical proportion. Now, of all 'simple, pure/Proportions and relations,' one of the simplest and most common in elementary geometry is continuous proportion or the golden section, as it is now called, which, with respect to Wordsworth's mind and poetry, has several qualities to recommend it to our attention. First, given the thoroughness of Wordsworth's exposure to geometry and the fact that continuous proportion appears at several points in Euclid's *Elements* – the work singled out for praise in Book V of *The Prelude* – it is unlikely that the poet would have been unaware of the ratio's existence and properties. To this, one may add that the ratio's existence beyond the realm of number and exact physical measurement is particularly well suited to Wordsworth's belief that geometry is a transcendental subject. As a concept and as a form, moreover, continuous proportion is to be valued for its simplicity in aiding a poet's habits of composition and in providing Wordsworth with a means of achieving the same literary purposes as his Miltonic blank verse sonnets but without restriction to a set number of lines. That is to say, a passage in continuous proportion may be as large or as small as the poet wishes, so long as its principal thematic and metrical division closely approximates the abstract geometrical existence of the ratio. Finally, because continuous proportion in Wordsworth's verse is limited to subjects which involve transcendental content and the relationship of timeless to temporal contexts, it is a symbolic pattern that concisely epitomizes Wordsworth's attributions of value to geometrical thought in general.

The symbolic value of continuous geometrical proportion in Wordsworth's poems is an understandable extension of its mathematical properties, which now need to be considered more closely. Divested of all non-mathematical value, continuous geometrical proportion indicates that a figure is divided at least once into two sections – a and b – the smaller of which is to the larger as the larger is to the whole – $a:b::b:a+b$. Recognizing that the extremes of the smaller sections are the means of the larger, the ancient Greek geometers developed what is still the best description of the proportion and termed it the cutting of a form into extreme and mean ratio. As Rudolf Wittkower has noted, 'It is well to remember that, unlike any other true proportion, the Golden Section contains only two magnitudes . . . mathematically speaking, this is indeed a proportion of extraordinary beauty and perfection.'[9] The extremes or outer limits of the two magnitudes share a common inner boundary that – without the intervention of a third part to moderate between the two – is also the same as the mean, or most equable internal division, of their combination. Because extremes become means, this proportion would appear to be mathematically suited to express the ethical notion of avoiding extremes and might have been so thought of in antiquity for the representation of the golden mean.[10] Because the ratio of magnitudes to each other is constant, whether they subdivide continuously down to a theoretical limit of zero or generate ever larger sections up to a theoretical limit of infinity, the golden section may be applied appropriately to a concept such as the scale of creation in order to show that all gradations of the scale, however humble or sublime, have a common characteristic. In this respect, as we saw was the case with the Pastor's blank verse sonnet from *The Excursion*, the links among God, man, and nature did not suggest dialectical tensions but a uniform interdependence maintained by a constant proportion: the ratio of the sestet to the octave was the same as that of the octave to the whole, and the quatrains of the octave, as well as the tercets of the sestet, observed the ratio with respect to one another.

What probably attracted Wordsworth to this particular ratio is not only its constant transformation of extremes into means – a feature which would accord with his fundamentally meditative and undramatic cast of mind – but also the fact that, although posing no difficulties whatsoever as an elementary geometrical concept and construction, the ratio cannot be represented perfectly by any numbers and therefore eludes exact measurement and reproduction in matter – a quality which would suit its transcendental symbolism in his verse. Nothing in the physical universe – according to this line of reasoning – would appear to account for knowledge of the ratio, which has been studied for millenia as a pure concept of abstract intellection but which has only recently been found to be approximated crudely by material objects, such as those – ranging from the relatively small size of the nautilus and other seashells to the vast expanse of spiral galaxies – in which the equiangular spiral is prominent. Because representations of the ratio which are perceptible to the senses must remain content with various approximations, great differences of interpretation may arise as a result of the way one chooses to approximate it. For example, one may find that the nature of geometry is not well served by algebraic and arithmetical attempts to fix the ratio. Putting aside the ancient Greek view of numbers as geometrical forms and adopting, instead, the modern use of numbers to signify discrete quantities, one learns that the golden section may be stated numerically by subtracting one from the square root of five and by dividing the remainder in half: $(\sqrt{5}-1)/2$. The result, like pi (for the circle) or the square root of two (for the square) is an infinitely non-repeating decimal fraction – what was called, by medieval mathematicians, an 'ineffable' number and, by their less exalted Renaissance descendants, an 'irrational' number. Those who think that modern arithmetic can do justice to the purely abstract spirit of geometry often approach the ratio by the cumbersome terms of 0.382 for the smaller section and by 0.618 for the larger (0.382:0.618::0.618:1.000). To those who realize that such a vexatious arithmetical pursuit of the geometrical *nous* is unnecessary, the simple whole-number fractions, three-eighths and five-eighths, although less precise in arithmetical terms, are no more imprecise in geometrical terms and are much easier to use – that is, the ratio may be expressed as 'three is to five as five is to eight,' a convenient approximation that avoids confusion with the common rational fraction, two-thirds. In the Appendix, we shall consider a musicologist's argument on the noted twentieth-century composer Bela Bartók, who purportedly favoured the inconvenient approximations of ruthless arithmetical precision in establishing golden sections for his compositions. Bartók's unwieldy computations must have cost him a good deal of trouble, for in his music the ratio is equated with unstable chromaticism and all that is sinister, infernal, and demoniac – a meaning, or possibly an understandable revenge, which is quite evidently antithetical to that held by Wordsworth and the old geometers. In analysing Wordsworth's poems, I have nevertheless assumed a sceptical stance by adopting strict arithmetical limits for approximations – $0.36:0.64::0.64:1.00$ and $0.39:0.61::0.61:1.00$. – in the supposition that any ratio within this range is no more than one to two per cent above or below the geometrically exact golden section. Such a narrow range of close approximations rarely presents difficulties, however, for Wordsworth seems usually to have relied on the simple rational fractions – three-eighths and five-eighths – which are, of course, extremely easy to use, are also arithmetically never more than a percentage point or two away from the geometrically exact ratio, and imply a sensible attitude towards the role of computation in what is, above all, the composition of poetry. In this regard, the meaning of Wordsworth's simple calculations does not reside in the numbers themselves but in the 'ineffable' and exclusively geometrical – and therefore poetical – concept they represent.

The preceding distinction between geometrical and arithmetical approaches to continuous proportion can also reveal a susceptibility or aversion to number symbolism. The numerological attitude – such as Bartók's – is likely to be distressed by the golden section's 'irrational' sequence of infinitely non-repeating numbers, which seem to suggest an open and restless system, and is likely to feel more comfortable with the closed and static tidiness of simple whole numbers and 'rational' proportions. By contrast, a strict geometer is likely to view continuous geometrical proportion as the essence of transcendental simplicity, elegance, lucidity, and perfection, to which the assignation of numbers – although not arbitrary – is nevertheless irrelevant and unnecessary. Wordsworth's employment of continuous geometrical proportion is based on a truly geometrical attitude and thus has no numerology associated with it. The issue becomes somewhat clouded, however, if an artist uses the Fibonacci series to construct the ratio. The Fibonacci series is formed simply by adding together successive pairs of numbers which are temporarily in ultimate and penultimate positions: 1, 1, 2, 3, 5, 8, 13, 21, 34 . . . The larger the numbers become, the more closely do the ratios of penultimate to ultimate numbers converge towards the golden section. A numerologist might attribute especial significance to these pairs of integers, but the geometer knows that the numbers are only pawns in a geometrical process; for any two numbers may be selected arbitrarily to start the series, which always leads to the same result – the golden section: for example, 6, 7, 13, 20, 33, 53, 86 . . . The problem for the critic is to decide whether an artist who uses the golden section is more attuned to the interrelationships of geometrical magnitudes or to the numbers which represent those interrelationships. In English poetry, the problem is greatly simplified because Wordsworth, so far as I know, is the only English poet to have used this proportion in the designing of poems. A partial explanation of why the appearance of continuous proportion may be restricted to Wordsworth is that previous English poets, whether they knew it or not, embraced a theory of proportion based on integers, whole numbers, and easily measured quantities.[11] Integers account for the arithmetical and geometrical aspects of all traditional verse forms. Renaissance thought, for example, was sensitive chiefly to the representation of geometrical forms by integers and tended to neglect certain proportions – such as the division of a form into extreme and mean ratio – that can be represented arithmetically only by 'irrational' or 'ineffable' numbers. Such a situation can give rise to much numerology, but the critic of Renaissance art must take care to distinguish between number symbolism which is divorced from geometrical forms and that which is subsumed by a larger geometrical purpose. In contrast to Renaissance artists, Wordsworth had an understanding of geometry that is at once purer and more comprehensive as the study of interrelationships among all forms, whether or not they can be easily measured. In this, he followed the lead of Euclid's *Elements*, which relies on diagrams rather than on numbers for its demonstrations. Wordsworth's exemplification of the ancient spirit of geometry is revealed in many poems and prose remarks, as in his impressions of mountains of varying heights: '. . . the sense of sublimity depends more upon form and relation of objects to each other than upon their actual magnitude.'[12] Thus, measuring the size of an object is secondary to considerations of its shape and of the context of other shapes in which it exists. Numerical magnitudes take second place to the geometrical interrelationships among those magnitudes.

In sum, then, the relationship of numbers to geometrical form in the golden section helps to explain why Wordsworth uses this proportion selectively and only for the expression of his most capacious thoughts. By definition, a passage in continuous proportion has an exact geometrical existence that can only be approximated by numbers. One might think of the numbers, or the measurable quantities in the passage, as the medium which conveys words in a temporal sequence. By comparison, the geometrical form of the passage is the non-temporal abstraction and empirically unattainable concept towards which the numbers nevertheless move. The physical senses perceive the language of the poem but neither see nor hear its abstract geometrical form, which is known only in reflection. The numerical behaviour of the passage calls upon the analytical or discursive faculty in the perception of temporally discrete events, just as the geometrical idea of the passage engages the synthetic or intuitive reason in the intellectual apprehension of how all those events behave in a timeless configuration ('discursive or intuitive': *Prelude*, 1805, XIII, 113; *Paradise Lost*, V, 488). As a result, it is not accidental that Wordsworth employs the golden section to relate the measurable numbers of time to the immeasurable geometry of eternity. The ratio thus embodies his thoughts on the scale of creation and shows the idea of the scale to be transcendental, immeasurable, yet rationally verifiable, as it lies behind and orders the easily measurable flow of sensory perceptions of objects on the scale. As a prime ingredient in Wordsworth's characteristically intellectual and rigorous interpretation of that cultural commonplace, the scale of creation, continuous geometrical proportion not only appears in the Pastor's blank verse sonnet but more extensively in *Tintern Abbey*, the Snowdon episode from *The Prelude*, and in other places in which Wordsworth attempts to assert the constant presence of an immaterial power in the perception of a wide range of objects.

Wordsworth's intense interest in geometrical thought and his development of continuous proportion as a symbolic form in the major poems reflect, of course, his educational background and his solution to the principal intellectual crisis of his life. His educational grounding in geometry began at grammar school, where a Cambridge mathematician, William Taylor, saw to it that his Hawkshead pupils studied Euclid's *Elements* carefully in preparation for a possible career at Cambridge, a primary requirement of which was the mastery of Euclid before analysing Newton's *Principia*, then the chief object of Cambridge's curriculum. So thorough was Wordsworth's preparation that, according to Mary Moorman, Wordsworth at Cambridge 'was much farther advanced in Euclid than most of the other men.'[13] It is also clear that, after Cambridge, Wordsworth's love of geometry continued to grow. The catalogue of the Rydal Mount Library reveals that, among the many works on astronomy, mathematics, and the natural sciences contained therein, he owned a copy of that other treatise which rivals Euclid's as one of the great achievements of Western culture – Descartes' geometry.[14] Without question, it is the post-Cambridge period which marks Wordsworth's most profound commitment to geometrical thought. Although it is difficult to characterize the role of mathematics for the youthful Wordsworth, we know that it held singular importance for him when, in his mid-twenties, he returned to an intensive study of Euclid as a means of preserving his sanity against his depression over the political and philosophical trends of his era. As Moorman puts it, geometry helped him 'to avoid complete mental chaos' during this period of his greatest intellectual despondency and recovery.[15] In theory, the empirical philosophers, associationist psychologists, and political scientists of the time had divested the human mind of its spiritual component; in practice, historical events such as the French Revolution also pointed to the hopelessness of human possibilities. In *The Prelude*, Wordsworth says he 'Yielded up moral questions in despair' and in his depression 'turned towards mathematics, and their clear/And solid evidence' – evidence that the human mind is not defined exclusively by materialist considerations (1805, X, 901, 904-5). In the words of B.R. Schneider, Jr, 'during his recovery from Godwinism, Wordsworth found great solace in geometry, the avocation of his Cambridge period: though moral questions had baffled his intellect, geometrical questions suited it perfectly, because they began and ended in the mind. Having discovered no justice in the political world, he was comforted to find perfect justice in the geometrical world. Geometrical study restored his faith that behind the inscrutable face of creation lay the benign system of order and justice which his reason had failed to compass.'[16] His recovery through geometrical inquiry soon enabled him to return to the composition of poetry, which resulted in the works of his first great period, 1797-1800. The symbolic geometrical form of his greatest poems and most important passages from *Tintern Abbey* onwards to the end of his life argues, however, that his immersion in the study of geometry was no mere psychological escape mechanism but a permanent element of his commitment to a philosophical idealism grounded in mathematical thought. The consistency of his thought and geometrical artistry is firmly established in the mid 1790s and thus challenges the view that his career may be divided into an early empirical or pantheistic phase and a less interesting transcendental period which settles in after 1800.[17] Wordsworth's crucial reassessment of geometrical thought in the mid 1790s is at the heart of a metaphysical attitude which interrelates the observer and the thing observed in accordance with objectively verifiable mathematical patterns and which therefore enables him to describe and respect the existence of external objects so faithfully that one might mistakenly think him to be an empiricist. What Wordsworth accomplished, in resolving his intellectual difficulties, was to stand the empiricism of his day on its head by restoring rationalism to a metaphysical foundation.

To Wordsworth, then, the study of geometrical thought was not simply a therapeutic diversion limited to a short period of his life but a key to his lasting recovery of rational idealism. In the context of intellectual history, his use of mathematical form depends on the notion that geometrical propositions are not derived from empirical experience but from innate ideas which reflect a metaphysical ontology. Because the mind can conceptualize abstract geometrical form and relationships that have no exact counterparts in the material universe, it has been suggested that the mind also has a component that does not originate in mutable circumstances but participates in a transcendental existence. Wordsworth's 'paramount belief' (*Prelude*, 1850, VI, 132) that geometry is imperishable a priori knowledge and also yields evidence of the imperishable nature of the soul is generically compatible with the views of such older mathematical philosophers as Descartes and Plato, who, in the *Meno* and in the *Phaedo*, argues that geometrical thought is the soul's recollection of knowledge from the direct contemplation of intelligibles in a prior existence. Wordsworth's attitudes towards geometry therefore look towards the past rather than anticipate the future, for they are not particularly compatible with those promulgated since the time of Kant. Geometry has left its Euclidean certainties, and modern philosophy has dealt rather harshly with metaphysics in general, although one of its most frequent debates concerns the possibility of innate or synthetic a priori knowledge, which Kant based partly on the existence of mathematics and which expresses the necessary conditions or laws governing the perceptions of all objects of all thought. The general trend of philosophical and cultural interests over the past two centuries has favoured rational empiricism over rational idealism, however, and, more broadly, has seen the gradual displacement of rationalism of any kind by the emergence of exclusively subjective and psychological principles. The modern mind is popularly defined by the thought of Freud, Jung, and the like, but respectable subjective, emotional, and psychological attitudes in the humanities go back as far as Burke's *Enquiry*, which includes attacks on the utility of mathematical order in art and architecture.[18] In literary studies, it is an understandable but mistaken consequence of the presuppositions of modern culture to be insensitive to Wordsworth's intense interest in the metaphysical role of geometrical thought – to ignore his interest, to deem it irrelevant or inimical to the nature of the imagination, rather than to understand it, along with the history of transcendental poetry, as one of the two keystones of his convictions and power of artistic expression. Standing in opposition to psychological and philosophical materialism, his evaluation of geometry assumes that the capacity of the mind to think in such abstract terms shows geometrical knowledge of any kind to be transcendental, innate, and independent of sensory impressions. That geometrical knowledge is 'in the Mind' (*Prelude*, 1805, VI, 153) is of vital interest to him, for such knowledge serves as a bridge to a transcendental order that is capable of rational representation and of, therefore, a significance which goes beyond individual subjectivism to comment on the nature of mind generally.

In the eighteenth century, Wordsworth's discovery of a spiritual dimension in mathematical thought would have associated him with many other minds. It was, after all, an age of mathematical adepts, whose activities in the life of the times – whether in court, church, university, or in the freethinking contexts of deism and freemasonry – were sufficient to catch the public notice of writers as different as Swift and Voltaire. Some of them carried on in the spirit of Jacob Bernoulli (1654–1705), the renowned late seventeenth-century mathematician, who ordered that his tombstone be engraved with equiangular spirals, figures based on continuous geometrical proportion and which symbolized to him, as continuous geometrical proportion would symbolize to Wordsworth a century later, the wedding of time and eternity.[19] When asked in the Russian court for a proof of God's existence, the Swiss mathematician, Leonhard Euler (1707–83), could reply by writing a simple algebraic equation. J.S. Bach could present the canonic and fugal glories of *The Musical Offering* to the court of Frederick the Great in the expectation that its mathematical triumphs, such as a fugue in six voices which was built on continuous geometrical proportion, would be appreciated. In his attempts to refute Hume, Kant would turn to mathematics for illustrations of synthetic a priori knowledge as a main element of his 'Transcendental Aesthetic.' In England, as elsewhere, it was, above all, an age in which geometry was the stepping-stone to Newton's 'great system' of the universe. As handmaiden to the classical mechanics of astronomy, geometry occupied a central position in many English schools, such as the one Wordsworth attended, so that even those who did not pursue mathematical studies later were thoroughly acquainted with this large body of disciplined speculation. It was also an age, however, which anticipated subsequent centuries and neglected the epistemological aspects of mathematical thought by taking it for granted merely as a tool. The cast of mind which treats many of J.S. Bach's canons and fugues as quaint and ingenious musical 'games' and 'puzzles' rather than as spiritual exercises is similar to the eighteenth-century custom of separating the *Principia* from the 'General Scholium,' in which Newton's deeply religious, Pythagorean spirit and idealist motivation for his work are revealed.

Wordsworth's interest in geometry was not only metaphysical but practical, and Newton was his guide to the rational apprehension of the external universe. The relationship of Euclidean geometry to Newtonian astronomy, the product of 'the great Newton's own ethereal self,' as Wordsworth, in one of his adulatory references to Newton, termed him (*Prelude*, 1805, III, 270), elicited enthusiastic commentaries in eighteenth-century texts of the *Elements*. For example, Book VI, on ratios and proportions, is introduced by this statement: 'Those things which are delivered in this Book are so necessary to be known, that without them no Man can penetrate into the Secrets of Geometry, and reap the sweet fruits of Mathematics. Each proposition deserves to have an Encomium annexed, so great is the Utility of all.'[20] The 'utility' of Book VI was of especial importance, for its abstract ratios and proportions, when applied to the motions of material objects, are at the heart of Newton's system of the world. Of particular interest to this study is the fact that proposition 30 of Book VI is what Johannes Kepler called one of the two great treasures of geometry: the division of a line into extreme and mean ratio.[21] Actually, the ratio occurs as early as Book II. 11 and is used as part of other propositions. It has a significant place in the whole of the *Elements*, for it inheres in the figure with which Euclidean geometry ends – the pentagonal dodecahedron.[22] Wordsworth's careful attention to Euclid over the years not only acquainted him thoroughly with the mathematical properties of continuous geometrical proportion in particular but generally impressed upon him the goal of understanding Newton's great system and the need to adopt a Newtonian outlook and apply geometrical thought to the natural universe.

The relationship of mathematics to Wordsworth's own system of the world involves the ways in which abstract geometrical forms correspond to 'the forms of nature,' a phrase which continually recurs in numerous variations throughout *The Prelude* and *The Excursion*. In Book III of *The Prelude*, shortly after the statue in the chapel of Trinity College, Cambridge, has occasioned lines in praise of Newton, Wordsworth recalls his first deliberate attempt to rationalize the universe by 'searching out the lines of difference/As they lie hid in all external forms' – an attempt both founded on and productive of 'perpetual logic' (1850, III, 160–1, 167). The most characteristically Wordsworthian attitude towards geometrical and natural forms is that the presence of one calls forth the other: 'the alliance of those simple, pure/Proportions and relations with the frame/And laws of nature' (*Prelude*, 1805, VI, 144–6). From nature's side of this alliance, 'the forms/Perennial of the ancient hills' influence the mind and enable it 'to move/With order and relation' (*Prelude*, 1850, VII, 756–7, 760–1). In the same way, the Wanderer clothes 'the nakedness of austere truth' in mathematics with nature's 'forms, and with the spirit of her forms' and thereby discovers that 'His triangles – they were the stars of heaven,/The silent stars!' (*Excursion*, I, 268–9, 272–3). What geometrical thought provides for Wordsworth is a mathematical ordering of the external universe – a union of abstractions and concretions that, in a way poetically parallel to Newton's, is not restricted to one individual's subjectivity but possesses a logic which may be tested and shared by others. Conversely, one of the principal virtues of the forms of nature is that their approximations to geometrical forms and relationships prompt the mind to recognize the existence of imperishable qualities in itself.

In Wordsworth's poems, the correspondences between natural forms and geometrical thought are often generally denoted by the poet's habit of perceiving objects along intersecting horizontal and vertical planes. As was noted in the Introduction to this study, the establishment of a geometrical 'frame' of perception by means of the horizontal 'length of street' and the vertical ascent of the cathedral is essential to the speaker's recovery of ordered consciousness in 'St. Paul's.' At the same time, there is often an abstraction of primary qualities of shape and magnitude from the secondary properties of colour and external appearance. Thus, in 'St. Paul's,' again, the external appearance of the scene is described – 'white with winter's purest white' and 'fresh and spotless' – before the primary shapes and natures of the street – 'This moveless and unpeopled avenue' – and of the falling snow – 'a veil' – become prominent in conjunction with the poem's general shift from concrete to abstract diction. What needs to be kept in mind is that Wordsworth's tendency to construct geometrical 'frames' of perception is a general habit that does not necessarily signify the presence of symbolic form in the metrical construction of passages. To put matters the other way around, however, a geometrical perception of the forms of nature always occurs when a passage is designed in symbolic geometrical form. There is here, moreover, a significant difference: unlike passages which have merely ornamental patterns, those with symbolic form do not simply present a geometrical mode of perception for the sake of clarity in one context but juxtapose different contexts whose values contrast and thereby exercise the full powers of imagination.

The consequential influence of symbolic geometrical design on Wordsworth's language of natural description and juxtaposition of contexts of perception may now be considered with regard to 'Yew-Trees' and *Tintern Abbey*, which not only summarize the more ambitious correspondences between natural and geometrical forms, but, as relatively short works in blank verse, provide useful stepping-stones to the more extended examples of their concerns in the major blank verse poems. The ingenious and complicated readings of 'Yew-Trees' by new critics, linguistic, structuralist, and phenomenological experts unfortunately seem to refer to essentially different poems, although everyone agrees that the work is clearly a masterpiece, whatever its basic argument.[23] My own view, which also concludes that 'Yew-Trees' is a masterpiece of the highest order, is relatively brief and simple: although not intended to displace the suggestions of others, it has the distinction of showing that the poem is undeniably by and characteristic of Wordsworth and that what one learns from 'Yew-Trees' is of general value in approaching the best of his blank verse. It seems to me that the poem is, in large part, a meditation on the common notion that yew-trees simultaneously and somewhat paradoxically represent both death and immortality. More specifically, contemplation of the yew-trees as forms of nature in historical time results in abstract thought and the perception of geometrical form, by which means the conditions of mutability and permanence are interlinked:

> THERE is a Yew-tree, pride of Lorton Vale,
> Which to this day stands single, in the midst
> Of its own darkness, as it stood of yore:
> Not loth to furnish weapons for the bands
> Of Umfraville or Percy ere they marched   5
> To Scotland's heaths; or those that crossed the sea
> And drew their sounding bows at Azincour,
> Perhaps at earlier Crecy, or Poictiers.
> Of vast circumference and gloom profound
> This solitary Tree: a living thing   10
> Produced too slowly ever to decay;
> Of form and aspect too magnificent
> To be destroyed. But worthier still of note
> Are those fraternal Four of Borrowdale,
> Joined in one solemn and capacious grove;   15
> Huge trunks! and each particular trunk a growth
> Of intertwisted fibres serpentine
> Up-coiling, and inveterately convolved;
> Nor uninformed with Phantasy, and looks
> That threaten the profane; – a pillared shade,   20
> Upon whose grassless floor of red-brown hue,
> By sheddings from the pining umbrage tinged
> Perennially – beneath whose sable roof
> Of boughs, as if for festal purpose decked
> With unrejoicing berries – ghostly Shapes   25
> May meet at noontide; Fear and trembling Hope,
> Silence and Foresight; Death the Skeleton
> And Time the Shadow; – there to celebrate
> As in a natural temple scattered o'er
> With altars undisturbed of mossy stone,   30
> United worship; or in mute repose
> To lie, and listen to the mountain flood
> Murmuring from Glaramara's inmost caves.
> (*PW*, II, 209–10)

As the opening lines on the Lorton Yew indicate, the tree has, in the profane or historical context, furnished materials for war and death while enjoying a longevity that makes it appear immortal. The remaining lines concern the Borrowdale Yews, establish a sacred and timeless context which exists to 'threaten the profane' and to encourage 'worship.' But the trees are common to both contexts, which are shown to be mutually interdependent inversions of each other.

The symbolic geometrical form of the poem becomes a key to the interrelationship of profane and sacred contexts. The poem divides asymmetrically by continuous geometrical proportion into two main parts. The first and minor section of the ratio describes the Lorton Yew, covers slightly more than twelve lines, and concerns historical time, in which the yew is a natural symbol of permanence. The longer or major part of the ratio extends from line thirteen to the end of the paragraph and celebrates the 'fraternal Four of Borrowdale' in a supernatural context aided by 'ghostly Shapes' from Vergil's underworld in Book VI of the *Aeneid*. The poem's form, then, shows its opening 12.4 lines to be approximately 0.62 of the remaining 20.6 lines, which are, in turn, roughly 0.62 of the verse paragraph's thirty-three lines – with the arithmetical approximations closely surrounding the geometrically exact and immaterial continuous proportion among the main sections of the work. The contrast between the Lorton and Borrowdale Yews reveals that what, in the opening temporal context, is concrete was also alive; what is abstract seems to be without life. Conversely, in the concluding supernatural context, that which lived concretely in time is now abstract and lifeless; but what was abstract is now concrete and seemingly vital. Another way of looking at the inverse relationship between the contexts in which the trees are presented is to take note of the conventional symbolism associated with circles and squares. The Lorton Yew is depicted in circular terms, and in the realm of historical time the living tree seems to partake more of the endless perfection of a circle and becomes an inanimate abstraction of eternity. As the four corners of a square – the traditional figure for the earth and its elements – the four Borrowdale Yews invert the popular view that the timeless realm in which they stand should be thought of as lifeless and abstract. In other words, although spiritual and geometrical concepts are the abstractions of time, they are the concretions of eternity.

The poem opens in a fictional present and in the everyday world, as if we were on a tour of the Lake District and were now standing in front of the Lorton Yew. The antiquity of the tree soon becomes apparent in the ever-backward movement of time through the English past, during which the tree 'furnished weapons' for various warriors. In lines nine to thirteen, the tree itself is described, but in exclusively abstract and geometrical terms – 'Of vast circumference,' 'Of form and aspect too magnificent/To be destroyed,' and is 'a living thing' which is so motionless and monumental that its life in any sense of the word seems paradoxical. What is abstract and geometrical in the temporal world is static and does not appear to be subject to time's laws of growth and decay. There is even a fine grammatical touch which subtly calls attention to the tree's resistance to time: this sentence of abstract description (9–13) is fragmentary, lacking that form of the verb which would complete the tree's existence and denote its state of being in the world of generation.

When the golden section of the paragraph is reached, however, a wide variety of images and motions animates the Borrowdale Yews so that they become the concretely active agents of their domain. These twenty-odd lines – as the superimposed dotted lines indicate – subdivide into simple binaries of approximately five lines each and create an ornamental pattern which contains the mathematically regulated perceptions that predominate in the supernatural context of the poem's major section. In the first five and a half lines (13–18), the principle of multeity in unity – of the four trees as one – imparts a sense of motion to them; and the same principle carries over into the phrase 'and each particular trunk a growth/Of intertwisted fibres serpentine/Up-coiling, and inveterately convolved,' as a vertical plane is also established. The next five lines (19–23) establish a horizontal plane of perception along the 'grassless floor of red-brown hue,' and the word 'perennially' has a literal meaning here in the supernatural realm.

The remaining ten lines of the major section unite planes of perception into single images. First, there is the 'sable roof,' from which hang 'unrejoicing berries,' so termed to distinguish them from other fruits associated with festal seasons and human passions. These berries, although solemn, nevertheless yield bright imagery and thus contrast with some 'ghostly Shapes' borrowed from Book VI of the *Aeneid*. Within the poem itself, however, the presence of fear, hope, silence, foresight, death, and time is more easily explained simply as a reflection of human and temporal qualities, which, in the historical context, animate life but which, being linked to the world of generation, are here bloodless and abstract personifications. In the final five lines of the poem, incomplete forms of verbs once again appear, but in this context the infinitives and present participles achieve a thematic propriety as a normal mode of the language of eternity and attend the shadowy condition of the 'ghostly Shapes,' which celebrate a rather listless united worship – as suggested by the altars which are 'undisturbed' – or merely lie 'in mute repose' and 'listen to the mountain flood/Murmuring from Glaramara's inmost caves.'

These last two lines are among the most highly charged that Wordsworth ever wrote. They best illustrate the working motif of the poem's major section – that what is most concrete is most symbolic – and should not be taken only as a literal description of an actual mountain or flood. They refer, instead, to the principle of interchange that weds time to eternity and completes the geometrical and spiritual pattern of the cosmos, just as they complete the mathematically transcendent form of the poem itself. The lines create a double motion: one with the stream down the mountain and the other back into the 'inmost caves.' Different contexts and different planes of perception are thereby combined in one principle of celestial, not fearful, symmetry. The mountain may signify space and the stream time, but the 'inmost caves' are eternal. It does not matter whether Wordsworth knew that the root of the word 'Glaramara' means 'of or by the sea.' Nor does it matter if the reader knows that the poet's beloved River Derwent originates in or near Glaramara, which is next to Sca Fell, the highest peak in England proper and the point from which most vales and mountains of the Lake District seem to flow. Such local details, occupying a privileged position anyway, are notable mainly not for their naturalistic interest but for the symbolic and abstract principles they suggest. Extremes meet, and the 'inmost caves,' as origin of the mountain flood, are inevitably linked to the sea, in which their waters terminate and which is, in the poem, an implicit presence of infinitude in relation to the explicit presence of the caves. One manuscript of the poem did not stop with these magnificent symbolic images but, in an addition made with another writing instrument and at a presumably different time, continued in a renewed direct address to the reader with a short fragment on 'Mona's Druid Oaks' and other images which invariably accompany further geometrical designs from the poet. The addition was halted in mid-line, deleted, and the golden section in the poem's first thirty-three lines was allowed, in the latest draft, to remain in its undistracted clarity. The decision strikes me as a happy one, for with the final lines on the Borrowdale Yews and the 'inmost caves' Wordsworth had completed one of his most profound and characteristic insights – that, by means of geometry, temporal and timeless contexts interpenetrate each other, not as antagonists, but as allies – and such an insight deserves to stand in a position of final prominence. Whatever tensions and oppositions other writers might find – usually between a distasteful earth and a blissful heaven – Wordsworth has an appetite for both realms, discovers how universal forms of the spirit inhere in the natural forms of common experience, and reveals how, in the well-known phrases from the 'Prospectus' to *The Excursion*, the vision of absolutes is to 'the discerning Intellect' a 'simple produce of the common day.' So many details of this remarkable poem could be pursued, but, for our purposes, it is perhaps sufficient to say that further consideration of this work's linguistic minutiae is most likely to be successful when it assumes that the poem is essentially metaphysical and recognizes that the forms of nature are not merely natural but also supernatural in relation to the abstract powers and the immaterial forms of geometrical thought.

Although serious interest in 'Yew-Trees' is relatively recent, the thousands of pages of commentary on *Tintern Abbey* would appear to make any addition superfluous. One item which has been insufficiently considered, though, is the metrical principle in Wordsworth's first major blank verse poem; and an account of its geometrical design may help to alleviate confusion over its basic nature. Now, it is obviously absurd to expect a poet to be a professional philosopher, but literary philosophizers have rushed into *Tintern Abbey* and have found instances of what are assumed to be Wordsworth's problematical and changing philosophical stances. Although the attainment of an idealist's position, however precarious, is usually conceded to the poet after 1802, *Tintern Abbey* is frequently assessed as a powerful counterstatement of his earlier materialist preferences. The characteristics of Hartleyan associationism, empiricism, animism, and pantheism – in the sense that Wordsworth's initial conception is of spiritual forces wholly contained by the physical universe – are variously discovered in line after line, taken as the point of the poem, and are sometimes even prized as the basis of the poet's imagination in its unsullied essence and at its uncorrupted apogee, from which his later excursions into idealism represent a decline. A main contention of this study, of course, is that from at least 1796 onwards the attitudes throughout the body of Wordsworth's work are consistently those of an idealist and transcendentalist and that these attitudes precede and enhance his empirical appreciation 'of all the mighty world/Of eye, and ear.' Whether, in *Tintern Abbey*, his views are founded on the priority of spirit or matter and whether his conception of spirit is of something exclusively immanent or of something which is also transcendent are both topics of such a general character that they do not require excessive philosophical refinement and, in their generality, even supply needful evidence of a much more practical cast which pertains to the nature of this poet's art.

Because Wordsworth's primary dedication was to the invention of poetry and not to the exposition of philosophy, it becomes important not to confuse a critique of his outlook with what are actually questions of poetic genre or type. He had an old-fashioned respect for the conventional genres, which he adapted in developing his own system of classification, and the fact that he mastered such an astonishing number of them only complicates the attempt to see any general uniformity of values in his works. Apparent inconsistencies in his poems are the result not so much of minor shifts in his philosophical position as of his adjustments to the changing requirements of the genre or type of poem undertaken. In *Elegiac Stanzas*, for example, the theme of fortitude has a heaviness appropriate to its presentation in 'Hammond's Measure' – the stanza of Gray's *Elegy* – but the same theme rises to brighter regions in conjunction with the equally grave but philosophically more capacious heritage of the rhyme royal and Spenserian Alexandrines of *Resolution and Independence*. The somewhat complex problem of inferring his leading ideas from the rhymed lyrics is nevertheless of secondary concern, for his chief metaphysical pronouncements occur most extensively and clearly in his blank verse. Any overview of his essential attitudes is thus almost inevitably founded on major similarities or discrepancies among *Tintern Abbey*, *The Prelude*, and *The Excursion*. Because *Tintern Abbey* has proved to be the most elusive of these poems, a strong case for the grounds of its expression would be desirable. Furthermore, because questions of genre are so important to an understanding of Wordsworth, it is proper to start this consideration of *Tintern Abbey* with some remarks on the kind of poem it is.

As it turns out, the geometrical basis of *Tintern Abbey* is intimately linked to the poem's fulfilment of generic requirements. In 1800, Wordsworth himself indicated the type of poem he had written: 'I have not ventured to call this Poem an Ode; but it was written with a hope that in the transitions, and the impassioned music of the versification, would be found the principal requisites of that species of composition' (*PW*, II, 517). Modifying its generic origin, much as the lyrical ballads transform their models, the poem in its 'transitions' and in the 'impassioned music of the versification' nevertheless follows the basic letter and spirit or 'principal requisites' of the sublime, greater, or Pindaric Ode, which places it in the same class as the *Immortality Ode* and requires from it a similar attempt at thematic loftiness. The main 'transitions' mark major changes of time and place in the poem's subjects. Wordsworth has divided the work into two large verse paragraphs (1-57; 58-159), the first of which has a principal subdivision separating the lines on the forms of nature (1-22) from those on the recollection of the forms in the city (22-57). The resulting three sections of the poem correspond to a strophe or turn (1-22), an antistrophe or counterturn (22-57), and an epode or stand (58-159). Each section, which has its own internal consistency based upon simple binary equivalences, has a different length from the others. Their interrelationships are not, however, haphazard but in accordance with continuous geometrical proportion. That is, the magnitude of the turn is to that of the counterturn as the counterturn is to both; similarly, the magnitude of the turn and counterturn together is to that of the stand as the stand is to the whole. The accuracy with which these main metrical divisions have been established may be easily checked by using the common rational fractions, three-eighths and five-eighths ($3:5::5:8$), as convenient numerical approximations to the geometrical concept on which the poem is based. Three-eighths of the initial fifty-seven lines yields a result close to the poem's opening 21.6 lines, which are 0.38 of the first paragraph; three-eighths of the entire poem is clearly contained by the first verse paragraph, which, at 0.36 of the whole, also falls within the range (0.36-0.39) of close approximations adopted in this study. The precision of the poem's physical structure, although an imperfect reflection of its geometrically exact abstract form, nevertheless shows how far Wordsworth has transformed loco-descriptive practices to meet the less leisurely demands of major lyric poetry symbolically designed.

The poem is, properly speaking, a modified Pindaric ode in the form of a double golden section, which is built upon the lesser details of repeated images and the ornamental pattern of simple binaries. The repeated images act as frames for the poem's major divisions. The turn begins with some lines on the Wye (1-4), and the counterturn ends with an address to the river (49-57). The stand concludes with a recapitulation of natural images (157-9) which were initially presented at the opening of the poem, the circular effect of which is important to M.H. Abrams' thoughtful treatment of this and other such poems of the period as 'greater Romantic lyrics,' a flexible and thematic definition which seems appropriate to Coleridge's efforts but misses the precision and rigour of Wordsworth's geometrical adaptation of the Pindaric ode.[24] With the exception of the lines which directly concern the Wye River, all other passages in the poem are simple binaries. In the turn, the repeated phrase 'once again' (4,14) introduces passages of approximately nine lines each (4-22). The counterturn uses the phrases 'I have owed' (26) and 'I may have owed' (36) to set up parallel passages of fourteen lines each (22-49). The epode, which helpfully has the phrase 'while here I stand' placed near its outset, falls into four simple binaries of approximately twenty-five lines each: lines 58-83; 83-111; 111-34; 134-59. In sum, every passage is shaped by simple binaries to fit the governing ratio of the completed poem so that Wordsworth's language could move in accordance with exacting relationships, fulfil the transcendental nature of continuous geometrical proportion, and thereby reveal the metaphysical ground of his philosophical and visionary sympathies.

To undertake a long and tedious reading of *Tintern Abbey* is not necessary here, but we should attend to some features of the poem which show how its language corroborates its geometrical design and which also point the way to similar, but more elaborate and highly developed, linguistic patterns in *The Prelude* and *The Excursion*. One of Wordsworth's most common uses of continuous geometrical proportion is to bring together temporal and timeless dimensions of a subject – a function which is also evident in *Tintern Abbey*. The turn is set in a fictional present, but its images are so treated that they appear to be ever-present forms of nature. The counterturn refers to the past and to the role the forms of nature have played in lightening the weariness of the temporal world. The stand has past, present, and future commingled with both natural and human realms, the entirety submitting to the long view in which the local forms of nature are now universalized as cosmic agents.

The turn confers geometrical significance on its images of nature by presenting them in horizontal and vertical planes of perception:

> Once again
> Do I behold these steep and lofty cliffs,
> That on a wild secluded scene impress
> Thoughts of more deep seclusion; and connect
> The landscape with the quiet of the sky.
> The day is come when I again repose
> Here, under this dark sycamore, and view
> These plots of cottage-ground, these orchard-tufts,
> Which at this season, with their unripe fruits,
> Are clad in one green hue, and lose themselves
> 'Mid groves and copses. (*PW*, II, 259)

The opening half of the turn's simple binary, these lines reveal a trait which is also prominent in *The Prelude*: that images along a vertical axis – the 'steep and lofty cliffs' with their 'wild secluded scene' – are suggestive of sublimity and that the horizontal plane is restricted more to what is familiar and beautiful – 'plots of cottage-ground' and 'orchard-tufts.' In the second half of the binary, the movement is reversed from a consideration of 'little lines/Of sportive wood' and 'pastoral farms' to the 'wreaths of smoke/Sent up, in silence, from among the trees.' While establishing geometrical frames for both powerful and gentle imagery, Wordsworth is simultaneously presenting a scale of life which ranges from the purely natural to the human, both in social and in solitary aspects. By its conclusion, the turn has fashioned a microcosm of the enduring forms of the landscape – an illusion of actuality perceived in a geometrical spirit which heightens its sense of permanence and harmonious stability. Finally, it may be added that, although the opening lines of *Tintern Abbey* rely on the poet's intimate knowledge of the Wye River valley, the scene he constructs does not, of course, exist there in any one place but is a conflation of the beautiful pastoral landscape above the ruins and the more sublime gorge below them. Here, as in the natural images with which 'Yew-Trees' ends, local details are not so important for their own sake as for the geometrical and symbolic patterns they fulfil.

The rest of the poem develops geometrically as a meditation on the opening scene. The argument of the counterturn is, of course, that 'these beauteous forms' of nature have confirmed the poet's ability to apprehend as a unity the continuum of perceptions, ranging from gentle 'sensations sweet' to awesome impulses 'of aspect more sublime,' and that the influence of the forms, awakening as they do the deeper and intelligible structures of the soul, is not confined to time or place but possesses a moral force in helping the poet survive in the literally and philosophically 'unintelligible world' of generation and decay. The stand continues with generalized observations on the efficacy of the forms and on their relation to the mind. In the first half of the stand (58–111), the poet considers the span of his own life and, in the second half (111–59), of his sister's – 'when thy mind/Shall be a mansion for all lovely forms,/Thy memory be as a dwelling-place/For all sweet sounds and harmonies.' The division of the stand and the direct address to an auditor seem calculated in part to show that what a poet says of the nature of nature and of the mind is true not only for himself alone but also for others – that his vision of things is not mystically private but is a discovery which has a wider and public value. The thematic and structural correspondences among the simple binaries of the stand indicate that the lines on his sister's knowledge of 'all lovely forms' are parallel to the most famous lines of the poem, which occur in the poet's half of the stand and reveal that contemplation of the forms of nature has been attended by

> a sense sublime
> Of something far more deeply interfused,
> Whose dwelling is the light of setting suns,
> And the round ocean and the living air,
> And the blue sky, and in the mind of man:
> A motion and a spirit, that impels
> All thinking things, all objects of all thought,
> And rolls through all things. (95-102)

In some of his later poems, perhaps most notably in *The Excursion*, Wordsworth often groups the traditional four elements together as a way of signifying the existence of a rational cosmic order as well as the principle of creation in the scale of being that is projected through the forms of nature. A related procedure is followed in these lines from *Tintern Abbey*. His choice of the sun, the ocean, and the sky to represent their elements is, of course, typical, as is Milton's selection of imagery for a corresponding passage in *Paradise Lost* which may, though, have more than a generic resemblance because of the additional stylistic similarity of repeating the word 'all' for its inclusive effect:

> . . . hope no higher, though all the Stars
> Thou knew'st by name, and all th'ethereal Powers,
> All secrets of the deep, all Nature's works,
> Or works of God in Heav'n, Air, Earth, or Sea . . .[25]

The poignant touch in Wordsworth's lines is that man, compounded of dust, is of the earth and represents the lowliest of the four elements; yet 'the mind of man' ranges back up to the highest element in contemplating 'the light of setting suns.' The three lines which depict the elements (97-9) have the further distinction of showing a congruence between the lengths of their phrases and the metrical line-lengths of the poem. As was true of 'St. Paul's,' in which the same agreement occurred as the thematic climax was reached, the regularity of phrasing at this point in *Tintern Abbey* heightens the influence of abstract metrical form and thought on the actual language perceived by the senses. The power of abstract principles in these lines is parallel to the poem's general discussion concerning the physical manifestations of the forms of nature and their metaphysical origins. Wordsworth's conviction that geometry issues from a transcendent source but is also approximated by nature becomes particularly effective when the immanent and transcendent dimensions of the forms of nature are most closely united. The design of the poem, representing an instance of transcendental geometry, has verbal counterparts in those images which complement the poet's consciousness in spanning the poem from outset to conclusion. Thus, just as the waters of the Wye River, 'rolling from their mountain-springs,' wind their way through turn and counterturn and through a geometrical description of local and concrete natural forms, so a 'motion and a spirit,' which 'rolls through all things,' is the corresponding abstraction in the stand which interlinks the forms of nature in their universal aspect as elements. By returning at its end to 'the banks of this delightful stream,' the poem merely strengthens what is already apparent: that the Wye and the 'motion and a spirit' are complementary agents on a scale which traverses the physical and metaphysical properties of the forms of nature. That the 'motion and a spirit' should not be identified with but taken as emanating from a transcendent Creator is fairly clear, just as Wordsworth asserts that geometrical thought is not God but an 'immaterial agent' of the supreme source of things. What is also clear is that the metaphysical language and symbolic geometrical form of the poem challenge the common view that at this period of his life Wordsworth believed material nature to be the ground of everything, including spiritual concepts and mathematical abstractions, or thought spiritual agencies to exist only within the material universe. As the poem's thought and form stand, Wordsworth's steadfast belief in the transcendental origins of geometrical thought is exemplified in *Tintern Abbey*'s geometrical design, which not only establishes a foundation for the confident assessment of semantic values but also surpasses the limitations of language by representing, ultimately, a form of communion with the Godhead.

In retrospect, then, *Tintern Abbey* is the poet's first major consolidation of his most ambitious themes and artistry. His principal purpose is to express gratitude to the 'beauteous forms,' for 'in the hour/Of thoughtless youth' the visionary power of sensibility takes in sensation after sensation in what may appear to be a totally empirical exercise – but, thanks to the geometry suggested by many of those sensations and forms of nature, the mature imagination and intellect come to recognize their own spiritual origins and are enabled to discern the rational and transcendental pattern which lies behind all creation. To put it another way, the famous 'impulse from a vernal wood' is valuable because it is a rational impulse which reminds man of a greater order both within and beyond himself. As a full expression of this theme, the argument of *Tintern Abbey* provides a synopsis of what essentially happens in *The Prelude* and of how the character of the Wanderer is built up in *The Excursion*. In fact, it may not be going too far to say that the momentous achievements of thought and artistry in *Tintern Abbey* made possible the composition of the long poems. Wordsworth's choices of blank verse and geometrical form for a Pindaric ode certainly become less startling if one surmises that he may have thought of his poem as being in some way preparatory to the writing of longer works which would employ the same metre and formal designs. Whatever the case, the meditative imagination achieved in Wordsworth's remarkable Pindaric ode clearly points the way to the long poems, of which it is the forerunner.

CHAPTER TWO

The Topologic Self of *The Prelude*

There are two main assumptions in this chapter. The first is that *The Prelude* has little to do with ordinary autobiographies, which attempt to disclose an individual's personality, but everything to do with Wordsworth's determination to create a poetic or literary self capable of writing an epic and of thereby extending the range of the most ambitious form in the history of poetry. *The Prelude* itself is not, of course, the epic Wordsworth had in mind but is a necessary examination of his suitability for a successful attempt at the supreme genre later in life. As the Preface of 1815 indicates, epic poetry presupposes the possession of the meditative or prophetical strain of imagination – the ability to relate, as Milton did, human concerns to a larger sense of cosmological design and spiritual pattern. Whether that larger sense is merely peculiar to the poet or can also be shared by his community becomes a principal challenge to his choice of language and to the attainment of a publicly credible mode of utterance. In this regard, we come to our second main assumption, which is that Wordsworth tried to bring his language into line with rational and logical procedures that are generally recognized to have a universal application. Among the passages to be considered later, we shall find, for example, that Wordsworth's first deliberate attempts to conceive of the scale of being are prefaced by a tribute to Newton, whose mathematical and scientific language gave public value to his vision of the universe, and are expressed by Wordsworth's corresponding reliance on 'strict analogies' and 'perpetual logic' in his vision of the same universe, so that a charge of arbitrary subjectivity on Wordsworth's part must contend with his use of rational principles adopted and sanctioned by the community at large (1850, III, 60-3, 127-69). The chief aim of this chapter is to demonstrate that Wordsworth's eventual achievement of a public language which is still worthy of the meditative imagination is at its highest level accomplished by his use of geometrical thought, the rational authority of which assists his private visions in their translation to credible public expression as it unites his individual self with the poetic self that belongs to literary tradition.

Although it cannot do justice to the historical and political subjects in which the poem is so firmly rooted, this chapter does contribute to the ways in which relationships between an individual's participation in time and his completed poetic self's reliance on timeless geometrical patterns constitute one of the poem's principal themes and define its metaphysical character. The design of *The Prelude* as a metaphysical poem emerges from a series of challenges to the poet's ability to bring together his individual and poetic selves – to incarnate or make immanent the transcendental abstractions of geometry in ordinary phenomenal experience. There would appear to be three main stages in the attainment of interchange between a priori and empirical knowledge. The first four books deal with the poet's early youth, his eventual dedication to poetry, and his confusion over what kind of poetry he is best equipped to write: that is, Wordsworth, in the fiction of the poem, indicates that he has not yet discovered the meditative imagination as his conscious goal. In this early part of the poem, his youthful attitude towards intellectual abstractions is depicted as one of suspicion. A little excerpt from Book II is a splendid instance of this wary frame of mind: 'But who shall parcel out/His intellect by geometric rules,/Split like a province into round and square?' (1805, II, 208-10). The gap between abstractions and sensory experience cannot, at this stage, be bridged, and Wordsworth represents himself as having disliked formal education while revelling in the tutelage of the natural environment. The next stage occupies the central section of the poem, Books V to XI. These books document his despairing reactions to the social realities of London and France, and also reflect the intellectual trends that promote his growing depression. As a countercurrent to his melancholic impressions of life, these central books also establish his partial success in uniting geometrical patterns with perceptions of the material universe. Wordsworth significantly attributes this positive achievement to literature rather than to life, for his study of geometry and poetry yields in Book V a dream-vision of an Arab, stone, and shell that encompasses and places in perspective all temporal activities. But to Wordsworth a dream-vision is at a remove from conscious life, and he therefore attempts to transfer the transcendental mode of his dream to his actual perception of daily objects. His failure to achieve a satisfactory resolution of transcendental and empirical knowledge is recorded most strikingly in incidents such as his view of Mont Blanc and his experiences on and below Simplon Pass. The final stage of the poem, Books XII to XIV, reveals the accomplishment and assured mastery of a mode of perception which conforms not to psychological, but to geometrical, patterns. As numerous paragraphs in the last three books show, Wordsworth now beholds the world in accordance with the objective laws of geometry, lining up objects of perception along vertical and horizontal planes, penetrating through their secondary qualities of appearance into their primary natures as shapes and forms, and establishing mathematically regulated habits of meditation that exemplify the permeation of the temporal by the spiritual universe.

The great reversal of the poem is that the transcendental imagination which Wordsworth struggles to affirm in his maturity is something which he already had in his youth without fully realizing it. Several of the most powerful and important passages in the first four books show nature's influence upon the growing boy to have had the geometrical features of form and vision, which, after one's merely sequential and chronological reading of the poem, would seem to be the exclusive achievement of the mature, intellectually self-conscious poet. The explanation of this apparently contradictory feature of the poem highlights one of Wordsworth's main ideas: that what he calls the 'forms of nature' embody the forms of geometry and are, in part, a natural geometry that conditioned his youthful mind to perceive rigorously and capaciously without recourse to the intellectual study of abstractions. The role of these 'forms' is thereby identical to that of the 'beauteous forms' in *Tintern Abbey* and provides a principle of continuity which links the young boy to the adult poet. Wordsworth's discovery of continuity between his past and present also explains the otherwise strange and deceptively ingenious title of this chapter. Topology concerns those properties of geometrical figures which remain constant despite any deformation of the figures. For example, a circle drawn on a rubber sheet will continue to separate what is inside the circle from what is outside no matter how much the sheet – short of tearing – is twisted, stretched, or deformed. Similarly, the constant deformations – or, rather, the growth and development – of Wordsworth's life show that the influence of the forms of nature is constant throughout and preserves the transcendental dimension of his mind even when his worldly experiences 'know it not.' In sum, the forms of nature would have *The Prelude* end where it began except that the poet is now fully conscious of their significance.

The formation of a poetic self, which was first presented incisively in *Tintern Abbey* before occupying the entirety of *The Prelude*, also appears in Book I of *The Excursion*. The opening pages of that poem deserve a few remarks here, for the portrait of the Wanderer reveals in miniature the geometrical and prosodic procedures which Wordsworth develops at length in the poem on his own career. On the propriety of comparing Wordsworth's descriptions of himself with those of his Wanderer, J.C. Maxwell has observed, 'For the study of the origins of *The Prelude*, what is interesting is that a number of passages originally written about the Pedlar . . . were eventually transferred, as self-portraiture, to *The Prelude* . . . This confirms both that the Pedlar is largely autobiographical, and that, at the time of writing, Wordsworth had no idea of composing a separate, overtly autobiographical poem.'[26] When, over the years, Wordsworth was differentiating materials for his two separate long poems in blank verse, he nevertheless imparted to both works the same profile of imaginative development, in which the youthful sensibility's response to natural forms eventually evolves into the mature intellect's understanding of their geometrical significance.

Of great assistance in delineating and in marking the main stages of the Wanderer's background is a series of blank verse sonnets, seven of which – of the kind Wordsworth identified with Milton's – appear at strategic places in Book I of *The Excursion*. None occurs in the story of Margaret; one, near the end, concerns the narrator; and the rest describe the Wanderer. These fourteen-line passages share the thematic and structural characteristics of Wordsworth's rhymed sonnets. They have clearly defined octaves and sestets, even to the point of being phrased in Wordsworth's enjambed style as two quatrains followed by two tercets. The octaves normally contain matter placed in a specific or temporal setting, and they contrast with the universal or timeless context of the sestets. Taken out of the book and viewed as a group, these blank verse sonnets constitute a sequence which summarizes the development of the Wanderer's character and also embodies the principal concepts, themes, and images to be found throughout the rest of the poem.

Before examining a few of these passages, we should note that they are not evident in the early drafts of the poem but were created after 1801, when Wordsworth rediscovered sonnet-form. Manuscript B, the first complete draft of 'The Ruined Cottage' – as well as the early versions of 'The Pedlar' and 'The Ruined Cottage' as separated and given in Jonathan Wordsworth's *The Music of Humanity* – shows its paragraphs and passages to be written throughout in simple binary form, the poet's habitual method of composition in the late 1790s. Thereafter, as his artistry developed, he recast many simple binary passages into more elaborate and structurally symbolic forms, among which blank verse sonnets are prominent. As such, the blank verse sonnets of Book I are major revisions and prosodic transformations of ornamental into symbolic patterns that point to the essence of what he has to say in the poem as a whole.

Three of the blank verse sonnets in Book I provide our first and last glimpses of the Wanderer and the narrator. The first (38-51) has a Miltonic inversion of syntax in its opening line – 'Him had I marked the day before, alone' – which is appropriate to the Miltonic sonnet-form of the entire passage. In the sestet, the Wanderer is placed 'Under the covert of these clustering elms,' the first of the poem's symbolic identifications between people and trees, qualities of which are meant to typify the outstanding features of the characters. Near the end of the book, just after the conclusion of the Wanderer's tale of Margaret, the narrator's reaction to the story is embodied in a blank verse sonnet (917-30). The divisions of the sonnet are perfectly regular: the first and second sentences are each exactly four lines long, and the six-line complex sentence of the sestet divides neatly into two tercets, as the narrator extols the permanence of the 'secret spirit of humanity.' The absence of enjambement between quatrains and between octave and sestet suggests a balanced utterance which matches the narrator's chastened sentiments and tone of tranquillity. Furthermore, by couching the narrator's remarks in a blank verse sonnet, Wordsworth has deftly indicated that the narrator now participates in the magnanimous and capacious imaginative character of the Wanderer, whose sensibility and spirit are normally presented in Miltonic blank verse sonnets. Finally, the last verse paragraph of the book (957-70) is fourteen lines along and gives us a parting look at the Wanderer. The paragraph divides into a regular octave and sestet, with sunset and birdsong depicted in the octave and the Wanderer's departure concluding the paragraph. Of these three blank verse sonnets, the one of greatest substance describes the narrator: it reveals his inner attitudes and character in a way denied to the descriptive sonnets on the Wanderer, which open and close the book in a remarkably and perhaps excessively unpretentious manner.

But the other blank verse sonnets on the formation of the Wanderer's character are another matter. Sharing the same form, they invite comparisons with one another and concern the developing visionary power of the Wanderer in his boyhood and youth. Originally written as passages in simple binary form, they finally attained the length of fourteen lines with their content organized into octaves and sestets. The first, eventually published as a separate verse paragraph, describes the Wanderer as a boy:

> From his sixth year, the Boy of whom I speak,
> In summer, tended cattle on the hills;
> But through the inclement and the perilous days
> Of long-continuing winter, he repaired,
> Equipped with satchel, to a school, that stood   5
> Sole building on a mountain's dreary edge,
> Remote from view of city spire, or sound
> Of minster clock! From that bleak tenement
> He, many an evening, to his distant home
> In solitude returning, saw the hills   10
> Grow larger in the darkness; all alone

Beheld the stars come out above his head,
And travelled through the wood, with no one near
To whom he might confess the things he saw.
(*Excursion*, I, 118–31)

The first line of the next paragraph – 'So the foundations of his mind were laid' – surely indicates that Wordsworth's depiction of the Wanderer is not exclusively along psychological, but architectural, lines, in which a blank verse sonnet has an appropriate role.

Although Wordsworth initially conceived of this paragraph as a thirteen-line passage in simple binary structure, he made very few revisions in adapting it successfully to its present form as a sonnet. In the octave, the schoolhouse is the dominant image. Standing at a distance from the spires and clocks of the human world, the school keeps the growing boy in contact with the natural world. The influence of nature on the boy as shepherd and as student thus extends throughout the year, establishing in the octave the external conditions that lead in the sestet to the boy's inner responses. The sestet is notable, first, for its depiction of the boy's solitude and the absence of any reference to the human world. Then one might note that the images in the sestet have counterparts in the octave: the octave's 'city spire' and 'minster clock' are images of space and time as measured on a human scale, and they are countered in the first tercet by the hills that 'grow larger in the darkness' and, in the final tercet, by the 'stars.' Seen through the boy's eyes, the hills and stars show the spatial and temporal scale of nature to be of another magnitude that approaches permanence and timelessness. In its early version as a simple binary form, this passage merely balanced two equivalent sources of imaginative stimulation by alluding to the boy's reading of 'his bible in a school' and then his reading of the hills and stars (*PW*, V, 380). Now, as a blank verse sonnet, the passage contrasts outer and inner worlds in accordance with the structural differences between octave and sestet. The passage now also has a form which relates it to other blank verse sonnets and to the sustained development of the Wanderer's imaginative character.

To turn a fifteen-line passage from manuscript B into the next blank verse sonnet, Wordsworth again relied on only minor revisions. One change is the opening line – 'Such was the Boy – but for the growing Youth' – which clearly indicates that a close comparison of the Wanderer's boyhood and his youth is appropriate:

> Such was the Boy – but for the growing Youth
> What soul was his, when, from the naked top
> Of some bold headland, he beheld the sun
> Rise up, and bathe the world in light! He looked –
> Ocean and earth, the solid frame of earth   5
> And ocean's liquid mass, in gladness lay
> Beneath him: – Far and wide the clouds were touched,
> And in their silent faces could he read
> Unutterable love. Sound needed none,
> Nor any voice of joy; his spirit drank   10
> The spectacle: sensation, soul, and form,
> All melted into him; they swallowed up
> His animal being; in them did he live,
> And by them did he live; they were his life.
> (*Excursion*, I, 197–210)

In the previous blank verse sonnet on the Wanderer's boyhood, his response to nature took place during darkness at the base of the hills. The youthful Wanderer, by comparison, has achieved a higher stage, metaphorically represented by his response to nature while on the 'top/Of some bold headland,' which he presumably climbed during nighttime so that he could see the sunrise. The occasion for this passage is thus similar to the ascent of Snowdon in *The Prelude*. The youth's greater stature is also marked by Wordsworth's employment of more abstract diction: the octave describes the actions of the Wanderer's 'soul,' and the sestet shifts contexts to the more comprehensive world of the 'spirit.' The contrast between the soul or sensibility and the higher mind or spirit receives further support from Wordsworth's characteristic technique of presenting images and then abstracting them into didactic relationships. In the octave, the sun, ocean, earth, and clouds call up each of the four elements – fire, water, earth, and air – and thereby yield in purely visual terms a compendium of nature. In the sestet, sight gives way to taste – 'his spirit drank/The spectacle' and 'they swallowed up/His animal being' – while the octave's images are internalized in an ascending order of spirit:

'sensation, soul, and form.' In short, this sonnet shows the Wanderer's increasing ability to link his perceptions together along a conceptual scale which extends far beyond the impact of immediate impressions.

As part of the chain of blank verse sonnets which help to build up the Wanderer's character, this passage has important echoes in Book IV. Near the beginning of that book, the Wanderer speaks in blank verse sonnets, the second of which – 'If the dear faculty of sight should fail' (109–22) – repeats two patterns of the passage before us: references to the four elements and the correspondence of human life to the course of the sun. There, as the Wanderer reviews his youth and age, both sunrise and sunset are present; here, because only the Wanderer's youth is relevant, sunrise alone appears.

The next blank verse sonnet in Book I – 'A Herdsman on the lonely mountain-tops' (219–32) – differs from its early versions by having the octave regularized at exactly eight lines and by turning the six lines of the sestet into one sentence. The passage fulfills Wordsworth's customary treatment of sonnet-form, for in the sestet there are abundant references to 'immortality,' sublimity, and the 'infinite' as the Wanderer discovers how his religious faith corresponds to his experiences of nature in the mountains. The most decidedly Miltonic and sublime of the blank verse sonnets in Book I, the passage denotes the culmination of the Wanderer's progress from the visionary power of sensibility to the transcendence of spiritual insight. The remainder of the paragraph adds, however: 'Low desires,/Low thoughts had there no place; yet was his heart/ Lowly' (234–6). The conjunction of sublimity and lowliness leads to 'wisdom' (239) and also marks the essential formation of the Wanderer's mature imaginative character, which is derived from Wordsworth's concept of his own artistic character and from the one he thought Milton possessed. Even the language of the present lines is remarkably similar to that of Wordsworth's earliest tribute, in sonnet-form, to Milton's spiritual majesty: 'and yet thy heart/The lowliest duties on herself did lay' (*PW*, III, 116: 'London, 1802,' 13–14). As is so often the case in Wordsworth's poetry, the most definitive moments are those which are most Miltonic.

In demonstrating the power of the Wanderer's imaginative character, Wordsworth came to invoke Milton in the next paragraph (244–79), the revisions of which are perhaps the most substantial, revealing, and significant that Wordsworth ever made. The final version has thirty-six lines. Its first fourteen lines show the works of Milton and mathematical texts to be sources of the Wanderer's imaginative strength. The rest of the paragraph contains an application of those sources to the Wanderer's experiences of external nature. In an early version, manuscript B, this section of poetry covered fifty-four lines and had no references to the poems of Milton. The allusion to Milton was incorporated later into manuscript D, which was also cut to a length of forty-five lines. After that, there was a further shortening of the passage, a major revision which has, as we shall see shortly, a mathematical basis. First, let us consider the opening fourteen lines of the paragraph:

> So passed the time; yet to the nearest town
> He duly went with what small overplus
> His earnings might supply, and brought away
> The book that most had tempted his desires
> While at the stall he read. Among the hills   5
> He gazed upon that mighty orb of song,
> The divine Milton. Lore of different kind,
> The annual savings of a toilsome life,
> His Schoolmaster supplied; books that explain
> The purer elements of truth involved   10
> In lines and numbers, and, by charm severe,
> (Especially perceived where nature droops
> And feeling is suppressed) preserve the mind
> Busy in solitude and poverty. (*Excursion*, I, 244–57)

Because it follows a succession of fourteen-line passages, these lines would appear, at first glance, to be another blank verse sonnet. Further support for that view comes from Wordsworth's habit of associating sonnet-form with Milton. But the passage is more accurately seen as a simple binary. There is no distinct division into an octave and sestet. Rather, the passage breaks into halves, with the lines on Milton's poetry balancing those on the schoolmaster's mathematical texts. And this is as it should be, for Wordsworth here depicts poetry and mathematics as equals and even goes so far as to characterize Milton's works with a geometrical image – 'that mighty orb of song' – and to describe aesthetically the 'charm severe' of mathematics. A division of the passage into an octave and sestet might have suggested a contrast between the powers of poetry and mathematics, but the simple binary emphasizes their similarities and equivalence. The function of great poetry and mathematics is, as the rest of the paragraph shows, to supply the Wanderer with abstractions and systems of permanence that enable him to comprehend the range of the world's flux and mutability. Whereas the Wanderer's books keep him in touch with divine and timeless contexts, the Solitary is, by contrast, associated with 'a Novel of Voltaire' and is, like his book, locked within time (*Excursion*, II, 443).

The first fourteen lines, then, provide spiritual forms for human nature that are, in the rest of the paragraph, measured against the forms of external nature. Although the substantial revisions of the paragraph apparently cost Wordsworth a great deal of trouble, he eventually designed its two parts as a golden section. That is, the opening fourteen lines on the forms of spiritual nature are to the twenty-two lines on the forms of external nature as this larger section is to the entire paragraph – 14:22::22:36. The construction of the paragraph in continuous proportion seems to have aided Wordsworth in several ways, for this is the first version to have a well-co-ordinated, coherent final section on the forms lodged in external nature:

> These occupations oftentimes deceived   15
> The listless hours, while in the hollow vale,
> Hollow and green, he lay on the green turf
> In pensive idleness. What could he do,
> Thus daily thirsting, in that lonesome life,
> With blind endeavours? Yet, still uppermost,   20
> Nature was at his heart as if he felt,
> Though yet he knew not how, a wasting power
> In all things that from her sweet influence
> Might tend to wean him. Therefore with her hues,
> Her forms, and with the spirit of her forms,   25
> He clothed the nakedness of austere truth.
> While yet he lingered in the rudiments

> Of science, and among her simplest laws,
> His triangles – they were the stars of heaven,
> The silent stars! Oft did he take delight   30
> To measure the altitude of some tall crag
> That is the eagle's birthplace, or some peak
> Familiar with forgotten years, that shows
> Inscribed upon its visionary sides,
> The history of many a winter storm,   35
> Or obscure records of the path of fire.
> (*Excursion*, I, 258–79)

The golden section not only links the spiritual systems of an eternal nature in the first fourteen lines to the concretions of external nature described in the twenty-two lines above but shows them to be interdependent. Without the 'sweet influence' of external nature, spiritual truth is austere, naked, and has a 'wasting power' over the Wanderer. At the same time, external nature is no longer a simple realm of sense impressions: 'with her hues, / Her forms, and with the spirit of her forms' she participates in the abstractions of spiritual nature. In fact, it is mathematical description that in large part confers on mutable nature an aura of timelessness. Added to this is the scale of time and space that these lines convey. They range from the small to the great: from 'listless hours' and 'daily thirsting' to 'forgotten years' and the 'history' and 'obscure records' of past events. Spatially, the passage moves upwards from the 'hollow vale' to a 'tall crag' and 'peak.' To depict time and space on their largest natural scale, the constellations are equated with geometrical triangles. John Jones aptly wrote of these lines, 'There is no passage in Wordsworth more important than this, for it makes the main argument of his poetry brilliantly clear . . . [The Wanderer] learns about a single world in which triangles march about the sky, in which mountainsides are suffering things, and also quietly, mathematically, eternal.'[27] Given the continuous proportion which governs the entire paragraph, these lines are more intensely mathematical and calculated than one might have thought. Their geometrical exposition of a scale of being brings them into line with the scale of creation in Milton's poetry and with the universal range of mathematical relationships. As such, they are a touchstone of the Wanderer's imagination and are also analogous to the Wordsworthian artistic self.

What the passages on the Wanderer's development show, then, is a sequence of increasingly Miltonic blank verse sonnets and, finally, a paragraph in continuous geometrical proportion in which Milton and geometry are principal subjects. The convincing way in which the sequence builds is, in large part, a tribute to the judicious and effective revisions of simple binaries into blank verse sonnets and geometrically symbolic paragraphs. One may easily imagine the gratification with which the revisions of 'The Pedlar' were undertaken to improve and clarify the portrait of the Wanderer and to enhance the main movement of the sequence: from a delight in natural objects for their own sakes to a more abstract spirit of contemplation, and from abstractions back to natural objects, the value of which is reaffirmed but in a meditative context. A similar movement is, of course, much more detailed and greatly elaborated in *The Prelude*, but without the same pattern of revisions. In *The Prelude*, the geometrical form of many paragraphs is part of Wordsworth's initial conception and is not imposed upon the text at a later date. Although much has been made of the revisions of this poem, they do not, unlike those of 'The Pedlar,' affect the essence of the poet's vision but are confined more to the superficies of stylistic preferences. With *The Prelude* – as is also true of the greater part of *The Excursion* – one is dealing with poetry in which fully developed geometrical procedures are inherent in the first attempts at composition.[28]

Of geometry itself, Wordsworth speaks most directly and extensively in Book VI (115-67) of *The Prelude*. These fifty-three lines are organized into three separate verse paragraphs which are so designed as to establish a double sequence of interlocking binary relationships and thereby demonstrate by structural means the principles of geometrical order and relation celebrated in the language of the verse. The first paragraph (115-28) has fourteen lines divided into a simple binary. The entire paragraph is itself in simple binary relationship with the second paragraph (129-41), which has a length of thirteen lines. Wordsworth then repeats this pattern of simple binary relationships. Paragraphs one and two, in binary form with each other, comprise twenty-seven lines and are balanced by the third paragraph (142-67), which has a length of twenty-six lines. Finally, the third paragraph exhibits another mathematical relationship within itself: its two sentences form a golden section and thus provide the most poignant expression of the poetical insight which informs the sequence – that geometry and poetry both bring the suffering of the temporal world into relationship with divine sustenance.

The first two paragraphs recount the descriptive and metaphysical values of geometry:

> Yet may we not entirely overlook
> The pleasure gathered from the rudiments
> Of geometric science. Though advanced
> In these enquiries, with regret I speak,
> No farther than the threshold, there I found   5
> Both elevation and composed delight:
> ....
> With Indian awe and wonder, ignorance pleased
> With its own struggles, did I meditate
> On the relation those abstractions bear
> To Nature's laws, and by what process led,   10
> Those immaterial agents bowed their heads
> Duly to serve the mind of earth-born man;
> From star to star, from kindred sphere to sphere,
> From system on to system without end.
> ....
>
> More frequently from the same source I drew   15
> A pleasure quiet and profound, a sense
> Of permanent and universal sway,
> And paramount belief; there, recognized
> A type, for finite natures, of the one
> Supreme Existence, the surpassing life   20
> Which – to the boundaries of space and time,
> Of melancholy space and doleful time,
> Superior, and incapable of change,
> Nor touched by welterings of passion – is,
> And hath the name of, God. Transcendent peace   25
> And silence did await upon these thoughts
> That were a frequent comfort to my youth.
> (1850, VI, 115–41)

The word 'pleasure' is common to both paragraphs. It occurs initially in the opening half of the first paragraph in accompaniment to Wordsworth's consideration of geometry in itself. The rest of the paragraph concerns his attempt to find an aesthetic value in mathematics, to co-ordinate geometrical with natural laws, to assign, in short, abstractions to the forms of nature. Of particular interest is the geometrical description of astronomy: 'From star to star, from kindred sphere to sphere, / From system on to system without end.' As G.H. Durrant has stated, 'This passage makes plain that "geometrical science" was, for Wordsworth, intimately linked with Newtonian astronomy and the natural laws – with that region of "science" for which Wordsworth so often expresses his deep admiration, and with which he records none of the dissatisfaction aroused in his mind by the biological, psychological, and social sciences as practised in his day.'[29] That is to say, astronomy and mathematics exercise the synthetic powers of reason which are synonymous with the rational imagination, but the life-sciences rely on merely analytical reasoning which breaks down and classifies things as particulars and loses the sense of interconnection among them. One might even add that Wordsworth's pleasure in geometry is partly attributable to his desire to employ its forms in the description of nature and the passions and thus to parallel Newton's achievement in using Euclidean proportions for an account of planetary and stellar motion.

The source of Wordsworth's greatest pleasure in geometry, however, is clarified in the second verse paragraph. It is here that he points to a philosophical dimension in geometry that yields evidence of the mind's participation in an immutable context. Concentrically designed, the paragraph begins and ends with the pleasures that have attended the poet's contemplation of geometry. At its centre, however, stands geometry's essential nature as a subject which originates in infinitude and lies beyond all human passion. The function of geometry in support of philosophical idealism is so important to him that he repeats the notion later in Book XI, when, after having 'Yielded up moral questions in despair,' he

> . . . turned to abstract science, and there sought
> Work for the reasoning faculty enthroned

> Where the disturbances of space and time –
> Whether in matter's various properties
> Inherent, or from human will and power
> Derived – find no admission. (1850, XI, 328–33)

Like the Pythagoreans and Platonists before him, Wordsworth reasons that geometry does not depend for its existence on the life of the mutable universe. Take away the whole of external and human nature, and geometrical relationships would continue unabated. This is, for Wordsworth, a 'paramount belief' and one of his profoundest convictions. In geometry, he recognizes 'a type, for finite natures, of the one/Supreme Existence,' in which mathematical thought is sustained; and although such thought does not require the existence of the human mind, the ability of the mind to conceptualize an abstract, semipiternal emblem of the Godhead is evidence that the nature of mind transcends temporal limitations.

In both paragraphs, Wordsworth insists on the eternal character of geometrical abstractions as 'immaterial agents' and as 'a type' of 'the surpassing life/Which . . . is,/And hath the name of, God.' Being so similar to each other, these attributions to geometry receive an appropriate presentation in the text of 1850, in which the two paragraphs constitute a simple binary form of equivalence. In 1805, however, the two paragraphs were not separated but joined together in lengths of fifteen and ten lines, a combination which suggests both a loose approximation to continuous proportion and Wordsworth's habit of comparing a subject in temporal and timeless contexts. That this may have been the case is borne out in the first fifteen lines by Wordsworth's omission of the 'immaterial' nature of geometry and his greater emphasis on his own 'dark guesses' about its use in the natural world (1805, VI, 149). The complete paragraph of 1805 thus shows the development of geometry from time and nature to eternity and God. This sense of development is virtually eliminated by Wordsworth's later decision to concentrate on the immaterial character of geometry throughout and to divide the paragraph into equal sections. This is a noteworthy revision that strengthens his celebration of geometry's essential character and keeps its timeless context always in the forefront.

The length of the third paragraph of the sequence places it in

83 THE TOPOLOGIC SELF OF *THE PRELUDE*

simple binary relationship with the first two, and there is now a contrast amounting to a little spot of time or a parable:

> 'Tis told by one whom stormy waters threw,
> With fellow-sufferers by the shipwreck spared,
> Upon a desert coast, that having brought
> To land a single volume, saved by chance,
> A treatise of Geometry, he wont,   5
> Although of food and clothing destitute,
> And beyond common wretchedness depressed,
> To part from company and take this book
> (Then first a self-taught pupil in its truths)
> To spots remote, and draw his diagrams   10
> With a long staff upon the sand, and thus
> Did oft beguile his sorrow, and almost
> Forget his feeling: so (if like effect
> From the same cause produced, 'mid outward things
> So different, may rightly be compared),   15
> So was it then with me, and so will be
> With Poets ever.⌋ Mighty is the charm
> Of those abstractions to a mind beset
> With images, and haunted by herself,
> And specially delightful unto me   20
> Was that clear synthesis built up aloft
> So gracefully; even then when it appeared
> Not more than a mere plaything, or a toy
> To sense embodied: not the thing it is
> In verity, an independent world,   25
> Created out of pure intelligence. (1850, VI, 142-67)

The golden section in this paragraph brings the lines on the shipwreck into relation with Wordsworth's praise for the 'clear synthesis' of geometry's 'independent world' – 26:16.5::16.5:9.5. As he implies, the shipwreck may be thought of as a metaphor for his own dashed hopes, which he restored by meditating on geometrical problems. In one unified perception, these lines convey the two aspects of geometry: its temporal function of restoration, which is related by the actual language of the verse, and its eternal nature, which the language fulfils by completing the mathematically transcendent pattern of the golden section. The most startling remark in the passage is his claim that all poets rely on the charm of geometry's abstractions: 'So was it then with me, and so will be/With Poets ever.' Such an assertion may seem peculiar, especially in the present age, in which the creative process is often held to be irrational, strange, or at least an expression of largely non-intellectual energies and drives. For historical reasons, however, Wordsworth is quite correct in assuming that the best poetical minds appreciate mathematical relationships, which are of course inherent in a full knowledge of metrical poetry and in the keen sense of number and symmetry found in the older cosmologies.[30] He may have been thinking of more than the proportion, order, and regulation of parts that mark the powers of abstract thought in the works of his favourite poets or have been going far beyond such specific things as Chaucer's treatise on the astrolabe or Milton's Urania, tributes to Galileo, and interest in cosmology. But whatever construction one may place on the passage, it is clear that Wordsworth believes poets need systems of permanent relationships by which the fluctuating passions of life can be countered or measured and that thoughtful poets are thus bound to be attracted to the consolations of geometry's world of 'pure intelligence.'

The paragraph itself shows Wordsworth's characteristic treatment of images in a geometrical context. The natural world is reduced to its barest features – sea and desert – which become elemental representations of time and space or of unaccommodated experience itself. In the same manner, the victim of the shipwreck is man reduced to naked austerity, destitute 'of food and clothing.' Beset by no worldly distractions and seeking solitude, the man proceeds to study pure geometrical relationships and exhaust his mind of images. The function of geometry here is mainly restorative. The next stage, which is not represented in this paragraph but in the first of the sequence, is to return to the world by clothing geometrical forms and abstractions with their kindred forms of nature. The function of geometry is no longer merely restorative but informs the mind's active, 'excursive' powers.

The reduction of the world to the elemental features of sea and desert, which is the first stage of Wordsworth's celebration of geometry, and the corresponding desire to clothe geometrical truth with lasting outward forms, which is the second stage, are processes which both occur near the beginning of Book V in Wordsworth's famous dream of the Arab, stone, and shell. The transformations and reductions of images in the dream are part of the mature poet's sense of spiritual pattern and derive from his literary and mathematical studies rather than from the natural geometry of the environment that helped to form and elevate his youthful perceptions, that period in which geometrical knowledge was 'a mere plaything' and 'not the thing it is/In verity, an independent world.' It would not be going too far to assert that the dream chiefly expresses a conflict between the mind's ability to dwell in the permanent realm of pure geometry, poetry, and spiritual truth and its inability to create temporal forms of that realm which are equally permanent. In trying to resolve the conflict, Wordsworth gives us the most poetry can offer: a dream-vision of such power that it may appeal to our instincts and which is designed in such a rigorously geometrical manner that it may elicit the admiration of the intellect. The dream, as we shall learn, unfolds as a triple golden section, a continuous proportion in three interlocking movements. By this geometrical means of imaging the spiritual in the material, the 'body' of literature, which exists in the physically perishable form of books, is returned to the spirit of literature, just as, in religious poetry, the word is absorbed into the Word.

The occasion of the dream apparently reflects Wordsworth's general notion that spiritual truths by themselves have no utility unless they are incarnated and that incarnated truths should take on outward forms as lasting as possible. It is unlikely that he would have held geometry in such high esteem, after all, if he had been unable to link its principles with those of nature. Geometry that resisted incarnation would have been for him, as it almost was for his Wanderer, 'a wasting power' (*Excursion*, I, 265). The incarnation of truth, however, leads to frustration. Although eternal truth 'fails not,' as Wordsworth writes later in the 'Mutability' sonnet, truth's 'outward forms' – even those 'that bear the longest date' – are all subject to 'the unimaginable touch of Time' (*PW*, III, 401). From this derives his concern for the fate of books, the nominal subject of Book V of *The Prelude*.

In lines preparatory to the dream, Wordsworth establishes some relationships between spirit and matter that powerfully emphasize his impatience with the transitory character of human effort and that suggest, furthermore, how far removed his thought was from the confidence in earthly fame asserted by many poets from Horace onwards. Nature, or the 'speaking face of earth,' is the 'bodily image' of the 'sovereign Intellect' of God (13ff). In like manner, human creations are the 'garments' of our 'immortal being,' but these works 'must perish' (22-4). It is here that Wordsworth's intense desire for lasting incarnations of the human spirit receives strong expression:

> . . . and yet man,
> As long as he shall be the child of earth,
> Might almost 'weep to have' what he may lose,
> Nor be himself extinguished, but survive,
> Abject, depressed, forlorn, disconsolate. (1850, v, 24-8)

The destruction of the world would not touch the 'living Presence' of spirit (34), which would work for a renewal of incarnations – 'kindlings like the morning – presage sure/Of day returning and of life revived' (36-7) – but all products of human effort and 'all the meditations of mankind' (38) would be extinguished:

> Oh! why hath not the Mind
> Some element to stamp her image on
> In nature somewhat nearer to her own?
> Why, gifted with such powers to send abroad
> Her spirit, must it lodge in shrines so frail? (1850, v, 45-9)

To rescue things such as books from mutability is desirable so long as there lives a 'child of earth' who needs spiritual development. Otherwise, the love for books in themselves would reveal an excessive attachment to the world, the existence of which is, properly speaking, no longer crucial once its role as an agent has been accomplished.

The dream itself brings into clearer focus Wordsworth's contending passions for things eternal and temporal. Having perused *Don Quixote* and then having meditated 'On poetry and geometric truth, / And their high privilege of lasting life' (64-5), the dreamer has a vision of eternal truth and of whether or not a mad mission could save books of poetry and geometry from disaster. The catastrophe, a deluge, emphasizes the dreamer's apocalyptic concerns and is suited to the ancient role of dreams as instruments of predictive prophecy. In this way, the dream is supposed to be primarily a revelation not of the dreamer's psychological patterns but of the operations of timelessness on temporality.

The structure of the dream is that of a golden section repeated three times. The texts of 1805 and 1850, although differing slightly in length, both show acceptable calculations of the proportion. The geometrical design calls attention to the dream's eternal character – that it is something sent. Its divisions are marked by breaks in the fictional time of the narration and in each instance by the repetition of the key images – the stone, the shell, and the Arab. The divisions exhaust the various ways in which time and eternity can relate to one another. There is a progression from a landscape of time to one of eternity in relation to time; then eternity itself is celebrated; finally, time in relation to eternity is placed against all that precedes it, and the dream is rounded off by a return to the original landscape of time, the magnitude of which provides the final fulfilment of the mathematical patterns governing the entirety of the vision.

The continuous proportion in the opening movement of the dream contrasts the desolate landscape (1–10) with objects of eternity (10–28) so that, approximately, $10:18::18:28$. Although this approximation is less precise than the others in the paragraph (being one per cent outside the strict range of close approximations used throughout this study), it should not be dismissed on such narrow grounds; for its literary function is the same as that of the other geometrical divisions of the dream:

> I saw before me stretched a boundless plain
> Of sandy wilderness, all black and void,
> And as I looked around, distress and fear
> Came creeping over me, when at my side,
> Close at my side, an uncouth shape appeared   5
> Upon a dromedary, mounted high.
> He seemed an Arab of the Bedouin tribes:
> A lance he bore, and underneath one arm

A stone, and in the opposite hand, a shell
Of a surpassing brightness. At the sight   10
Much I rejoiced, not doubting but a guide
Was present, one who with unerring skill
Would through the desert lead me; and while yet
I looked and looked, self-questioned what this freight
Which the new-comer carried through the waste   15
Could mean, the Arab told me that the stone
(To give it in the language of the dream)
Was 'Euclid's Elements'; and 'This,' said he,
'Is something of more worth'; and at the word
Stretched forth the shell, so beautiful in shape, 20
In colour so resplendent, with command
That I should hold it to my ear. I did so,
And heard that instant in an unknown tongue,
Which yet I understood, articulate sounds,
A loud prophetic blast of harmony;   25
An Ode, in passion uttered, which foretold
Destruction to the children of the earth
By deluge, now at hand. (1850, V, 71-98)

The minor part of the ratio – the opening ten lines – is in a temporal setting. As is usual when Wordsworth creates a landscape for geometrical purposes, nature is reduced to elemental austerity: 'a boundless plain / Of sandy wilderness.' While in the realm of time, the dreamer experiences discomfort. The only contrast to his 'distress and fear' in the desolation 'all black and void' is the shell 'of a surpassing brightness.' Nevertheless, the stone and shell remain, in this temporal context, natural objects and nothing more. Similarly, the Arab is localized in time and space as a member of 'the Bedouin tribes.' In the major section of the proportion, the dreamer rejoices, and the stone, shell, and Arab are presented again but are now renamed as objects of eternity in relation to time. The Arab is transformed into a 'guide' of 'unerring skill.' Appearing first in the simple binary division of this section, the stone becomes 'Euclid's Elements,' which, as we noted earlier, contains several explanations of continuous geometrical proportion. The shell is logically associated with a deluge, but Wordsworth's finest touch in writing this passage is the transformation of 'an unknown tongue' into 'articulate sounds' and then into a 'blast of harmony' and an 'Ode, in passion uttered.' Each successive stage represents the dreamer's increasing apprehension of the sounds, the meaning of which depends solely on their attainment of form. The most specific designation of form is, of course, the last – 'an Ode, in passion uttered' – and such a poem was considered in Wordsworth's time to be an ideal vehicle for sublime expressions of transcendent themes. By showing the dreamer's successive responses to the sounds from the shell, these transformations are similar to the challenge of understanding Wordsworth's poetry properly: ultimate meaning may reside not so much in individual words and phrases as in the patterns and structures in which the words are arranged.

The opening twenty-seven and a half lines of the dream comprise the major section of a continuous proportion with the following passage of sixteen and a half lines, which chiefly concern things eternal – 44:27.5::27.5:16.5 –

>   No sooner ceased
> The song, than the Arab with calm look declared
> That all would come to pass of which the voice   30
> Had given forewarning, and that he himself
> Was going then to bury those two books:
> The one that held acquaintance with the stars,
> And wedded soul to soul in purest bond
> Of reason, undisturbed by space or time;   35
> The other that was a god, yea many gods,
> Had voices more than all the winds, with power
> To exhilarate the spirit, and to soothe,
> Through every clime, the heart of human kind.
> While this was uttering, strange as it may seem,   40
> I wondered not, although I plainly saw
> The one to be a stone, the other a shell;
> Nor doubted once but that they both were books,
> Having a perfect faith in all that passed. (1850, V, 98–114)

This passage, the minor part of the golden section that governs the first forty-four lines of the dream, is in simple binary form. The central portion of the entire dream, the passage presents the Arab, stone, and shell for the third time; but here the stone and shell attain their most definitive transcendental form as books, and the dreamer, although mentioning their double character, concentrates on the celestial sources of their content. The tributes to geometry – its astronomical function, its world of pure intelligence, and its independence of space and time – are a condensation of Wordsworth's remarks in Book VI (115–67). The Newtonian character of all these tributes has often led me to wonder if Wordsworth were acquainted with Newton's famous and oft-quoted final assessment of his enormous achievements: 'I do not know what I may appear to the world, but to myself I seem to have been only like a boy playing on the seashore, and diverting myself in now and then finding a smoother pebble or a prettier shell than ordinary, whilst the great ocean of truth lay all undiscovered before me.'[31] The main images of Wordsworth's dream-vision are here, as if, by the happiest of coincidences, his dream were, in large part, a meditation on Newton's sentiment. Whatever the case, the geometrical faith of both the scientist and the poet unites them in a common pursuit. Just as geometry represents the 'purest bound/Of reason,' so poetry has the power to 'exhilarate . . . and to soothe . . . the heart of human kind.' Once again, we find an instance of Wordsworth's characteristic union of intellect and instinct – reason and passion – and his refusal to separate the two or to exclude one for the sake of the other. The book of poetry is spoken of purely as something to be celebrated, a fact which does not seem consonant with its earlier function as a bearer of apocalyptic tidings. In the present context, however, it is solely an object of eternity. Earlier, it existed in relation to time, and the message which all eternal objects bring to time is simply that time must perish. In time, the dreamer may experience 'distress and fear.' By contrast, in these lines on eternity, he is content with 'a perfect faith in all that passed.' The only reminder of the imminent deluge is the Arab, who intends 'to bury those two books,' presumably in a vain attempt to save them from the catastrophe.

Of the dream's first forty-four lines, then, the greater part concerns eternity in itself or as the prior element in relation to time. The timeless dimension of the stone and shell thus predominates in the opening three movements, which, as a unit, constitute the major section of the continuous proportion in the entire seventy lines of dream. The fourth movement of the dream, its last twenty-six lines, returns to the temporal setting of the opening landscape and presents time in relation to eternity. This final movement is the minor section of the continuous proportion that governs the entire dream, and time, rather than eternity, is its point of departure. The stone and shell, for example, are no longer sublime sources of geometry and poetry but are merely a 'twofold treasure' or a 'twofold charge.' The major and minor sections of the continuous proportion in the entire dream – its first forty-four lines in relation to its last twenty-six – comprise a great ratio of eternity to time – 70:44::44:26. At the beginning of the dream, the dreamer is still in a realm of time, but he soon enters a timeless kingdom, which becomes most purely eternal in the central portion of the dream, and then, in the final movement, returns to the realm of time, in which, inevitably, he must wake up:

> Far stronger, now, grew the desire I felt 45
> To cleave unto this man; but when I prayed
> To share his enterprise, he hurried on
> Reckless of me: I followed, not unseen,
> For oftentimes he cast a backward look,
> Grasping his twofold treasure – Lance in rest, 50
> He rode, I keeping pace with him; and now
> He, to my fancy, had become the knight
> Whose tale Cervantes tells; yet not the knight,
> But was an Arab of the desert too;
> Of these was neither, and was both at once. 55
> His countenance, meanwhile, grew more disturbed;
> And, looking backwards when he looked, mine eyes
> Saw, over half the wilderness diffused,
> A bed of glittering light: I asked the cause:
> 'It is,' said he, 'the waters of the deep 60
> Gathering upon us'; quickening then the pace
> Of the unwieldy creature he bestrode,
> He left me: I called after him aloud;
> He heeded not; but, with his twofold charge
> Still in his grasp, before me, full in view, 65
> Went hurrying o'er the illimitable waste,

> With the fleet waters of a drowning world
> In chase of him; whereat I waked in terror,
> And saw the sea before me, and the book,
> In which I had been reading, at my side. 70
> (1850, V, 115–40)

As the dreamer slowly returns to consciousness in the final movement of the dream, he clarifies the double sequence of images that have appeared throughout. The Arab, geometry, the stone, and the desert are balanced by Quixote, poetry, the shell, and the sea. That the Arab has been associated with the text of Euclid may owe something to the fact that geometry originated in Egypt, and the bond of imagination between Cervantes' knight and poetry needs little elaboration. One might add that, since Wordsworth's time, it has become commonplace to describe the curves of seashells geometrically as equiangular spirals, or coils of figures in relationship to one another as golden sections.[32] Such descriptions, most probably unknown to Wordsworth although recognized earlier by Christopher Wren, have, of course, no bearing on the strongly transcendental and non-empirical character of the dream-vision. Such knowledge nevertheless attests to a lingering influence of geometrical inquiry which links Wordsworth and his mathematically-minded contemporaries to later eras and which may also enhance, for some, the credibility of the union between geometry and poetry – stone and shell – that Wordsworth has accomplished.

The dreamer's desire to assist the Arab, 'to share his enterprise,' and preserve geometry and poetry from the deluge may refer to more than a mission of rescue. Wordsworth returns to this theme in the verse paragraph immediately following the dream-vision. The paragraph's subject is similar to the last twenty-six lines of the dream, as is its length and simple binary form. At the end, the poet states:

> . . . I could share
> That maniac's fond anxiety, and go
> Upon like errand. Oftentimes at least
> Me hath such strong entrancement overcome,
> When I have held a volume in my hand,

> Poor earthly casket of immortal verse,
> Shakespeare, or Milton, labourers divine! (1850, V, 159-65)

The desire to save works of Shakespeare and Milton or to bury books of geometry and poetry strongly attests to Wordsworth's love of books, but one suspects that he is also concerned to preserve the intellectual traditions he cherished most, knowing that they would pass away. It would seem that awareness of the geometrical nature of Wordsworth's poetry, for example, disappeared rather quickly – if, indeed, it were ever established – but to those who are sensitive to the mathematical character of his, and many earlier, works of art, nothing is more transparent or less hidden than the existence of great principles of symmetry and proportion, although the interpreter is still left with the considerable task of understanding their particular significance and aesthetic impact for each individual artist. The mad mission of the Arab would seem to be a way of countering such losses of tradition – in this instance, the specific tradition which shows poetry and geometry to be indissolubly united. In the prologue to the dream, apocalypse would be followed by renewed 'kindlings like the morning.' Transferring the notion of renewal to the dream in an inappropriately literal way, one might hope that the 'bed of glittering light' may show the ocean to be the agent of eternity, destroying all in its path, but also that the waters would eventually ebb away or evaporate. The buried books would be there as hidden treasure, which, once rediscovered, would nourish new life with testaments to the greatness of the human spirit and with the consolation that eternity exists.

In sum, the dream of the Arab, stone, and shell attests to the existence of transcendental knowledge and also concerns the possibility of conferring permanence on temporal objects such as books. It is Wordsworth's view that mathematical relationships and proportions are, like great poetry, indestructible. As principles of permanence, they all tell us that eternity exists. Because they are objects of eternity, however, they of necessity signify that all objects of time must pass away, and this notion accounts for the apocalyptic element in the dream-vision. Eternal principles are thus unable to confer permanence upon an object in time and thereby frustrate an aspect of the poet's main desire, which is to incarnate eternal truths. The most the poet can do is to bury eternal principles in the 'poor earthly casket' of a book – just as the Arab planned to bury his books in the desert sand – but this is, paradoxically, an attempt to protect the book from its own content, which says that the physical form of the book must perish. At the same time, however, the book has a continuing existence on the eternal plane, can direct others to that transcendent plane, and will not utterly perish on both planes as will books that are not informed by principles of eternity. Hence, Wordsworth exerts his artistic powers to the full in constructing a dream-vision that gives us great poetry geometrically designed.

The main consequence of this analysis is that Wordsworth's dream-vision exclusively concerns its announced subject – the perishable nature of books – but in ways hitherto unrecognized. Either because the dream is so transparently clear or because it seems fraught with covert difficulties, it has elicited few extensive commentaries from critics. Of the few recent discussions of the dream, Geoffrey Hartman's and Frank McConnell's are conspicuous and are also notable for failing, as does previous criticism, to explain – or to mention at all – the geometrical component of Wordsworth's thought. Hartman announces, 'I shall propose that the dream is sent by Imagination to lead the poet to recognize its power, and that what the dreamer fears is a direct encounter with Imagination.'[33] Of course, the dream is, first of all, not about imagination but concerns an ontological question – the relationship of eternity to time and the fact that time must perish in order for the concept of eternity to be taken seriously. Hartman's insistence on a psychological interpretation is misleading because a principal aim of the dream is the abandonment of the psychological for the mathematical realm. Although 'distress,' 'fear,' and 'terror' beset the dreamer on the edge of time and consciousness, peace, a 'calm look,' and 'a perfect faith' attend him in the heart of eternity. The distinction between temporal and timeless conditions shows that the dreamer's direct encounter with eternity (Hartman's 'Imagination') is at the basis of the dream's philosophical tranquillity. Despite his avowed criticism of Hartman, McConnell likewise subscribes to a psychological view that does not account for the mathematical content of the dream: ' . . . the dream of the Arab, which certainly represents Wordsworth's growing enslavement to the visual and the daemonic, is nevertheless presented in the form of an allegory – that very form which he elsewhere eschews so vigorously and which is the most blatant manifestation of the visual and the daemonic as literary resources.'[34] What is most interesting about McConnell's remark is that he finds the dream-vision to show its author in a false and inferior mode, unlike most of *The Prelude*, the thought and style of which McConnell approvingly relates to salvationists' pamphlets.

What could be argued about the dream of the Arab, stone, and shell, however, is that it is one of the greatest passages in the entire *Prelude* and is also utterly characteristic of its author at his best. Its general theme, the relationship of time to eternity, is basic to all Wordsworth's major poems. Its form, although mathematically elaborate, is not unique. Large passages of verse, which divide into multiple golden sections, also occur elsewhere. In the last chapter, the principal passage analysed was *Tintern Abbey*, which has the form of a double golden section. In the next chapter, we shall examine what is arguably the most substantial and thematically comprehensive set of lines Wordsworth ever composed: from Book IV of *The Excursion* (32–122), the Wanderer's address to the Supreme Being on the relationship of things temporal to things eternal. Those lines, as is true of the dream in Book V of *The Prelude*, are designed as a triple golden section. The formal similarities shared among that prayer, the dream-vision, and *Tintern Abbey* also extend to the way in which the theme of eternity is placed. In all three instances, the poems begin and end in the realm of time, and the passages in continuous proportion are so designed that the purest evocations of eternity are in the central sections. In the Wanderer's prayer, meditations on his span of life surround the passage that describes the transcendent source of the scale of creation. The central section of the dream-vision similarly concerns its subjects in a purely eternal context. The 'sense sublime' of *Tintern Abbey* occurs shortly after the midpoint of the poem and – in a manner directly anticipatory of the Wanderer's prayer – intervenes between reflections on human life-spans. Despite all these similarities, there is a distinguishing feature of the dream-vision: in few other passages does Wordsworth indicate so clearly that mathematics is a keystone of his intellectual traditions and that his poetry not only discusses the subject but also embodies and expresses it as part of his content.

That the dream-vision is not an aberration but an apogee of Wordsworth's art is supported by its role in the sequence of the entire poem. The dream is a repository of purely transcendental and geometrical knowledge which the poet may now attempt to apply to his perceptions of the material world, and his failures and successes in arriving at a correlation between transcendental and empirical knowledge comprise many of the remaining principal episodes of the work. The successful episodes show many characteristics of the dream. They represent consolidations of his thought, engage the whole of his being, take the form of golden sections, and culminate significantly in the vision on Snowdon so that the geometrical triumph of his art also sustains, as a goal and mark of imaginative perfection, the conclusion of the poem. The less successful episodes reveal a partial attainment of geometrical procedures and thereby contrast with some passages from the first four books which show that the youthful Wordsworth had already participated in a natural mode of geometrical perception, one which the mature poet must toil to find and re-establish. The simplicity of the whole – that of a paradise naturally acquired, lost, and then regained by the strenuous exercise of the literary and mathematical intellect – appears to be the main fiction of the completed poem of 1805. The clarity of this fiction has been obscured, of course, by the extensive research into the chronology of Wordsworth's experiences, which does not accord with his presentation of them in the poem, and by incessant dabbling in early drafts and fragments, the status and dates of composition of which also prove that Wordsworth cheated in taking them out of their order of composition, in revising them, and in rearranging them to suit the plan of the 1805 text. To take seriously that text, however – or, better still, its successor of 1850 – opens up the possibility that one may understand to what purpose the alterations and elaborations were undertaken. It is in this light that the overall fiction of the poem and the crucial role of Book V's dream-vision yield an argument which seems eminently worthy of pursuit.

A brief look at some incidents from Books VI–XIII (1850) illustrates how Wordsworth's geometrical mode of perception gradually acquires confidence and mastery. Difficulties accompany the

alpine tour recorded in Book VI, in which Wordsworth simply –
and not without humour – describes how nature educates an
imagination given to preconceptions about the sublime and the
aesthetic qualities assumed to reside in the geometry of landscapes. The main preconception touches on eighteenth-century
notions of the picturesque: that mountains, being elevated, impart
sublimity and that valleys, having the lower perspective, are associated with more modest and beautiful impressions. The first disappointment which Wordsworth and his companion sustain is
their view of Mont Blanc:

> That very day,
> From a bare ridge we also first beheld
> Unveiled the summit of Mont Blanc, and grieved
> To have a soulless image on the eye
> That had usurped upon a living thought
> That never more could be. (1850, VI, 523–8)

The actual appearance of Mont Blanc, which becomes just
another mountain, dashes the expectations of the sublime, and the
tourists retrieve what they can of the scene by placing the mountain in the larger context of the 'wondrous Vale/Of Chamouny'
(528–9), the beauty of which reconciles the travelers 'to realities'
(533). The second disappointment of sublime hopes attends their
crossing of the continental divide: unwittingly, they '*had crossed the
Alps*' (591) and had experienced no transports of imagination. The
failure of nature to produce the desired effects impels Wordsworth
to turn against her and say, in his frustration 'Our destiny, our
being's heart and home,/Is with infinitude, and only there'
(604–5).

What ensues shows that nature has not read pamphlets on the
aesthetic properties and geometry of landscapes. Abject,
depressed, and with slackened senses, the travellers descend,
expecting no imaginative stimulation along the stream-beds at the
lower altitudes. It is here that the poet is taken completely by surprise in a chasm along a brook:

> The immeasurable height
> Of woods decaying, never to be decayed,

> The stationary blasts of waterfalls,
> And in the narrow rent at every turn
> Winds thwarting winds . . .
> The unfettered clouds and regions of the Heavens,
> Tumult and peace, the darkness and the light . . . (1850,
> VI, 624-35)

The effect of nature, which so shortly before was rejected in favour of 'infinitude,' is now so overpowering that the poet sees in the scene 'Characters of the great Apocalypse, / The types and symbols of Eternity' (638-9). In thereby prompting an analogue to the poet's thirst for sublimity and infinitude, external nature also, of course, counters his preconceptions about her imaginative possibilities. The startling scene occasions verse of great power which Wordsworth himself acknowledged in his decision to include these lines among his *Poems of the Imagination* (*PW*, II, 212-13). Some readers have nevertheless made too much of this passage by acclaiming it to be perhaps the greatest and most important vision in *The Prelude*. Despite its self-evident power as a magnificent piece of almost pure sublimity, it is, along with the contrasting disappointment of Mont Blanc, a spectacular instance of the imagination's failure to discipline the poet's perceptions into a constructive order. The imagery is uncontrolled, 'immeasurable,' and 'unfettered,' indicating a want of what the Danish Wordsworthian Flemming Olsen calls the ordered geometrical 'frames' of the poet's preferred landscapes.[35] Intersecting geometrical planes are absent in the passage. The horizontal view, which gives mankind a place in the scheme of things, is missing. The main principle of organization amid the welter of conflicting imagery is the vertical plane, which usually provides a sublime impulse but which is here a virtually vertiginous axis, suggestive of an uncontrolled sublimity that has a limited use for the human mind, although it may be comprehensible to the Deity. The passage thus forestalls the geometrical sublime which informs many other utterances in *The Prelude*, most notably that which occurs during the ascent of Snowdon and which, in one stroke, resolves the excesses and deficiencies presented separately in the views of Mont Blanc and of the chasm below Simplon Pass. In this regard, the twenty-four-line paragraph which concerns the chasm is without any internal proportions of a geometrical nature; and far from consolidating the poet's thoughts, as do paragraphs which are geometrically designed, this passage leads nowhere; the next passages in Book VI turn to other topics associated with the continuation of the tour. In the larger context of Book VI, however, this paragraph is highly significant as one of several instances recorded which show how drastically out of phase are Wordsworth's imagination and the workings of nature at this stage of his development and that the dislocation results primarily from his failure to construct geometrical correspondences between nature and mind.

In saying that Wordsworth's occasional failures of imagination are specifically allied to an inability to perceive geometrically, I am not attempting to be reductive but to call attention to one of the principal goals of *The Prelude*: the establishment, by means of geometry, of a relatively objective mode of perception that shares the authority and force of the laws of nature. Although a geometrical mode of thought is not at this stage complete when the objects of perception reside on a grand scale, its relative success is present from the outset in the texture of the poem's lesser passages. Such passages include minor scenes memorialized in *The Prelude* and in which descriptive details appear along geometrical planes. For example:

> In summer, making quest for works of art,
> Or scenes renowned for beauty, I explored
> That streamlet whose blue current works its way
> Between romantic Dovedale's spiry rocks. (1850, VI, 190–3)

The horizontal ('blue current') and the vertical ('spiry rocks') aspects of the scene create a frame for perception and a formula which is repeated later in the paragraph:

> The varied banks
> Of Emont, hitherto unnamed in song,
> And that monastic castle, 'mid tall trees,
> Low-standing by the margin of the stream . . .
> . . . that river and those mouldering towers
> Have seen us side by side, when, having clomb

> The darksome windings of a broken stair,
> And crept along a ridge of fractured wall,
> Not without trembling, we in safety looked
> Forth, through some Gothic window's open space,
> And gathered with one mind a rich reward
> From the far-stretching landscape, by the light
> Of morning beautified, or purple eve. (203-19)

Bit by bit, details of the scene are built up into a perception of interlocking lines of the vertical and the horizontal, with the 'windings of a broken stair' connecting the lower and higher perspectives. A similar approach to descriptive poetry organizes the sights on the Rhone river (VI, 378ff), thoughts on the Grande Chartreuse (VI, 418ff), the groves of Vallombre (VI, 480ff), or later, in London, the ways in which crowds of people and buildings are perceived (for example, VII, 129ff).

The techniques employed in the minor passages of *The Prelude* are developed more fully in its major efforts, especially near the end of the poem, in which Wordsworth integrates his thoughts, for the last time, into a final vindication of the imaginative procedures he has attempted to establish throughout the poem. The concluding three verse paragraphs of Book XIII, for instance, reveal what theme will occupy the poet in his future work, reassert the forms of nature and forms of perception that have animated *The Prelude*, and celebrate his discovery of a new poetic mode. Furthermore, all three paragraphs are constructed as examples of continuous geometrical proportion and thereby call attention to their role of embodying the poet's main themes in the most significant form he can devise.

The first of the three paragraphs (1850, XIII, 221-78) is architecturally elaborate. Its fifty-eight lines are in simple binary form and have twenty-nine lines in each half, but each half is itself divided by a golden section and shows – in both cases and in both the 1805 and 1850 texts – a minor section of eleven lines followed by a major section of eighteen lines – $11:18::18:29$. The structural parallelisms in this passage indicate that not only are the minor sections of the ratio linked to the major sections but that, because of the simple binary form of the entire paragraph, the minor and major sections in one half should also be compared with their counterparts in the other half.

The remarkable construction of this paragraph is borne out in its language, as Wordsworth proposes the theme of his future work and meditates on the relationship of words to the human heart. In the minor section (221-31) of the continuous proportion in the paragraph's first half, Wordsworth defends his preference for rural humanity – 'How oft high service is performed within,/When all the external man is rude in show' – and illustrates his choice by contrasting 'a temple rich with pomp and gold' with 'a mere mountain chapel, that protects/Its simple worshippers from sun and shower' (227-31). Shifting to the future tense in the major section (232-49), the poet says of these people: 'Of these, said I, shall be my song . . . my theme/No other than the very heart of man,/As found among the best of those who live . . .' If we now compare the minor section of the paragraph's first half with the minor section of its second half (250-60), we see that Wordsworth's choice of language for his subject of simple humanity is also presented as a contrast of inner and outer values: his preferred language is 'to be heard by those/Who to the letter of the outward promise/Do read the invisible soul' (254-6). His language is outwardly austere, like his subject, but it attempts to convey such inward grandeur that the poet's 'familiar circuit of my home' (223) becomes, in this second minor section, 'holy ground,' on which the poet is 'speaking no dream, but things oracular' (252-3). In the major section of the paragraph's second half (261-78), Wordsworth turns from his own language to consider the relationship of his subjects to their language. He finds that 'among the walks of homely life' there are 'men for contemplation framed' whose outward reticence hides an inner eloquence:

> Theirs is the language of the heavens, the power,
> The thought, the image, and the silent joy:
> Words are but under-agents in their souls . . . (271-3)

Identifying with such people and speaking on their behalf, Wordsworth thereby suggests that his private language is publicly shared. In formal terms, the geometrical design of the entire paragraph shows the ratios of continuity between the internal and the external, the poet and his subjects, his language and theirs, and how a common theme of inner merit – 'the very heart' – unites them all.

Having resolved upon both theme and language, Wordsworth considers in the next verse paragraph (1850, XIII, 279-349) their relationship to the workings of external and human nature. The complex architecture of this paragraph is similar to its predecessor's; it is in simple binary form with thirty-four lines followed by thirty-seven, and each half is divided by continuous proportion, but this time the major sections appear before the minor – 34:21::21:13 and 37:23::23:14. The paragraph's first half (279-312) is set in the fictional present, and Wordsworth, in the major section of the continuous proportion (279-99), examines the relationship between 'the forms/Of Nature' and 'those works of man/To which she summons him.' In the minor section (299-312), Wordsworth addresses Coleridge and expresses the hope that the poet's insights, which are 'Heaven's gift,' may be one with the forms of nature and that those perceptions 'may become/A power like one of Nature's.' That this power is able to encompass both savage and enlightening extremes of human behaviour is illustrated in the paragraph's second half (313-49), which leaves the fictional present for antiquity. The description of old 'Sarum's Plain' is divided by continuous proportion to contrast echoes of barbarism, war, and sacrifice in 'Our dim ancestral past' – the major section of the ratio (313-35) – with the civilizing powers of intellectual enlightenment represented in the minor section (336-49) by the Druids. In the major section (313-35), the 'Briton clothed in wolf-skin vest,' the 'voice of spears,' 'barbaric majesty,' and the 'sacrificial altar' all prompt Wordsworth to call on 'Darkness' in accordance with the assertion made in the parallel major section of the verse paragraph's first half:

> . . . that the Genius of the Poet hence
> May boldly take his way among mankind
> Wherever Nature leads; that he hath stood
> By Nature's side among the men of old,
> And so shall stand forever. (295-9)

The plain, however, has also witnessed enlightenment: in the minor section of the paragraph's first half (299-312), Wordsworth described poets; and their ancient counterparts, the Druids, appear in the minor section of the paragraph's conclusion (336-49). It is appropriate that the Druids, who are depicted as purveyors of mathematical wisdom, should appear at a precise geometrical division of the paragraph, thereby exemplifying Wordsworth's characteristic union of poetry and mathematics:

> At other moments (for through that wide waste
> Three summer days I roamed) where'er the Plain
> Was figured o'er with circles, lines, or mounds,
> That yet survive, a work, as some divine,
> Shaped by the Druids, so to represent
> Their knowledge of the heavens, and image forth
> The constellations; gently was I charmed
> Into a waking dream, a reverie
> That, with believing eyes, where'er I turned,
> Beheld long-bearded teachers, with white wands
> Uplifted, pointing to the starry sky,
> Alternately, and plain below, while breath
> Of music swayed their motions, and the waste
> Rejoiced with them and me in those sweet sounds.
> (1850, XIII, 336-49)

As was true for the shipwrecked geometer in Book VI or for the dreamer of the Arab, stone, and shell in Book V, so it holds true here that the poet, in presenting a landscape for purely geometrical purposes, reduces it to the stark and austere condition of a waste. In that condition, it is an elemental plane on which abstractions can be inscribed. The abstract forms appear – the 'circles, lines, or mounds' – and the next stage is to show their application to the forms of nature, 'to represent . . . the heavens, and image forth/The constellations.' The final stage shows how geometrical abstractions and the forms of nature establish principles of perception. The Druids are teachers of those principles, and, as in a ritual, guide perceptions up and down, to the heavens and to the earth, to the far and the near, to the forms of nature and to the abstractions lodged within them. The interchange between the horizontal axis of the waste plain and the vertical movement 'to the starry sky' becomes a perception of the whole, of cosmic harmony, and produces oscillations that receive an aesthetic dimension in the accompaniment of music and dance. In the form of the entire paragraph, the verses on the poet's powers (300–12) geometrically parallel those on the mathematical Druids, through whom he has just projected himself. What distinguishes this 'waking dream' from the dream of the Arab, stone, and shell in Book V is that the poet's vision is now firmly identified through the Druids with his nation's history and with the local geography which greets his conscious mind. The gap between his realm of vision and his world of daily affairs has closed upon those forms of nature which are at once the particulars of his existence and through which the intimation of universals is assured.

Further recognition of this new and now localized mode of perception occupies the concluding paragraph of Book XIII (1850, 350–78). Addressed to Coleridge, it was revised so that its twenty-nine lines would divide by continuous proportion into sections of eleven and eighteen lines – 11:18::18:29. Its minor section (350–60) recounts Coleridge's estimate of Wordsworth's mind and is followed by the major section (361–78), in which Wordsworth assesses his own value. Some of the revisions affect the final part of the major section:

> I seemed about this time to gain clear sight
> Of a new world – a world, too, that was fit
> To be transmitted, and to other eyes
> Made visible; as ruled by those fixed laws
> Whence spiritual dignity originates,
> Which do both give it being and maintain
> A balance, an ennobling interchange
> Of action from without and from within;
> The excellence, pure function, and best power
> Both of the object seen, and eye that sees.

In 1805, there was no reference to 'those fixed laws,' an addition which is more specific than the earlier text and which – coming as it does just after the description of the Druids – suggests that the fixed laws are mathematical and that this is the objective basis of Wordsworth's 'clear sight/Of a new world.' At the very least, the revised paragraph fulfils a geometrical concept – that of the golden section – and its form is now consonant with that of the other paragraphs near the end of Book XIII. It represents an instance of revision undertaken not so much for stylistic as for mathematical reasons, showing, by means of both form and language, that Wordsworth has allied himself with a geometrical mode of perception.

The preceding account, albeit highly condensed, may suggest that much of the verse from the dream-vision in Book V to the waking dream of the Druids on 'Sarum's Plain' in Book XIII describes the poet's developing meditative and mathematical discipline and his intellectual struggle to recover the forms of nature for use in a mature context. The absolute accomplishment of that discipline yields its greatest proof in Book XIV, but, before turning to the conclusion of the poem, a summary of the geometrical contributions of the first four books is needful. The only direct reference to geometry in those books is, as was noted at the beginning of this chapter, the dismissive comment in Book II (1850, 203–5). This is as it should be, for in the fiction of the poem the poet is therein depicting experiences which are prior to his later and self-conscious dedication to the abstractions of geometrical thought. Although most of the verse paragraphing in the first four books relies, understandably enough, on simple binaries, continuous geometrical proportion – which is one of the gifts of the dream-vision in Book V – is virtually absent. That simple, yet sophisticated, proportion is more appropriate as a tool for the mature poet, and its relegation to three instances – two in Book III and one in Book IV – is, as we shall surmise, an illustration of how the natural geometry of the landscape encourages geometrical procedures in the unwitting devotee. In this way, the geometrical power inherent in the forms of nature becomes premonitory of the poet's future endeavours.

It would be amiss, then, to attribute an anti-mathematical bias to the first four books. The golden section plays only a small role there, but the poet's prevailing geometrical habits take less rigorous forms which are still consonant with the general characteristics of the entire *Prelude*. In the first book, for example, Wordsworth's use of such a potent symbolic form as the golden section would be out of keeping with the representation of his indecision about what to write or with his re-creation of events from childhood which antedate his conscious appropriation of geometrical knowledge. Despite the absence of strict geometrical procedures, Book I nevertheless has a form that is suited to the synthetic powers of imagination and reveals, in a context other than in a purely geometrical one, how conscious and deliberate Wordsworth is in matters of artistry. The form of Book I is cyclical. Few readers have missed in the line 'The earth is all before me' (I, 14) the allusion to the situation of Adam and Eve at the end of *Paradise Lost*. Wordsworth continues, 'whither shall I turn,/By road or pathway, or through trackless field' (27-8), and the answer appears at the end of Book I – 'The road lies plain before me' (640) – as the conclusion of the book circles round to meet its beginning. Similarly, the cycle of time involves the seasonal round:

> Not uselessly employed,
> Might I pursue this theme through every change
> Of exercise and play, to which the year
> Did summon us in his delightful round. (475-8)

The four spots of time in Book I which have so enchanted readers occupy the four seasons of the year and extend through night, day, and twilight: the snaring of woodcocks on an autumn evening (306ff), the stolen eggs on spring days (326ff), the stolen boat in a summer's twilight (357ff), and the winter's skating episode at night (425ff). Wordsworth repeats that these events show nature's influence 'through all seasons' (582) and then relates them to the seasons of life: 'Until maturer seasons called them forth/To impregnate and to elevate the mind' (595-6). In sum, although individual passages are less capacious and metaphysically charged than the more rigorous geometrical designs of paragraphs in later books, the circular form of Book I and its seasonal cycle of time establish an effective context of the whole which shows that the strength of the poet's final goals resides in his original indecision – a motif which is also at work in the entire poem.

Although other generally formal habits of mind in Books II-IV could be demonstrated, of more specific concern to the present argument is the appearance in the third and fourth books of paragraphs which clearly have the symbolic form of continuous geometrical proportion. The first instance of symbolic geometrical design in *The Prelude* occurs near the beginning of Book III (1850, 127–69). Wordsworth identifies the passage as having great significance, for he writes immediately thereafter, 'And here, O Friend! have I retraced my life/Up to an eminence . . . ' (170–1). Summarizing and consolidating the best of what Wordsworth has to say about his early intellectual maturity, it fittingly appears shortly after he has contrasted the social and academic milieu of Cambridge with his esteem for the kind of thought represented by one of the university's most famous figures – Newton. Wordsworth's unstinted praise for Newton (1850, III, 60–3) suggests that the rational apprehension of the external universe is what really interests the poet, who, in a Newtonian spirit, arrives at the verse paragraph in question (127–69) and, in the first deliberate attempt of his early maturity to apprehend the scale of creation, applies abstract principles to the ordering of the material universe.

Continuous proportion divides the forty-three lines of the paragraph into sections of sixteen and twenty-seven lines – 16:27::27:43 – by which means Wordsworth contrasts the influence of nature in a fictional present with her operations in antiquity and in a timeless context. The relationship of minor to major sections of the proportion shows the evolution of the poet's mind from what would later be called romanticism into the more objective and classical mode of his maturity. The first sixteen lines (127–42) are the minor section of the ratio and develop as a simple binary form. In the first part of the binary (127–35), Wordsworth recounts how 'To every natural form, rock, fruit or flower,/Even the loose stones that cover the highway,/I gave a moral life.' In the second half the binary (136–42), 'Nature's daily face' yields impressions that keep the mind of the poet as 'obedient as a lute/That waits upon the touches of the wind.' The mild animism of assigning life to external objects and then of finding life in them joins the trope of the aeolian lute in imparting to these lines their romantic traits. But to stop at this point in the paragraph would be to distort the complete picture of the mind that Wordsworth constructs. The major section of the continuous proportion (143–69) is, like the minor section, in simple binary form. It shows a development from the subjective and private insights of the minor section to the universal and public laws of logic enunciated at the conclusion of the paragraph. In the major section, the first half

(143-57) opens by recounting the private nature of the poet's insights, but now they are placed in an eternal context of deific presence:

> Unknown, unthought of, yet I was most rich –
> I had a world about me – 'twas my own;
> I made it, for it only lived to me,
> And to the God who sees into the heart. (143-6)

Of his response to this world, the poet says, 'Some called it madness' (149); but he changes the time-scheme of the paragraph and appeals to antiquity, asserting that his madness was prefigured 'By poets in old time, and higher up/By the first men, earth's first inhabitants' (155-6). By touching covertly on the Adamic springs of his thought, he is emboldened, in the final section of the binary, to assert the public and permanent strengths that govern his development:

> But leaving this,
> It was no madness, for the bodily eye
> Amid my strongest workings evermore
> Was searching out the lines of difference
> As they lie hid in all external forms,
> Near or remote, minute or vast, an eye
> Which from a tree, a stone, a withered leaf,
> To the broad ocean and the azure heavens
> Spangled with kindred multitudes of stars,
> Could find no surface where its power might sleep;
> Which spake perpetual logic to my soul,
> And by an unrelenting agency
> Did bind my feelings even as in a chain. (157-69)

As his language attains public confidence, his terms of discourse become more logical and conventional. His discovery of 'the lines of difference/As they lie hid in all external forms' – a phrase which anticipates the relationship of geometrical forms to the forms of nature – gives rise to abstract concepts and their 'perpetual logic.' The next phrase, 'Near or remote, minute or vast,' introduces an examination of perspectives and magnitudes; and these additional treatments of space are then exemplified in an appropriate range of imagery that brings together the small and the large, the near and the distant, to complete the formation of Wordsworth's early artistic character. The entire passage is thus similar to descriptions of the Wanderer's early poetical character as it is presented in Book I of *The Excursion*. The seamless continuity of the paragraph's governing geometrical ratio perfectly complements the gradual and apparently inevitable processes of the poet's maturation – a subtle and smooth pattern of growth and development from concretions to abstractions that shows this paragraph to represent in miniature all that has happened throughout the poem up to this point and to foreshadow the mature poet's expression of the scale of creation.

Continuous proportion builds up the delicate thought of this verse paragraph in both the texts of 1805 and 1850, despite the differences of their lengths. In 1805, the paragraph had forty-seven lines, divided by continuous proportion into sections of eighteen and twenty-nine lines – 18:29::29:47. In the course of revision, Wordsworth shortened the paragraph to forty-three lines but adjusted the lengths of both its sections so that an extremely accurate calculation of the golden section would be retained – 16:27::27:43. Although the text of 1805 sets off its forty-nine lines as a separate paragraph, the text of 1850 – thanks to faulty editorial work by Wordsworth's relatives – runs its paragraph into the preceding one. The error in the 1850 text has been repeated until the recent edition by J.C. Maxwell, who, by studying the manuscripts anew, has restored the proper paragraphing to the 1850 text and brought it back into a coherent relationship with the boundaries of thought delimited in the version of 1805. Maxwell's correction of the 1850 text is also upheld in the new edition by Jonathan Wordsworth, M.H. Abrams, and Stephen Gill – another instance in which the poet's paragraphing and punctuation have been soundly ascertained.[36]

Wordsworth's ability in this paragraph to range from a private to a universalized description of his modes of thought and of his developing artistic character carries over into the next paragraph (170–96), which is *The Prelude*'s second example of symbolic geometrical form. That the poem's first two examples of geometrical design should be adjacent is not surprising in view of their thematic importance in characterizing the essential nature of Wordsworth's mind. Of the twenty-seven lines of the second paragraph – their length in both 1805 and in 1850 – the first ten are addressed to Coleridge, and the remaining seventeen change the mode of address to include all mankind – 10:17::17:27. In the minor section (170–9), the poet reminds his friend that he has been speaking 'Of genius, power,/Creation and divinity itself . . . for my theme has been/What passed within me' – a recapitulation which recalls the consolidating power of the previous paragraph and its point of rest in a logical and public mode of language. The major section of the continuous proportion (180–96) begins, 'O Heavens! how awful is the might of souls,' and later states, 'Points have we all of us within our souls/Where all stand single.' These 'points' – later to be called 'spots of time' – comprise the 'god-like hours' which, the poet asserts, everyone has felt. The tone of the entire paragraph is public, widening in its scope as it goes from Coleridge to mankind in general, and it thus extends the movement from private to public which was developed in the previous paragraph of forty-three lines. The conjunction of these two verse paragraphs, both of which have the form of continuous proportion and the first of which is set in a fictional past before giving way to the fictional present of the mature poet in the second, argue through form and language the continuity which has become the main theme of the poet's life.

    The quietly geometrical precision with which Wordsworth binds together an enormous range of feelings and thoughts also controls the gentle passions that accompany one of his excursions recorded in Book IV. The event is described in a verse paragraph of sixty lines (1850, IV, 131–90), which, in both 1805 and 1850, is divided by golden section into twenty-two lines followed by thirty-eight 22:38::38:60. Furthermore, the twenty-two-line passage (131–52), the minor section of the ratio, is in simple binary form, having two eleven-line parts. The major section of thirty-eight lines (153–90) is likewise a simple binary with nineteen lines in each half. The extreme regularity of proportion throughout the paragraph suits its calm and balanced sentiments. The minor section of the ratio contains imagery which depicts an evening twilight and concludes with a tranquil revelation of the poet's soul: 'Gently did my soul/Put off her veil, and self-transmuted, stood/

Naked, as in the presence of her God' (150-2). In the major section of the ratio, the poet proceeds to review his situation – 'with firm hand weighed myself' – and the twilight imagery is first abstracted and then reconstituted into geometrical components. Time is frozen in the twilight setting, and the poet turns his thoughts away from the scene:

> Of that external scene which round me lay,
> Little, in this abstraction, did I see;
> Remembered less; but I had inward hopes
> And swellings of the spirit, was rapt and soothed,
> Conversed with promises, had glimmering views
> How life pervades the undecaying mind;
> How the immortal soul with God-like power
> Informs, creates, and thaws the deepest sleep
> That time can lay upon her . . . (160-8)

In the second half of the major section of the continuous proportion, he augments a capacity for sublime feelings with a celebration of more familiar and beautiful impulses: 'Nor was there want of milder thoughts, of love, / Of innocence, and holiday repose . . .' (172-3). Finally, he returns to the outward scene, rounding off his meditation with a mysterious interchange between his forms of thought and the forms of nature:

>   the slopes
> And heights meanwhile were slowly overspread
> With darkness, and before a rippling breeze
> The long lake lengthened out its hoary line . . . (178-81)

Vertical and horizontal directions in the heights and in the line of the lake recompose the scene, and in this naturally geometrical context the breath of wind and the spirit of the poet complement one another as correspondent breezes. That the abstract power of geometry does not here possess the full prominence and role it will have after Book V is evident in the conclusion of the paragraph:

> Now here, now there, moved by the straggling wind,
> Came ever and anon a breath-like sound,

> Quick as the pantings of the faithful dog,
> The off and on companion of my walk;
> And such, at times, believing them to be,
> I turned my head to look if he were there;
> Then into solemn thought I passed once more. (184–90)

The confusion of spiritual promptings – 'a breath-like sound' – with 'the pantings of the faithful dog,' representing the world of generation, is typical of the poet at this stage of his life. It remains ambiguous whether the source of his meditation is physical or metaphysical – an issue which, in later books, is resolved in the clear interdependence of both by means of geometry and the forms of nature.

Continuous proportion in this paragraph enhances the smoothness of style and the tone of tranquillity which are attained when all parts of an utterance are perfectly disciplined and regulated. The convincing resolution of sublime impulses and gentle, delicate revelations provides a comprehensive foundation for the youthful Wordsworth's dedication to poetry later in Book IV (333ff). The chastening of sublime impulses and their co-ordination with more gentle states of mind anticipate his tributes in Book XIV to his sister and to Coleridge, both of whom helped Wordsworth to humanize his basically Miltonic capacity for beauty that 'hath terror in it' (XIV, 246). What results is a vision of the whole, to which the sublime and beautiful each contribute as parts. Each is distanced in the larger context, but what may be sacrificed in immediate intensity is restored in the capaciousness of the vision and in its relative objectivity, that quality, so prized by Wordsworth, which is marked by the geometrical union of nature and mind.

All that is given to the youthful Wordsworth in the early books of the poem and is laboriously re-established by the mature poet throughout the middle books points to the ascent of Snowdon at the beginning of Book XIV and to the realization of a geometrical union between mind and nature which is so convincing that the full power of the meditative imagination seems at last to possess a force like that of nature. The apparent purpose of the climb is 'to see the sun/Rise from the top of Snowdon' (5–6), but in the attainment of this goal, which is not the poet's alone but is to be shared, the climbers are frustrated. Throughout Wordsworth's poetry, the sun symbolically represents the absolute principle of creation, and a direct view of it is rarely permitted. Even in the culminating sunset of *The Excursion* – to be discussed in the next chapter – the sun itself is hidden: 'but rays of light –/ Now suddenly diverging from the orb/ Retired behind the mountain-tops or veiled/ By the dense air . . .' (*Excursion*, IX, 592–5). The most the poet is allowed to see on Snowdon is the light of the sun reflected from the moon. What all this suggests is that Wordsworth's conception of the source of creation is of a truly transcendent being and that a direct vision of the Absolute would, in the temporal world, constitute a self-contradiction. The existence of that source is nevertheless affirmed in the design of things by the scale of life, which ranges from the animal to the human, and by the scale of perceptions, which progressively rise to higher levels throughout the paragraph. Physical movements and non-geometrical incidents slowly give way to a more intellectual movement and, finally, to the geometrical mode of apprehension which, after the physical climbing has stopped, organizes the vision from the top of Snowdon:

> It was a close, warm, breezeless summer night,
> Wan, dull, and glaring, with a dripping fog
> Low-hung and thick that covered all the sky;
> But, undiscouraged, we began to climb
> The mountain-side. The mist soon girt us round,   5
> And, after ordinary travellers' talk
> With our conductor, pensively we sank
> Each into commerce with his private thoughts:
> Thus did we breast the ascent, and by myself
> Was nothing either seen or heard that checked   10
> Those musings or diverted, save that once
> The shepherd's lurcher, who, among the crags,
> Had to his joy unearthed a hedgehog, teased
> His coiled-up prey with barkings turbulent.
> This small adventure, for even such it seemed   15
> In that wild place and at the dead of night,
> Being over and forgotten, on we wound
> In silence as before. With forehead bent

> Earthward, as if in opposition set
> Against an enemy, I panted up 20
> With eager pace, and no less eager thoughts.
> Thus might we wear a midnight hour away,
> Ascending at loose distance each from each,
> And I, as chanced, the foremost of the band;
> When at my feet the ground appeared to brighten, 25
> And with a step or two seemed brighter still;
> Nor was time given to ask or learn the cause,
> For instantly a light upon the turf
> Fell like a flash, and lo! as I looked up,
> The Moon hung naked in a firmament 30
> Of azure without cloud, and at my feet
> Rested a silent sea of hoary mist.
> A hundred hills their dusky backs upheaved
> All over this still ocean; and beyond,
> Far, far beyond, the solid vapours stretched, 35
> In headlands, tongues, and promontory shapes,
> Into the main Atlantic, that appeared
> To dwindle, and give up his majesty,
> Usurped upon far as the sight could reach.
> Not so the ethereal vault; encroachment none 40
> Was there, nor loss; only the inferior stars
> Had disappeared, or shed a fainter light
> In the clear presence of the full-orbed Moon,
> Who, from her sovereign elevation, gazed
> Upon the billowy ocean, as it lay 45
> All meek and silent, save that through a rift –
> Not distant from the shore whereon we stood,
> A fixed, abysmal, gloomy breathing-place –
> Mounted the roar of waters, torrents, streams
> Innumerable, roaring with one voice! 50
> Heard over earth and sea, and, in that hour,
> For so it seemed, felt by the starry heavens. (1850, XIV, 11–62)

The golden section in this verse paragraph separates the first thirty-two lines, which describe the ascent of the mountain and the poet's struggle with nature, from its last twenty and the presentation of the vision of union with nature at the top – 52:32::32:20. The contrast between the major and minor sections heralds a shift from the physical and temporal world to a timeless realm of geometrical forms. In the major section, the poet constantly refers to his steps and to the act of climbing, as if measuring the time given for the ascent, but in the minor section is at a condition of rest and is no longer concerned with bodily movement. In the major section, moreover, there are common psychological perceptions of the secondary qualities of images, for the moon has the outward appearance of being 'naked' and is 'in a firmament/Of azure.' But the description of secondary qualities disappears in the minor section and is replaced by primary qualities as the firmament becomes 'the ethereal vault' and as the moon becomes a geometrical shape – 'full-orbed.' The same transformations, it may be added, accompany descriptions of the sunset at the end of *The Excursion*: the 'blue firmament' changes into the geometrical image, 'half the circle of the sky,' and the 'multitudes of little floating clouds' are abstracted into an 'innumerable multitude of forms' (*Excursion*, IX, 596–602). On Snowdon, the impact of sounds likewise differs in the major and minor sections of the proportion. In the major section, the barking of the shepherd's dog is merely a source of distraction, and the unearthed hedgehog is a reminder of animal life in the world of generation. In the minor section, however, the roaring sounds of streams and torrents support the vision: like rivers of time, they are distanced within the larger geometrical configuration of the cosmos and help to knit its vast fabric together.

The actual structure of perception involves successions of downward, upward, and horizontal movements. These motions indicate the rising scale of the poet's apprehensions throughout the paragraph. At the beginning of the major section, perception is undifferentiated, but he thereafter specifies that his gaze is directed 'earthward.' Then, as light strikes 'the turf,' he looks up and sees the moon in the heavens, after which he considers the horizontal plane, on which 'Rested a silent sea of hoary mist.' The sequence of downward, upward, and horizontal movements is, in the minor section, reversed and greatly elaborated to extend in equal lengths throughout the entire passage. Of the twenty lines in the minor section, the first seven are devoted to the horizontal plane and the appearance of hills and 'shapes' in the ocean of mist; the next six and a half lines concern the poet's upward view of the moon and stars; in the last six and a half lines, his attention is directed downward to the noise of streams, which are then diffused throughout a recapitulation of geometrical planes – 'Heard over earth and sea, and, in that hour, / For so it seemed, felt by the starry heavens.'

It is to the streams that Wordsworth gives credit for the final establishment of horizontal and vertical geometrical planes. The streams are thereby linked to the poet's own imaginative processes, and their geometrical function may help explain why there is here no conflict between visual and auditory images. Some readers have made too much of the alternation of sensory impressions in Wordsworth's poetry. G.H. Hartman, for example, argues that in the Snowdon episode the poet does not hear the streams until the end because 'his senses were fixed by an obsessively visual image.'[37] A psychological interpretation of alleged obsessions and fixations in Wordsworth's poetry simply does not explain the structure of his perceptions, however, which carefully build up the subjective and psychological mode so that it may be transformed into the more objective and absolute pattern of mathematical principle. For that matter, the transition from psychological to geometrical perceptions is a fair way of summarizing what happens in the Snowdon episode. The minor section of the paragraph is the key to the geometrical correspondence between eye and ear. The opening perceptions of the ocean of mist and of the heavens are visual because it is through the eye that Wordsworth establishes geometrical planes. Once those planes are set, other senses – such as the auditory – pick up further details of perception and relate them back to the geometrical frame, assisting, as they do in the last two lines of the Snowdon episode, in the reassertion of the geometrical context. The alternation of Wordsworth's senses occurs not for psychological but for mathematical reasons. The same mathematical structure of his perceptions was noted earlier in his depiction of the Druids on Sarum's Plain: not until the horizontal and vertical planes were established did musical sounds accompany the Druids, and then as a way of supporting the geometrical content of the passage. The same structure informs the excursion in Book IV, discussed earlier in this chapter:

'a breath-like sound' is heard only after the heights and the line of lake have created a geometrical frame for the scene. The same pattern extends to Wordsworth's understanding of the geometrical possibilities of traditional poetic forms: in the sonnet 'Composed by the Side of Grasmere Lake' the visual images in the octave and in the first part of the sestet correspond to planes of perception, and the voice of Pan is not heard until the end (*PW*, III, 127). Likewise, the sounding of Triton's horn at the end of 'The world is too much with us' becomes a way of interlinking the horizontal and vertical planes of the seascape, which was depicted visually in the earlier parts of the sonnet (*PW*, III, 18-19). In these and in numerous other instances of Wordsworth's poetry it is now possible to understand the mathematical basis of his meditative habits. Psychoanalytical, psychological, and phenomenological criticism of his poems may find its best remaining outlet in a general consideration of the psychology of mathematical form. Any resulting discovery of obsessions that lead the artist to simplicity, coherence, and lucidity, however, will be hard pressed to shed more than a tangential light on poetry that is so exquisitely clear and shows its poet to know precisely what he was doing and why.

The mathematically elegant simplicity of the Snowdon episode is found in the texts of both 1805 and 1850. In 1805, the paragraph had fifty-six, rather than fifty-two, lines and was divided into sections of thirty-five and twenty-one lines, which is, of course, exactly what the most convenient approximation of the golden section – five-eighths and three-eighths – yields. The revised paragraph retains the extremely close approximation to the ratio and introduces various other improvements in phrasing. Perhaps the most substantial improvements are to be found in the minor section of the proportion. In 1805, Wordsworth had not allotted equal attention to the ocean of mist, the moon, and the noise of waters but had divided the minor section into a simple binary form so that the lines on the torrents and streams occupied the second half of the passage:

> . . . and from the shore
> At distance not the third part of a mile
> Was a blue chasm; a fracture in the vapour,
> A deep and gloomy breathing-place through which

> Mounted the roar of waters, torrents, streams
> Innumerable, roaring with one voice!
> The universal spectacle throughout
> Was shaped for admiration and delight,
> Grand in itself alone, but in that breach
> Through which the homeless voice of waters rose,
> That dark deep thoroughfare, had Nature lodged
> The soul, the imagination of the whole. (1805, XIII, 54-65)

The purpose of the simple binary in the text of 1805 is to call attention to a balance between the details of the external scene – the moon and sea of mist – and those of the waters, which are treated as an internal activity. Having observed the geometrical framework of the macrocosm, the poet then perceives these large forms of external nature to be lodged in the 'fracture in the vapour' and concludes that the internal scene now contains 'the imagination of the whole.' The entire process shows how the workings of nature illustrate Wordsworth's familiar theme that there is a correspondence between the external and the internal, between – in his terms – the forms of nature and those of mind. The text of 1850, by comparison, is not so limited in its treatment of this theme. Its goal is not merely to internalize the forms of nature but to have them return to their cosmic setting in a unification of external and internal forces within the initial geometrical frame of the whole. The later version thus has the advantage of taking the earlier text one stage further and, by reasserting the macrocosmic framework, achieves a more complex and objective resolution of the processes of interchange that bind all forms of nature together.

Far from being, in Hartman's words, 'a unique rather than a characteristic Wordsworthian moment,' the Snowdon episode is the logical culmination and representative of all the principal themes and strategies of perception and of artistry that have been built up throughout the poem.[38] The geometrical design of the passage and the mathematical configurations of its content recall other sections of the poem which similarly present instances in which the poet sums up his thoughts and attempts to show how his mental constructions 'may become / A power like one of Nature's'

(1850, XIII, 311-12). What perhaps distinguishes the Snowdon episode is the degree to which the geometry of external nature and the geometry of the poet's perceptions and artistry are thought to be interlinked. So intimate is the alliance that distinctions between subject and object tend to dissolve in a common pattern regulated by mathematical principles. This is frequently the condition of religious art. In Wordsworth's case, however, the purpose of the mathematical pattern is not to reject the chaos of this world for the compensations of an ideally ordered spiritual realm but to incarnate and to discover a spiritual order in the very texture of the temporal world. In Book II, as we have noted, Wordsworth asks, 'But who shall parcel out/His intellect by geometric rules,/Split like a province into round and square?' (1850, II, 203-5). By the end of the poem, the answer is quite obvious: Wordsworth would, but only if the geometric rules can be incarnated in actuality itself, in the forms of nature. Abstractions that cannot be incarnated hold no lasting interest for the poet. It is on this point that the Snowdon episode is the best of all possible conclusions to the poem. More than any other passage of *The Prelude* - and in this respect one can compare it with the more literary and abstract qualities in the dream of the Arab, stone, and shell - it represents the utmost of geometrical incarnation that the poet, at this stage of his life, could devise.

The distinctively mathematical construction of Wordsworth's imagination may be unusual, but it is also a key to the success his poetry enjoys in measuring up to traditional literature. Perhaps the major triumph of the Snowdon episode, after all, is that it shows Wordsworth's capacity to deal with an unoriginal and conventional topic - the instructive and panoramic view from the heights that, whether in the Bible or in *Paradise Lost*, marks a climactic vision. The relationship to Milton's poem is especially relevant, for it emphasizes that Wordsworth has formulated an artistic character which can participate in the traditions of great meditative poetry and satisfy, at the same time, an epic ambition. The emblem of that artistic character is to be found not only in the geometrical secrets of the golden section, by which Wordsworth intertwines the temporal with the timeless, but also in the sonnet, a form which Wordsworth uses to a similar purpose and which associates him directly with Milton. How appropriate it is, then, that

Wordsworth, who discovered the existence of the blank verse sonnet in *Paradise Lost*, should begin the concluding paragraph of his own poem with the same form:

> Oh! yet a few short years of useful life,
> And all will be complete, thy race be run,
> Thy monument of glory will be raised;
> Then, though (too weak to tread the ways of truth)
> This age fall back to old idolatry,
> Though men return to servitude as fast
> As the tide ebbs, to ignominy and shame
> By nations sink together, we shall still
> Find solace – knowing what we have learnt to know,
> Rich in true happiness if allowed to be
> Faithful alike in forwarding a day
> Of firmer trust, joint labourers in the work
> (Should Providence such grace to us vouchsafe)
> Of their deliverance, surely yet to come. (1850, XIV, 430–43)

Similarly, the final speech by a character in *Paradise Lost* is a fourteen-line passage. Spoken by Eve, it concludes:

> This further consolation yet secure
> I carry hence; though all by mee is lost,
> Such favor I unworthy am voutsaf't,
> By mee the Promis'd Seed shall all restore. (*Paradise Lost*, XII, 620–3)

Wordsworth and Coleridge are to be 'joint labourers,' as are Adam and Eve – and, for that matter, Wordsworth and Milton – knowing that through providential help they all may work for the redemption of the fallen world.

With a geometrical vision of creation on Snowdon to initiate Book XIV of *The Prelude* and with a prophetic message in the blank verse sonnet to conclude it, Wordsworth begins by celebrating his own distinctive contribution to poetic tradition and ends by allying his poetical character with Milton's. In a similar fashion, as we saw at the beginning of this chapter, the Wanderer's character in Book I of *The Excursion* is built up in a series of Miltonic blank verse sonnets which culminate in continuous geometrical proportion. At the outset of *The Excursion* and at the conclusion of *The Prelude*, the two symbolic forms of geometrical design and sonnet-form are of paramount significance. This is as it should be, for these symbolic forms have the task of paying tribute to the Wanderer's love for the poems of Milton and for books on geometry and to Wordsworth's belief that 'poetry and geometric truth' are the two chief treasures of the mind. With regard to *The Prelude*'s role in evaluating Wordsworth's qualifications for composing an epic, his symbolic forms have pride of place in proving that he had finally arrived as a great poet.

CHAPTER THREE

The Geometrical Imperative of *The Excursion*

Custom suggests that discussions of *The Excursion* should begin with a rehearsal of its shortcomings. Although acknowledging the reservations of readers from Coleridge onwards by touching at the outset on the poem's weaknesses, I shall then proceed to offer a fresh look at its considerable strengths and at those aspects of theme and artistry which have not received much attention. A thorough catalogue of the poem's deficiencies is not needed here – that sort of endeavour one may find elsewhere – but it is just as well to start with what may be thought of as the principal objection to the poem: that it neglects to give sufficiently the direct experience of vision which could serve as the basis of its rhetoric of transcendence and hope. That is to say, the scenes of rural life and the recollections of the lives of those buried in the churchyard constitute the bulk of the poem's length and comprise a wealth of imagery and immediacy which does not appear to have an adequately counterbalancing sequence of evidence to show concretely the workings of the meditative imagination. Perhaps the most thoughtful condemnation of the poem along these lines is that of Geoffrey Hartman, who says that the work's 'visionary element is almost denuded of visual supports,' that its defect 'is to *show* us death and to *word* hope,' and that the main reason for its aridity of imagination resides in Wordsworth's fear of imagination, 'a fear of the power of vision that is his very subject.'[39] What one is left with is merely a visionary voice – didactic, somewhat disembodied, and unable to practise what it preaches.

A contrasting account of the visionary voice emerges, however, if one recalls that the overarching task of *The Excursion* – and of all

Wordsworth's major poetry – is not the pursuit or avoidance of imagination in itself but the employment of imagination in the definition of being and that the key word in the first phrase of that definition is geometry. First of all, those who take imagination – whether in a Coleridgean, psychological, aesthetic, or any other sense – to be the principal subject of Wordsworth's poetry are in danger of confusing the means with the end, which is the correct apprehension of being. Of course, Imagination, in the loftiest Wordsworthian sense, is implicit in Being; but the word 'imagination' is so promiscuously and also restrictively used in discussions of art and of the creative process that its application to Wordsworth's poetry is best accomplished by the addition of a qualifier, such as 'meditative,' which indicates that, as an agent in the world of becoming or mutability, it exists chiefly to serve a higher ontological purpose. Second, those who claim Wordsworth fears imagination need to recognize that it is futile to try to determine whether he thought the imagination to be inherently alarming, for the issue of imagination itself is again secondary to its moral and spiritual function in the world of being, which he does not fear but in which he obviously rejoices. It could even be argued that, of all the Romantic poets, Wordsworth is the one who most effectively mastered the imagination, was thereby the least likely to take it as an end in itself, and, looking upon its most powerful and apocalyptic manifestations, could 'pass them unalarmed' (*PW*, v, 4). Third, although it is not therefore obligatory for Wordsworth, in his greatest verse, to glorify the imagination as such, it is necessary for him to assert and to describe the source and range of his conception of being. This he does comprehensively in *The Excursion*, not only through such specific items as the 'scale of being' and the principle of immortality but also more generally in the order and quality of the narrations and their imagery. The psychological experience of imagination is also present, but not in so great a proportion to the poem's entirety as it is in *Tintern Abbey* and *The Prelude*. Now, it is utterly unfair to separate the visionary experiences of Wordsworth's imagination from their ontological purposes, for imagination is the means to being. It nevertheless seems to be true that in *The Prelude* the means are more prominent than the end but that the primary emphasis of *The Excursion* is on the ontological point of it all. If we take the poet's great theme to be how, on the scale of being, the language of the sense leads gradually and inevitably to a disciplined contemplation of the universe, mankind, and, finally, the Supreme Being, it is apparent that *The Excursion*, assuming and building upon the work of the imagination in *Tintern Abbey* and *The Prelude*, concentrates more fully on the higher reaches of that scale and becomes the most mature formulation of the theme. As such, *The Excursion*, despite having a generally lower poetic intensity and less sense of discovery than its great companion, remains the clearest consolidation of all that Wordsworth has to say and provides ways of substantiating what might be perceived with less certainty elsewhere. Finally, the relative clarity of *The Excursion* is to be expected in view of its generic tendencies. Although *The Prelude* and *The Excursion* share loco-descriptive roots, *The Prelude*'s more exalted tone reflects, in part, a desire to deal with an epic ambition. *The Excursion*'s more austere tone attempts no such ambition but, by establishing the debate as the mode of the poem, makes it a poetic successor not only to *Paradise Regained* but also, even more, to the philosophical dialogue, in which difficult themes may be developed discursively and at leisure. Here, then, is a genre congenial to meditative repose, into which the customary enticements to artistic achievement and the compressions of imaginative brilliance could be admitted only as distractions to the deliberate and collective examination of the varieties of perception and ideas of being that sustain or impair the individual and the community.

Differences of genre and thematic emphasis in *The Excursion* and *The Prelude* do not, however, extend to their common reliance on geometry, which interlinks the two poems just as it bridges the gap between imagination and the poet's conception of being. As the previous two chapters have probably made clear, the psychological workings of imagination in the temporal world attain their greatest power by submitting to the discipline of geometrical form. According to *The Prelude*, moreover, geometrical form is transcendental, provides a direct and certain knowledge of a divine order, establishes a fixed basis of all knowledge and being, and lends support to Wordsworth's belief in the imperishable nature of mind. Because the nature of geometrical thought, as Wordsworth interprets it, depends upon a transcendental ontology, it is possible that the traditionally psychological interpretations of his works have undershot the mark and have missed the essential point and purpose of what he was doing – which is, in negative terms, to transcend mere psychology. An awareness of the role of geometry in *The Prelude* may clarify one's sense of the poem's ultimate greatness, but its evident and compelling merits hardly need to be encumbered by this or any other critical argument in support of its reputation. By comparison, appreciation of geometrical procedures can only strengthen the case to be made for *The Excursion*, for they appear to be crucial to a basic understanding of its arguments. Unfortunately for the intelligibility of the poem, such an appreciation can be cultivated only if the habit of reading the work as though it were a dull novel is abandoned in favour of a careful analysis of its prosody. This poem, perhaps more than any other by its author, derives it very life and substance from the fact that it is composed in metrical form. The interrelationships of the poem's metre and language are extremely precise, economical, and perspicuous – especially at those points of greatest geometrical significance. Even in general, the poem's artistic excellence is something Wordsworth was always willing to defend: '. . . the Excursion has one merit if it has no other, a versification to which for *variety* of musical effect no Poem in the language furnishes a parallel.'[40] With regard to the poem's economy of language and the charge that it lacks imagery, he granted that it did not show the usual kind of poetical imagery but added: '. . . I am far from subscribing to your concession that there is little imagery in the Poem; either collateral in the way of metaphor colouring the style; illustrative in the way of simile; or directly under the shape of description or incident: there is a great deal; though not quite so much as will be found in the other parts of the Poem where the subjects are more lyrically treated and where there is less narration . . .'[41] The relationship of prosodic structures to the imagery of the poem is a subject of considerable importance, for the passages to be examined show not only that Wordsworth's conceptions of geometry and being are inseparable but also that these abstractions acquire purpose only through their extension to the life and imagery of the mutable world. As we discovered in the previous chapter, geometry that resists incarnation is of no use to the poet.

Of course, much of the poem's imagery contributes to descriptions of the four principal characters – Wanderer, Solitary, Pastor, and Poet/narrator – each of whom is, furthermore, associated with major passages of a geometrical nature. That the most ambitious thoughts of these figures should all rely on geometry may come as something of a surprise, for one might assume that Wordsworth would reserve the definitive status of geometrical utterances solely for those characters whose viewpoints are to be preferred. A facile division of these figures into the mathematically enlightened and benighted, however, would have detracted from the more complex issue of the poem, which is not simply to choose one system of thought over all others but to take the main idealist tradition of Western thought and show what qualities of belief are necessary for its translation into ethical conduct and use by the individual in his daily perceptions. By complicating the interrelationships among characters who share a common culture, Wordsworth focuses his concern not only on the perennial challenge of correlating principles with actions but on the possibilities of retaining a core of traditional values in common – a topic which was becoming increasingly acute at the beginning of the modern era before an almost total fragmentation had become the norm. At the same time, these four figures are, in a biographical sense, all aspects or projections of Wordsworth's own character in different stages and capacities and thereby continue the self-examination and integration of sensibility that was begun in *The Prelude*.

What distinguishes the main characters of *The Excursion*, in part, is that each approaches geometry from a different direction. The Wanderer's appreciation of the universe is primarily intellectual, and he seems, at times, to be a natural and living embodiment of a Pythagorean and Platonic outlook. Wordsworth's close identification with his Wanderer suggests that he is not merely presenting an idealized self-portrait but is describing a character he has, in many ways, already become: '. . . I am here called upon freely to acknowledge that the character I have represented in his person is chiefly an idea of what I fancied my own character might have become in his circumstances' (*PW*, v, 373). Both poet and character are, as we noted in the previous chapter, linked to Milton, whose theme of how evil is converted into good lies behind the Wanderer's role of establishing a cosmological vision which subsumes the tragic limitations of an exclusively human perspective. In the development of his comprehensive standpoint, the Wanderer reveals that his conception of geometry is part of his conception of a transcendent creator, whence issues the scale of creation or being that in the forms of human and external nature circulates throughout the universe. His geometrical vision shows that all things from the abstract to the concrete are interrelated, that the golden mean is the salient virtue which promotes a sense of participation in the larger universal context, and that isolation of being is the principal vice which distorts the imagination and leads to a rejection of community. That geometry should not only be an abstraction but become a living force is fundamental to the Wanderer's argument, as it is reported to be for a famous geometer who is one of his ancient moral counterparts:

> – Call Archimedes from his buried tomb
> Upon the grave of vanished Syracuse,
> And feelingly the Sage shall make report
> How insecure, how baseless in itself,
> Is the Philosophy whose sway depends
> On mere material instruments; – how weak
> Those arts, and high inventions, if unpropped
> By virtue. – He, sighing with pensive grief,
> Amid his calm abstractions, would admit
> That not the slender privilege is theirs
> To save themselves from blank forgetfulness! (*Excursion*,
> VIII, 220-30)

A warning against any form of materialism, these lines allude to the unfortunate consequences which attend a rupture between practical conduct and the idealist imperatives of the highest cultural aspirations. By the same token, what is needed is an idealism that exists not as a compensation for the disappointing panorama of actual affairs but as an active support for moral law so that the forces of intellectual and ethical ideas are united in an organic application to the world. In echoing the commonplaces of ancient philosophy and religion – and in his regard for Christianity's perfect relationship between abstract principle and concrete act – the Wanderer becomes subject to the obvious literary risks of conventionality and piety, the very form of behaviour which he tries to rescue from flatness and to reinvigorate as the heart of his argument. In so doing, therefore, he ranges widely, taking the whole of nature as his domain, and relies on a geometrical presentation of the forms of nature to provide a distinctive, yet philosophically unimpeachable, basis of his reconsideration of convention.

The domain of the Solitary is, by contrast, restricted to a virtual hiding-place in a valley in which he effectively isolates himself from both man and nature. Although he follows the Wanderer in having an intellectual outlook, his idealism has been impaired by the narrowness of his assimilation of the Enlightenment, of which he is a product, and by the personal and public disasters he has sustained. His attitude towards systems of thought suggests that they are nothing more than toys of the fancy, and, in his observations of geometrical objects, his treatment of geometry itself resembles that of the youthful Wordsworth, to whom, in the words of *The Prelude*, 'it appeared / Not more than a mere plaything, or a toy / To sense embodied' (1850, VI, 163-5). Some rocky configurations in a dark nook near the Solitary's abode become the occasion for a summary of his limitations. To the Wanderer, the rocks, which appear to be an overturned ship and an altar, prompt him to speculate 'That in these shows a chronicle survives / Of purposes akin to those of Man' (*Excursion*, III, 89-90) and that from this place, which shows the mutually interdependent designs of nature and man, a cosmic meditation emerges 'until the scale / Of time and conscious nature disappears, / Lost in unsearchable eternity!' (III, 110-12). To the Solitary, the rocky shapes 'doubtless must be deemed / The sport of Nature, aided by Blind Chance / Rudely to mock the works of toiling Man' (III, 125-7). Playfully naming the rocks after great architectural monuments, he then adds,

> Forgive me, if I say
> That an appearance which hath raised your minds
> To an exalted pitch (the self-same cause
> Different effect producing) is for me
> Fraught rather with depression than delight . . .
> (III, 152-6)

Favouring chance over cosmological design, the Solitary has found himself in an intellectual malaise into which the geometrical vision of the Wanderer may enter as just another fanciful toy. In all this, the characterization of the Solitary clearly owes a great deal to Wordsworth's own despondency in the several years preceding 1796, just as the Wanderer represents the triumphant poet, who, after re-evaluating geometry in the mid-1790s, was able to restore his sensibility and return to an active career.

The Pastor's relationship to the Wanderer is, unlike the Solitary's, obviously complementary and is indebted to Wordsworth's habit of uniting intellectual and instinctual dimensions of his thought. In contrast to the Solitary's affinity for darkness and confinement, both Pastor and Wanderer are associated with sunlight and expansive domains; the Wanderer, providing his individual and intellectual vision, becomes the first of those to illustrate 'love and immortality' (V, 1002), the main theme of the Pastor, who is spokesman for the communal and public legacy of instincts, intuitions, and collective wisdom which have fallen into his care. In assessing general humanity, the Pastor understandably does not appeal directly to the somewhat specialized reaches of geometrical thought, which is nevertheless exemplified in his situation and in his most forceful utterances. His church and parsonage, for example, both share the same architectural character which the Wanderer finds in external nature at large. Bold, massive, asymmetrical, and organically at one with their natural surroundings, the structures are also paired by being described in verse paragraphs of the same size and in which symbolic geometrical form organizes their disposition of content. The first paragraph concerns the Pastor's church and divides by continuous proportion into a minor section of twelve lines followed by twenty-one lines in the major section (*Excursion*, V, 138–70) – 12:21::21:33. The minor section, itself a simple binary with six lines in each half, contains an overall view of the interior of the church, depicting it as if it were part of external nature: '. . . naked rafters intricately crossed, / Like leafless underboughs, in some thick wood . . .' (147–8). The major section of the continuous proportion, which – with ten and a half lines in each half – is also a simple binary, focuses on architectural detail and ranges from 'rudely-painted Cherubim' (153) to the 'Sepulchral stones' (169) on the floor. What the golden section in the paragraph evidently shows is that the church organically interlinks natural and human worlds, representing in miniature the scales of life which traverse nature and human culture. A similar harmony of natural and architectural elements marks the description of the parsonage in Book VIII (459-90). Again, continuous geometrical proportion separates a minor section of twelve lines from a major section of twenty lines. An exterior view of the parsonage is sketched in the minor section (459-70) with the purpose of calling attention to the structure's reconciliation of contrasts: 'with bold projections and recesses deep;/Shadowy, yet gay and lightsome . . .' The major section of the proportion (471-90) is notable as description, for it almost wholly neglects features of the house in favour of the flowers and trees which surround it. The vegetation is described, however, in precisely the same spirit as the architecture of the place:

> . . . and every flower assuming
> A more than natural vividness of hue
> From unaffected contrasts with the gloom
> Of sober cypress, and the darker foil
> Of yew . . . (471-5)

By suggesting that here is a place in which conflicting images are resolved into rich contrasts, the description of the parsonage fulfils the chief mathematical property of continuous geometrical proportion, which takes its form from the principle of similitude and continuity that links its parts together on the same scale or continuum.

It is highly appropriate, of course, that the Pastor's utterances sometimes reflect the geometrical qualities associated with the architectural structures in which he works and lives. In the first chapter, for example, we looked at his Miltonically impassioned prayer occasioned by the sunset scene in Book IX: a blank verse sonnet which has its internal divisions regulated by continuous geometrical proportion (IX, 614-27). His customary mode of discourse, however, is much less intellectually insistent and is directed more to the reconstitution of basic human sympathies. Such, at least, is the purpose of his initial comments on the churchyard (V, 515-57), a scene which aptly prefaces the 'Authentic epitaphs' (V, 651) he will relate. The churchyard, viewed 'from the sullen north' (532) on an April morning, will appear 'unillumined, blank, and dreary' (537); but sunlight on the 'southern side' will promote 'a vernal prospect . . . green and bright,/ Hopeful and cheerful (534-7) and thus point the moral:

> – This contrast, not unsuitable to life,
> Is to that other state more apposite,
> Death and its two-fold aspect! wintry – one,
> Cold, sullen, blank, from hope and joy shut out;
> The other, which the ray divine hath touched,
> Replete with vivid promise, bright as spring. (552-7)

In its simple way, the passage illustrates the Wanderer's response – 'We see, then, as we feel' (558) – although it also derives much of its quiet force from its tribute to the sun, 'the lord of light' (540), the poem's major and sustained symbol of spiritual presence. Perhaps, for some, the unusual prominence of directions – north and south – may be explicable as a typically Wordsworthian way of naturalizing classical analogues such as the 'Cave of the Nymphs' episode from the thirteenth book of *The Odyssey* in which the northern entrance of the cave leads mortals downwards to the world of generation and woe but the southern entrance, facing the sun, is passed through only by the undying. However straightforward or complicated one's interpretations of the passage might be, it nicely suggests the elemental language Wordsworth usually attempts for his Pastor, who is, more than any other figure in the poem, a projection and continuation of the poet who wrote the Preface to *Lyrical Ballads*. Each of the other characters can respond to the Pastor's illustrations in his own way – the Wanderer taking up the southern view, the Solitary the wintry consequences of the north, and the Poet/narrator adding, by turns, to the sentiments of the Pastor and the Wanderer. Of the Poet/narrator's language and, specifically, his attitude towards geometry, nothing more need be added except to note that his comments on the Wanderer's thoughts – which are often geometrically fashioned – or on the Pastor's – which appeal more to broad human sympathies – tend to adopt similar forms and sentiments.

The twofold view of the churchyard, besides having an interest of its own, also partakes of the larger movements and overall divisions of the poem, which are based chiefly on the differences between private and public histories and on the contrast between subjective and objective perceptions of those histories. The objective or northern attitude treats both the objects of perception and other perceiving subjects as objects. A literal *spectator ab extra*, the aloof and isolated Solitary is aware chiefly of a statistical and unrelieved procession of death, of the frustration of any constructive hopes, and of himself as the principal object in a universe of objects. To the Wanderer, all objects of perception and all other perceiving subjects are perceived in the fullness of his own subjectivity. Even mathematical patterns, which have as much claim as anything else to be considered absolutely objective, are not thought of as being external but become living and animate forces in helping the Wanderer attain that form of comprehensive subjectivity which is least arbitrary and self-indulgent and most attuned to the cosmological order. The same dynamic subjectivity applies to the categories of moral law:

>   Moral truth
> Is no mechanic structure, built by rule;
> And which, once built, retains a stedfast shape
> And undisturbed proportions; but a thing
> Subject, you deem, to vital accidents;
> And, like the water-lily, lives and thrives,
> Whose root is fixed in stable earth, whose head
> Floats on the tossing waves. (*Excursion*, V, 562-9)

Because the way in which one perceives is obviously the source of debate in the poem, the division of the work into private and public histories is necessarily superficial but perhaps worthwhile for indicating its impressive range. The Wanderer, exploring private revelations grounded in his interpretation of nature, and the Pastor, considering the public knowledge derived from a descent into the underworld and an analysis of the lives of those at rest in the churchyard, establish the two major parts of the poem, which is a massive example of simple binary form: Books I-IV and V-VIII, with Book IX serving as a coda. The two great binary sections of the poem are each in chiastic form. Books I and IV directly concern the Wanderer, and they frame Books II and III on the Solitary and his individual despondency. Books V, 'The

Pastor,' and VIII, 'The Parsonage,' flank their central section, the two books on 'The Churchyard Among the Mountains,' in which the collective impact of death is narrated. Like the conclusion of a syllogism, or, perhaps more aptly, a *peroratio*, Book IX, which contains various recollections of the main arguments and images, focuses largely on the Wanderer's reconciliation of private and public attitudes towards the challenge of establishing hope in a world of generation and decay.

At the other end of the poem, Book I prefigures all that happens. It is, of course, a conflation of 'The Pedlar,' which concerns the growth and development of an individual mind, and the great elegy, 'The Ruined Cottage.' Composed of two roughly equal parts, it is thus in simple binary form. Perhaps, as the first book to have been completed, it even suggested the simple binary form of thought and sequence that governs the entire poem: the studies in character of the Wanderer and the Solitary in Books I-IV, and the narratives of the dead and concern for social welfare in Books V-VIII. Besides affording a contrast between the characters of the Wanderer and Margaret, the two parts of Book I also provide the poem's first major instance of the relationship between a geometrical mode of perception and the moral evaluation it entails. The Wanderer's character, as we may recall from the opening section of the previous chapter, is built up in a series of blank verse sonnets which culminate in a verse paragraph designed in accordance with the golden section (*Excursion*, I, 244-79). What that geometrical paragraph makes clear is that the essentials of the Wanderer's character are now complete and that his mind is prepared to apprehend the range of being along the full scales of space and time as measured by the timeless principles of mathematics and the greatest poetry. By assigning the tale of Margaret to the Wanderer, Wordsworth is able to suggest how the disciplined meditative imagination approaches a tragic instance of the frustration of hope. To the Wanderer, it is apparent that to dwell on any one part of the scale of being too exclusively and with excessive intensity is to cut oneself off from the rest of the scale, and that the consequent isolation of being is the inevitable precondition of suffering and of impairment of the imagination. Always mindful of the transcendental order behind appearances, the Wanderer locates in a larger context 'all the grief/That passing shows of Being leave behind'

(I, 960-1). By comparison, Margaret's obsession with the 'one torturing hope' (913) of her husband's return is what dissociates her from the continuum of being and literally deprives her of life, as if she were like certain animals that, having lost their companions, waste away. Her disease has a different origin, however, for it results from her 'excess of love' (514), from the creation of an abstract idea, to which she actively clings with an unwavering faith, and shows how a narrow pursuit of something good can produce undesirable consequences. Although her behaviour is clearly not to be condoned or emulated, it is never subjected to overt criticism or to the stronger critique of a satirical temperament, which Wordsworth so thoroughly despised. Much of the meditative pathos of the elegy is attributable to the respect with which her plight is presented: not only is the narrator's capacity to understand her misery without question, but his presentation also reveals that her very capacity for hope, however misplaced and abused, is evidence of a spiritual agency counterbalancing the immediate circumstances of her suffering. The refusal to indulge in the dramatic, sentimental, and tragic possibilities of her situation and the employment, instead, of a vast and slow-moving framework for the tale promote that sense of distance and participation which raises a pathetic illustration of common life to a higher level of speculation. Here, the claims of the individual self and of the tragic perspective are qualified and made to serve the more universal purposes of first and last principles of being. This is surely the justification at the conclusion of the tale for the explicit reference to the Crucifixion (936-9) – a reference which has often, of course, been decried, although not always for the correct reasons – for the Wanderer's view of Christ is equally superpersonal and beyond tragedy. Despite the overwhelming disorder of her affections, then, Margaret has, even at the end, some remnants of an active soul – 'yet still/She loved this wretched spot, nor would for worlds/Have parted hence' (910-12) – and her unbidden traces of obstinacy, even in the worst of circumstances, show that her story strengthens the Wanderer's faith in the ultimate sources of the human spirit.

Having presented studies in souls of greater and lesser proportions than ordinary and having attempted a common ground of reconciliation between them, Book I yields to its successor, which concerns what may be done for an extraordinary soul now dormant. 'The Soul . . . may be re-given when it has been taken away,' writes Wordsworth; 'my own Solitary is an instance of this . . .'[42] I shall discuss later the degree to which the Solitary's soul is 're-given'; it suffices for the moment to note that, although Wordsworth's view in the preceding quotation obviously misrepresents on the side of optimism what is actually contained in the poem, comprehensive grounds for the Solitary's restoration are carefully established. In this regard, Books IV and VIII deserve particular attention, for their task is to summarize and extend the perspectives and primary thoughts of their respective halves of the work. Book IV, following two books on the private and public occasions for the Solitary's despondency, is especially pertinent and has, like the tale of Margaret, the additional virtue of undoubted greatness which would perhaps make it – were it not embedded in *The Excursion* – the most accessible and clearest consolidation of the poet's major themes. A large part of poetic excellence in this case stems from the fact that geometry, although significant throughout *The Excursion*, is pre-eminently conspicuous in Book IV. Numerous passages in the book bear out a geometrical influence, but, for the sake of relative brevity, we shall dwell chiefly on three of them taken from the beginning, middle, and near the end. These verse paragraphs, like most of Book IV, were, it is conjectured, composed after 1806 and therefore represent highly refined versions of the train of thought which began with *Tintern Abbey*.[43] Because all three show a relationship between geometry and the nature of the soul, they have, finally, as prominent a role as any passages can have in asserting the principal assumptions of the entire work.

The argument of *The Excursion*, requiring that many of its most important speeches be placed in Book IV, 'Despondency Corrected,' meets its responsibilities by relying on rhetorical schemes which highlight its geometrical design. The three passages to be examined most thoroughly are from the book's *narratio*, *refutatio*, and *peroratio*. The first paragraph of Book IV, however, prefaces a sustained utterance of several hundred lines with the Wanderer's statement of his thesis or *propositio*, from which the following lines are taken:

> One adequate support
> For the calamities of mortal life
> Exists – one only; an assured belief
> That the procession of our fate, howe'er
> Sad or disturbed, is ordered by a Being
> Of infinite benevolence and power;
> Whose everlasting purposes embrace
> All accidents, converting them to good. (10–17)

These lines, which contrast with the paragraph's opening narrative remarks on the Solitary's history (1–9), also conclude the first part of the entire paragraph's simple binary division. In the second part of the paragraph, the Wanderer includes among appropriate attitudes towards the Deity an 'habitual dread/Of aught unworthily conceived' (24–5), an admonitory sentiment which heightens expectations and prepares for what Wordsworth, in his original argument to Book IV, once called the 'Wanderer's ejaculation to the Supreme Being – Account of his own devotional feelings in youth involved in it – Implores that he may retain in age the power to find repose among enduring and eternal things – What these are' (*PW,* v 109n). What the argument or synopsis indicates is, in other words, that the Wanderer is to begin his speech with a *narratio*, a review of his background and qualifications for dealing with the Solitary's despair.

Our first example of geometrical thought in Book IV is found in the Wanderer's *narratio*, and, in accordance with Wordsworth's synopsis, we shall concentrate on the heart of that *narratio*, the prayer which is in the second and third paragraphs of the book (32–122). In those two paragraphs, the Wanderer expresses the relationship of his personal life to the general course of life in the universe and indicates further the relationship of time, as it affects both personal and general life, to eternity and God. All these relationships are governed by the divisions within and between the two paragraphs, and the divisions involve the major binary forms Wordsworth had mastered: the symbolic patterns of continuous geometrical proportion and the blank verse sonnet and the ornamental pattern of the simple binary. The largest divisions rely on continuous proportion. The two paragraphs are in continuous proportion with each other: the magnitude of the first is to that of the second as that of the second is to both – 34:57::57:91. The first paragraph (32–65) basically reflects the temporal existence of nature and of the Wanderer himself; the second (66–122) chiefly concerns permanent and eternal concepts, and its major divisions are themselves generated by continuous proportion. By dividing the two paragraphs as a golden section, Wordsworth has provided a mathematically logical expression which symbolizes the relationship of the lesser to the greater – of time to eternity.

Other comparisons between the two paragraphs are strengthened by Wordsworth's use of blank verse sonnets and simple binary forms. The Wanderer's reflections on his own life are embodied in blank verse sonnets, one of which inhabits each paragraph. The first (43–56) is a summary of the Wanderer's life from the standpoint of the strength that may be found in age; the second (109–22) also concerns his span of life but focuses on the visionary powers of youth. The two sonnets are the most lyrical parts of their respective paragraphs, and their similarities and differences will deserve a full examination. By contrast, simple binary forms are the smallest and most numerous formal divisions within the paragraphs. To be aware of them is necessary, however, for they indicate parallelisms in the greater contexts of each paragraph and thereby enable the reader to apprehend the larger units of thought more easily and accurately. Most important, they build up the minor and major sections of each instance of continuous proportion and interrelate its parts so that the mathematical continuity of the ratio is affirmed as clearly as possible in the language of the poem.

In sum, three examples of the golden section account completely for the overall construction of these two paragraphs. As a result, they form a triple continuous proportion, which is the most grandiose kind of architecture to be found in Wordsworth's blank verse and which occurs, so far as I know, in only one other place: the dream-vision of the Arab, stone, and shell in Book V of *The Prelude*. In the Wanderer's prayer, the second and larger of the paragraphs is composed of three main sections, all of which are in continuous proportion with one another; and the entire paragraph is, as has been noted already, in continuous proportion with the first paragraph. In order to show how the ratio interlinks the thought of these passages, let us begin with the second paragraph,

THE GEOMETRICAL IMPERATIVE OF *THE EXCURSION*

working systematically from its smallest example of the golden section to its larger ones and then, finally, taking the largest example of the ratio that binds the two paragraphs together.

The three major divisions of the second paragraph concern: 1/ the Wanderer's opinion of what, in this mutable world, may be thought of as permanent; 2/his direct address to the supreme creator; and 3/his reflections on the termination of his own life. The continuous proportion binding the fifty-seven lines of the three sections together works in the following manner: the ratio interrelates the first (1-14) and second (14-37) sections as a unit that marks the principal division of the paragraph – 14:23::23:37 – and the personal meditation in the third section (38-57) establishes the ratio in relation to all that precedes it – 57:37::37:20. The smallest instance of the ratio, to which we now turn, occurs in the thirty-seven lines that lead up to the paragraph's major division. In this, as in all other passages, the same typographical marks are imposed on the text: a series of dots separates the two parts of a simple binary form, and a solid line indicates the conjunction of two parts in golden section:

> 'And what are things eternal? – powers depart,'
> The grey-haired Wanderer stedfastly replied,
> Answering the question which himself had asked,
> 'Possessions vanish, and opinions change,
> And passions hold a fluctuating seat: 5
> But, by the storms of circumstance unshaken,
> And subject neither to eclipse nor wane,
> Duty exists; :– immutably survive,
> For our support, the measures and the forms,
> Which an abstract intelligence supplies;   10
> Whose kingdom is, where time and space are not.
> Of other converse which mind, soul, and heart,
> Do, with united urgency, require,
> What more that may not perish? – Thou, dread source,
> Prime, self-existing cause and end of all   15
> That in the scale of being fill their place;
> Above our human region, or below,
> Set and sustained; – thou, who didst wrap the cloud
> Of infancy around us, that thyself,

> Therein, with our simplicity awhile   20
> Might'st hold, on earth, communion undisturbed;
> Who from the anarchy of dreaming sleep,
> Or from its death-like void, with punctual care,
> And touch as gentle as the morning light,
> Restor'st us, daily, to the powers of sense   25
> And reason's stedfast rule. :- thou, thou alone
> Art everlasting, and the blessed Spirits,
> Which thou includest, as the sea her waves:
> For adoration thou endur'st; endure
> For consciousness the motions of thy will;   30
> For apprehension those transcendent truths
> Of the pure intellect, that stand as laws
> (Submission constituting strength and power)
> Even to thy Being's infinite majesty!
> This universe shall pass away – a work   35
> Glorious! because the shadow of thy might,
> A step, or link, for intercourse with thee.   (66–102)

As the divisions indicate, the Wanderer's comments to his auditors take nearly all of the opening fourteen lines or minor part of his remarks and stand in continuous proportion with the major section, slightly more than twenty-three lines of direct address to God – 14:23::23:37. Within both the minor and major sections, simple binary forms demarcate further interrelationships in the sequence of his thought. In the minor section of the proportion, the Wanderer considers what immutable laws may be discerned in the temporal world. His observations, separated in the binary form of the passage, suggest that there are two such laws: one, duty, which engages the heart and the instincts; the other, mathematical thought, which appeals to the intellect. Of duty as law for possessions, opinions, and passions, one thinks, I suppose, of the 'Ode to Duty' – in which moral and astronomical gravity are interlinked – or of the milieu of Kantian and post-Kantian thought with which the Wanderer's concept probably has affinities, despite Wordsworth's general dislike of all things Germanic. But one need look no further than at the procession of simple binaries within the paragraph itself, for, alternating between passages which allude to moral instincts and those which allude to reason, the total pattern shows that the concept of duty derives from a source anterior to self-conscious rationality: the intimations of absolute order, as the major section of the proportion will describe more fully, attend a sense of obligation to the 'scale of being' and are also related to the poet's treatment of childhood as a transcendental theme. With regard to 'the measures and the forms' of 'an abstract intelligence' that exists 'where time and space are not,' the Wanderer is more explicit right from the outset. The reference here is clearly to mathematics – geometry in particular – and the language is the same as that employed in Wordsworth's other descriptions of geometrical concepts. From *The Prelude*, we may recall that geometry's 'abstractions' are 'superior' to 'the boundaries of space and time' and are 'incapable of change' (1850, VI, 123, 135, 137). Further, those geometrical 'abstractions' are 'created out of pure intelligence' (1850, VI, 159, 167). And in the 'abstract science' of mathematics, the 'reasoning faculty' is 'enthroned/Where the disturbances of space and time . . . find no admission' (1850, XI, 328, 329-30, 333). In all these passages, as well as in the Wanderer's esteem for 'measures' and 'forms' in his comments from Book IV of *The Excursion*, it is proper and important to state the obvious: that geometry is a prop for philosophical idealism and is not significant for its mechanical utility alone as a means of parcelling out bits of matter. What needs to be added is that in *The Excursion* a greater emphasis is placed on the proximity of geometry's role in transcendental thought and the moral imperatives it augments. In Book VIII, as we saw before, Archimedes, working 'Amid his calm abstractions,' urges the necessity of finding a moral component, a form of duty, which is compatible with geometrical insight (228). The present lines from Book IV, moreover, separate the laws of duty and of mathematical thought only to indicate that they are equals, for they are united later in the paragraph to forge a common bond between the creation and the creator.

A unifying principle for all aspects of the cosmos is not apparent in the minor part of the golden section, which merely calls attention to the presence of moral and mathematical law in the temporal perspective, but in the twenty-three lines of the major part of the ratio the Wanderer considers things eternal in their timeless context and presents them in accordance with a penetrating reevaluation of the scale of being. This, his address to the supreme creator, is in simple binary form, which places the thought of the two sections in parallel not only with each other but also with the binary form of his opening remarks on duty and mathematics so that the continuity of his thought is matched by the non-verbal, geometrical continuity between the minor and major components of the proportion. The Wanderer, in the first half of his address to God, asserts the existence of 'the scale of being' and then justifies its given propriety by referring to the scale of life as it runs from 'infancy' to 'reason's stedfast rule' – in other words, from instinct to intellect. No one could miss the thematic resemblance of these lines to the *Immortality Ode*, which presupposes that children are, of all humanity, closest to the eternal realm in which mathematical thought originates, but here the union of instinct and intellect has the additional function of revitalizing and imparting a new dimension to the conventional scale of creation. The same difference distinguishes the Wanderer's prayer from Wordsworth's most elaborate expression of the union of instinctive and intellectual capacities – *The Prelude*'s dream-vision of the Arab, the stone (Euclid's *Elements*), and the shell (poetry). What the Wanderer's prayer and the great dream-vision have in common, however, is that they, more fully than any other passages, establish the principal imaginative assumptions on which their respective poems turn. Within the context of the Wanderer's *narratio* itself, there are two other references to the span of life that may be compared with the present lines. Both are blank verse sonnets, which we shall examine in due course, and both are on the Wanderer's own life; the present statement, which is collective and applies to life in general, is properly the ground or basis for these more personal passages. As a general basis, lines 66-102 preserve the interdependence of instinct and intellect which the Wanderer prefigures at the beginning of the paragraph. 'The cloud/Of infancy' permits God's 'communion undisturbed' with 'our simplicity,' which has a heavenly origin; and the process continues sacramentally in the influence of the dayspring, 'the morning light,' which ranges across a scale of perceptions from 'the anarchy of dreaming sleep' to 'the powers of sense/And reason's stedfast rule' and which, as a symbol of the ordering spiritual presence, occupies the highest place on the scale.

143 THE GEOMETRICAL IMPERATIVE OF *THE EXCURSION*

In the second half of his address to God, the Wanderer considers 'the blessed Spirits' on the upper reaches of the scale of being as well as its eternal source. He views the creator as the origin of duty – 'endure/For consciousness the motions of thy will' – and of mathematical relationships – 'those transcendent truths/Of the pure intellect.' Both terms, which have wound their way through the paragraph, are thereby conjoined for the last time, but as closely as possible. In the opening thirty-seven lines of the paragraph, then, the Wanderer has traced the presence of instinct and of intellect up through the scale of being: from the mutability of the temporal world to the godhead itself. The Wanderer sums up his attitude towards the Deity in the word 'adoration.' It is an important term to the tenor of his argument, for it clearly encompasses both instinctual and intellectual motivations. As he observes later in Book IV, his thoughts on the scale of being have a decidedly intellectual aspect and are thus better characterized by adoration than by love, a word which might appear to be misleadingly restricted to a merely emotional context:

> 'Happy is he who lives to understand,
> Not human nature only, but explores
> All natures, – to the end that he may find
> The law that governs each; and where begins
> The union, the partition where, that makes   5
> Kind and degree, among all visible Beings;
> The constitutions, powers, and faculties,
> Which they inherit, – cannot step beyond, –
> And cannot fall beneath; that do assign
> To every class its station and its office,   10
> Through all the mighty commonwealth of things;
> Up from the creeping plant to sovereign Man.
> Such converse, if directed by a meek,
> Sincere, and humble spirit, teaches love:
> For knowledge is delight; and such delight   15
> Breeds love:: yet, suited as it rather is
> To thought and to the climbing intellect,
> It teaches less to love, than to adore;
> If that be not indeed the highest love!' (332–50)

A beautifully turned passage of didactic writing, these lines on the scale of being attain a clarity which is enhanced by the positioning of the simple binary divisions of the paragraph in continuous proportion with one another – 19:12::12:7. In the first twelve lines, which comprise the major section of the continuous proportion, the Wanderer considers that part of 'the mighty commonwealth of things' which exists in a temporal context. In the concluding seven lines – the minor section of the proportion – he discusses the purpose of the mind's powers in the proper understanding of the scale of being. The opening halves of the two simple binaries of the paragraph contrast with each other: the 'visible Beings' of the first binary give way to the 'spirit' of the second. Similarly, the concluding halves contrast: the 'creeping plant' – the only concrete image in the passage – is in parallel with the 'climbing intellect,' as the paragraph shifts from consideration of the scale of being below man to that which is superior to him. As the minor part of the golden section, the last seven lines also provide an example of the type of imaginative character which is best suited to apprehend the scale of being and to interrelate its humble and sublime elements. The 'meek,/Sincere, and humble spirit' called for should enable one to appreciate the lower forms of life, for humility, in Wordsworth's diction, always retains its Latinate connection with lowness – things on the ground. At the same time, the humble spirit leads to adoration, the highest form of love, which takes one to the sublime source of the scale of creation. The Wanderer seems to suggest that love is appropriately extended to each part of the scale and that adoration attends contemplation of the whole. As Wordsworth writes in the 'Essay, Supplementary to the Preface' of 1815, no doubt thinking of the scale of being which interlinks all things, 'In nature everything is distinct, yet nothing defined into absolute independent singleness' (*PW,* II, 423). The hierarchical context for all things is revealed, however, only to the synthetic apprehension which is represented here in a transcendental geometrical form.

The transcendental nature of geometry is what, of course, justifies and coherently explains the intellectualism with which these discussions of the scale of being are presented and also with which, at the end of the Wanderer's prayer to the Supreme Being, the eventual death of the entire universe is predicted: 'This universe shall pass away . . .' (100). For some, such as G.H. Hartman, 'the concept of the Chain of Being . . . is superfluous' in this poem and, furthermore, does not square with 'the apparently contrary affirmation that the world shall pass away,' a contradiction which denies to Wordsworth any philosophical acumen and results in only 'a personal and moody digest of ideas.'[44] The main thrust of Wordsworth's presentation of the scale of being, however, is to argue that it inevitably leads to knowledge of a transcendent source, from which it issues but which, being eternal, does not depend on the scale of creation for existence. The point here, as in the dream-vision of the Arab, stone, and shell in Book V of *The Prelude*, is entirely ontological and is based on the distinction between time and eternity – a distinction which Wordsworth repeatedly employs the golden section to express. Just as the words on a page are a temporal, inexact, and mutable form of evidence of the timeless geometrical proportion which orders them but which does not exist because of them, so the universe by definition must pass away in order to uphold the distinction between time and eternity. This assumption enables the Wanderer to assert, as absolutely as possible, the transcendent nature of the Supreme Being and to reach the logical point at which to conclude his ascent up the scale of being to its source. To the time-bound, a universe perceived without benefit of the concept of a scale of being would remain a universe of dead objects. Wordsworth's concept, especially in the transcendental gradations of its geometrical expression, is hardly 'superfluous' but 'glorious' because, as 'a step, or link,' it gives the climbing intellect and intuition of the human spirit a way of conversing with God.

Having finished the prayer in the first thirty-seven lines of the paragraph, the Wanderer turns in the last twenty lines to a meditation on his own span of life. Of the new typographical marks in the text, a bracket indicates the presence of a blank verse sonnet, and a broken line distinguishes the octave from the sestet:

> Ah! if the time must come, in which my feet
> No more shall stray where meditation leads,
> By flowing stream, through wood, or craggy wild,
> Loved haunts like these; the unimprisoned Mind
> May yet have scope to range among her own,   5

> Her thoughts, her images, her high desires.
> If the dear faculty of sight should fail,
> Still, it may be allowed me to remember
> What visionary powers of eye and soul
> In youth were mine; when, stationed on the top   10
> Of some huge hill – expectant, I beheld
> The sun rise up, from distant climes returned
> Darkness to chase, and sleep; and bring the day
> His bounteous gift! or saw him toward the deep
> Sink, with a retinue of flaming clouds   15
> Attended; then, my spirit was entranced
> With joy exalted to beatitude;
> The measure of my soul was filled with bliss,
> And holiest love; as earth, sea, air, with light,
> With pomp, with glory, with magnificence! (103–22)   20

Built upon two 'if-then' clauses, these twenty lines form a golden section with the rest of the paragraph and provide, incidentally, a suggestive calculation of the ratio.[45] As the minor section of the proportion, they mark a return of the Wanderer's thoughts from the timeless setting of the major section to a temporal context. They carry, however, the burden of incarnating eternity in time, as foreshadowed by the parallelisms in the first six lines: stream, wood, and craggy wild – objects associated with the Wanderer's physical movements – should be in balance with the mind's thoughts, images, and high desires.

A balance between contexts of eternity and time is attained in the second clause, a fourteen-line sentence that follows the form of a blank verse sonnet and thereby makes explicit the Miltonic inspiration of the passage: the Wanderer even touches first on the Miltonic theme of blindness before associating the springs of vision with a Wordsworthian childhood. All of this is balanced magnificently within the blank verse sonnet: the Miltonically enjambed quatrains of the octave, which runs continuously into the sestet, give way to the final tercet and its regular measures, rhetorical parallelisms, and strength of thought in a summary vision of the cosmos as the full powers of imagination unite in an affirmation of the transcendental nature of the scale of being. In its concrete expression of the incarnation of eternity in time, the language of the blank verse sonnet is perforce symbolic. The Wanderer establishes eternal intervals figuratively by correlating the span of his own life with the course of a day from sunrise to sunset, and the two twilights govern, respectively, the octave and sestet. Age is also here, as in Book IX, 'a final EMINENCE' (52); and age circles back to youth as the Wanderer recalls watching the sun when, standing on 'some huge hill,' he possessed the 'visionary powers' of youthful sensibility. As the symbolic presence of spirit in human life, the sun draws some of its attributes from the earlier section of the paragraph in which, during his address to the supreme creator, the Wanderer alludes to the gentle touch of 'the morning light' as the deific way of restoring the 'powers of sense/ And reason's stedfast rule.' The parallelisms in the major and minor sections of the continuous proportion of the paragraph suggest further that both the span of life and the diurnal course are manifestations of the scale of being as it is internalized by the scale of perceptions. Just as the sun, in the major section of the paragraph, brings life back from darkness and sleep to the senses and reason, so in the blank verse sonnet the sunrise banishes darkness and sleep, leads on the 'visionary powers of eye and soul,' and, by sunset, has supervised the maturing of the soul into a spirit, which is 'entranced/With joy exalted to beatitude.' The course of an ideally well-ordered life, such as the Wanderer's, conforms to the contemplative gradations of the Wordsworthian continuum, on which there are no dialectical extremes and opposites to be reconciled but a smooth expansion of knowledge and an ascent to the transcendental source in which the life originates.

The meditative climax of the paragraph occurs in the sestet of the blank verse sonnet. In each tercet, images balance abstractions. First, the sunset exalts the Wanderer's spirit – just as it does for all the poem's characters at the end of Book IX (590–608) – and it is worth repeating that the word 'spirit' is chosen whenever the soul, or the power of sensibility, is to be placed in a timeless perspective. Then, in the last three lines, images take the form of a simile: 'as earth, sea, air, with light.' By this means, each of the traditional four elements is invoked in accordance with the Wanderer's expanded comprehension of the limits of the temporal universe. The elements are also cited in their scale of ascending order and thereby re-establish, for the last time, the scale of being that has informed the entire paragraph. 'The measure of my soul' is, on the face of it, a strange phrase which suggests that the stature of the Wanderer's sensibility is intended to fulfil some specific qualifications. Just as it is utterly characteristic of Wordsworth to use mathematical terms, so it would be uncharacteristic of him to use such terms without implying their specific mathematical significance. The geometrical sense of measure – and this is the meaning that would have been dear to Wordsworth – involves symmetry and proportion. Not surprisingly, then, 'the measure of my soul' echoes an earlier section of the paragraph: 'the measures and the forms,/Which an abstract intelligence supplies;/Whose kingdom is, where time and space are not.' But now the Wanderer has imposed those abstract measures and forms on the extent of time and space – earth, water, air, and fire – in accordance with the constitution of his own sensibility. The incarnation of eternity in time has been achieved both semantically and structurally, for the continuous geometrical proportion that interrelates all sections of the paragraph also provides an objective framework for the poetical measures of the verse.

The major and minor sections of the third paragraph, then, contain fifty-seven lines and form, as was noted earlier, a golden section with the thirty-four lines of the entire second paragraph – $34:57::57:91$. The third paragraph concerns 'things eternal' and their relationship to things temporal; the second paragraph largely restricts itself to the temporal context. The continuous proportion interrelates the two paragraphs, as do the blank verse sonnets embedded in each. Here, then, is the second paragraph, which opens the Wanderer's *narratio* and which is discussed now rather than earlier because its internal proportions derive not so much from Wordsworth's knowledge of geometry as from his experience in writing sonnets. Again, the sonnet is indicated by a bracket and the division between octave and sestet by a broken line:

> Then, as we issued from that covert nook,
> He thus continued, lifting up his eyes
> To heaven: – 'How beautiful this dome of sky;
> And the vast hills, in fluctuation fixed
> At thy command, how awful! Shall the Soul,   5
> Human and rational, report of thee

> Even less than these! :– Be mute who will, who can,
> Yet I will praise thee with impassioned voice:
> My lips, that may forget thee in the crowd,
> Cannot forget thee here; where thou hast built, 10
> For thy own glory, in the wilderness!
> Me didst thou constitute a priest of thine,
> In such a temple as we now behold
> Reared for thy presence; therefore, am I bound
> To worship, here, and everywhere – as one 15
> Not doomed to ignorance, though forced to tread,
> From childhood up, the ways of poverty;
> From unreflecting ignorance preserved,
> And from debasement rescued. – By thy grace
> The particle divine remained unquenched; 20
> And, 'mid the wild weeds of a rugged soil,
> Thy bounty caused to flourish deathless flowers,
> From paradise transplanted: wintry age
> Impends; the frost will gather round my heart;
> If the flowers wither, I am worse than dead! 25
> – Come, labour, when the worn-out frame requires
> Perpetual sabbath; come, disease and want,
> And sad exclusion through decay of sense;
> But leave me unabated trust in thee –
> And let thy favour, to the end of life, 30
> Inspire me with the ability to seek
> Repose and hope among eternal things –
> Father of heaven and earth! and I am rich,
> And will possess my portion in content! (32–65)

The internal proportions of the paragraph show that the blank verse sonnet in its central section is flanked by nine lines of the Wanderer's monologue and that each of the nine-line passages is in simple binary form. The symmetry of the Wanderer's speech is related to the concept of architecture presented and would also appear to draw on Wordsworth's notions of architectural and of 'orbicular' or 'sphere-like' form in the sonnet. As he said of sonnet-form, when finding metaphors for its structure, 'Instead of looking at this composition as a piece of architecture . . . I have been in the habit of preferring the image of an orbicular body, – a sphere – or a dew-drop' (*PW*, III, 418). Here the comparison is to the 'temple' of nature with its 'dome of sky.' Perhaps it is not too fanciful to see in the architecture of this paragraph an orbicular sonnet symmetrically enclosed in a way that corresponds to the domed natural temple which is celebrated.

After some opening remarks on the argument from design, the Wanderer reviews his life, using the blank verse sonnet for this purpose. He speaks throughout from the standpoint of 'wintry age' – as befits a paragraph that generally has a temporal context. The sestet, however, contains a reference to timelessness: a 'particle divine' has sustained the Wanderer, and he has Edenic promptings from 'deathless flowers, / From paradise transplanted.' In one of Wordsworth's customary treatments of sonnet-form, the octave presents a subject in its temporal setting, and the sestet supplies a spiritual or timeless reality. The octave and sestet of this blank verse sonnet fulfil that pattern, with each part clearly delimited by a complete sentence. In the sestet's sentence, the 'particle divine' – the Wanderer's minute portion of spiritual fire – does not seem remarkable by itself, even though it has continued to shine throughout his life. But the geometrical interdependence and parallel blank verse sonnets of the second and third verse paragraphs indicate that the humble 'particle divine' in the first sonnet has its cosmic counterpart in the second sonnet's majestic rising and setting sun, which, as we have seen, is not only a metaphor for the course of the Wanderer's life but also a symbol of eternal fire. Depending almost entirely on the differences in their points of view – age versus youth recollected in age – and in their contexts – temporal versus timeless – the contrast between the two blank verse sonnets does not impair their unity of purpose, which is to show the spiritual continuity of the Wanderer's life. In the same way, these passages are elaborations of the form, function, and imagery of the blank verse sonnets in Book I which depict the Wanderer's development amid the vales, mountains, and sunrises of his childhood and youth. In Book I, as the opening pages of the previous chapter demonstrated, the blank verse sonnets are presented separately from the culminating description of his development, which is a verse paragraph in golden section (I, 244–79). In the second and third paragraphs of Book IV, however, the two forms – blank verse sonnet and continuous geometrical proportion

– are not separated in time but are combined and presented simultaneously, an effect which, in the prosody of the work, perfectly complements the thematic transition from a discussion of things separated in time to a consideration of them under the eye of eternity.

In sum, the second and third paragraphs of Book IV provide the quintessence of the Wanderer's *narratio* and are also among the most revealing and grandly conceived lines Wordsworth ever wrote. Judged by their architectonic features alone, these paragraphs become a model for what can be accomplished in English blank verse: Milton himself never designed blank verse paragraphs superior to these. Judged in terms of their significance to Wordsworth's thought, these two paragraphs constitute the poet's own *narratio* and review of his leading ideas. They recapitulate all his major themes, and nowhere else can one find such a condensed and yet comprehensive summary of what this poet has to offer. The level at which thought and form are here combined is astonishing in the course of a long didactic poem, and Wordsworth was not insensitive to the difficulties for art or for life which the achievement of such excellence poses. As he has the Wanderer say, in the lines following the third paragraph of Book IV:

> 'Tis, by comparison, an easy task
> Earth to despise; but, to converse with heaven –
> This is not easy: – to relinquish all
> We have, or hope, of happiness and joy,
> And stand in freedom loosened from this world,
> I deem not arduous; but must needs confess
> That 'tis a thing impossible to frame
> Conceptions equal to the soul's desires;
> And the most difficult of tasks to *keep*
> Heights which the soul is competent to gain. (130–9)

Acknowledging that it is difficult to love the whole scale of being from earth to heaven, to sustain a vision of 'ideal form' – which is what the geometry of these passages essentially concerns – and, moreover, to relate such a vision to the quotidian humility of the world, the Wanderer nevertheless would not live in a realm of vision to the denigration of the material universe. To do so, to long

'To realize the vision, with intense / And over-constant yearning; – there – there lies / The excess, by which the balance is destroyed' (IV, 176-8). Rather, the scale of being, which through its golden mean is a cure for such excesses, and the great deductions stated at the outset of Book IV must now be applied to general problems of conduct.

The ease with which the world may be despised and the difficulty of keeping heights to which the soul ascends are conditions exactly characterizing the Solitary's plight; an analysis of these conditions accompanies the Wanderer's attempt, in the middle of Book IV (466-504), to help the Solitary relate an epiphanic experience to daily life. The occasion for the Wanderer's speech is an incident related by the Solitary, who is given his finest moment in the poem at the end of Book II. The Solitary has joined some neighbours in a search for an old man who, while gathering fuel one night, was lost on a mountain during a storm. The next morning, despite an impenetrable mist, the Solitary and his companions discover the old man near a mountain chapel. As his companions carry their burden down the mountain, the lingering Solitary suddenly emerges from the dull mist and has a vision which shows the aftermath of the storm to resemble a celestial city. His vision occupies a verse paragraph of sixty-nine lines (II, 827-95) which has two main parts in golden section – the first, a major section of forty-three lines (827-69), which precedes a minor section of twenty-six lines (870-95) – 69 : 43 :: 43 : 26. The major section of the ratio contains descriptions of the 'mighty city,' 'A wilderness of building.' The section is subdivided into simple binary forms of twelve and thirteen lines followed by two nine-line passages as the Solitary notes first the exterior architecture of the structures and then their interior features. In contradistinction to the mountain-visions in Books I and IX or to that on Snowdon in *The Prelude*, everything here is glossily inorganic, metallic, and bejewelled: the architecture is of diamond, gold, alabaster, and silver, all of which is 'Molten together' with the 'emerald turf' and the 'sapphire sky.' The Solitary's vision seems closer to Mammon's Pandaemonium than to the City of God, for, whatever the Solitary thinks he sees, its effect on him is to disturb adversely his relationship to all that is living. For his part, he concludes by saying that these things are 'Such as by Hebrew

Prophets were beheld/In vision – forms uncouth of mightiest power/For admiration and mysterious awe.' The next line, 'This little Vale, a dwelling-place of Man,/Lay low beneath my feet,' marks the beginning of the minor section of the continuous proportion; and the Solitary, leaving the visionary realm on the heights, turns his thoughts towards the familiar, mutable world. This minor section of twenty-six lines is also subdivided into a simple binary form, as the Solitary considers first his own spiritual life and death in contrast to the vision – 'the revealed abode/Of Spirits in beatitude' – and then the death of his counterpart in this tale – of the old man who had been rescued:

> This little Vale, a dwelling-place of Man,
> Lay low beneath my feet; 'twas visible –
> I saw not, but I felt that it was there.
> That which I *saw* was the revealed abode
> Of Spirits in beatitude: my heart   5
> Swelled in my breast. – 'I have been dead,' I cried,
> 'And now I live! Oh! wherefore do I live?'
> And with that pang I prayed to be no more! –
> – But I forget our Charge, as utterly
> I then forgot him: – there I stood and gazed: 10
> The apparition faded not away,
> And I descended.
>   Having reached the house,
> I found its rescued inmate safely lodged,
> And in serene possession of himself,
> Beside a fire whose genial warmth seemed met   15
> By a faint shining from the heart, a gleam
> Of comfort, spread over his pallid face.
> Great show of joy the housewife made, and truly
> Was glad to find her conscience set at ease;
> And not less glad, for sake of her good name,   20
> That the poor Sufferer had escaped with life.
> But, though he seemed at first to have received
> No harm, and uncomplaining as before
> Went through his usual tasks, a silent change
> Soon showed itself: he lingered three short weeks;   25
> And from the cottage hath been borne today. (II, 870–95)

What is evident in the design of the entire paragraph is the discontinuity between the visionary ecstasy recorded in the major section and the disappointments recorded in the minor section – the Solitary's unwillingness to connect the vision on the heights with the life of the vale, his intense yearning for death in the vision, and his complete forgetfulness of the occasion for the climb. The thematic discontinuity is paralleled in the prosody: the minor section's two parts, the first of which concerns the Solitary on the heights and the second of which concerns the old man in the vale, are separated by a break in the text.

Countering the Solitary's response to his vision, the Wanderer attempts to show how the extremes of the scale of being may be brought together and, in fulfilling this purpose, resorts to an elaborate *refutatio*, in which the principal subdivisions are appropriately in continuous geometrical proportion with one another but are also skilfully interlinked by a blank verse sonnet. In the typography, the lighter solid line indicates the golden section up to the heavier solid line, which gives the proportion for the entire paragraph. The presence of the sonnet is here, as before, indicated by a bracket; a broken line denotes the division between octave and sestet:

> 'How bountiful is Nature! he shall find
> Who seeks not; and to him, who hath not asked,
> Large measures shall be dealt. Three sabbath-days
> Are scarcely told, since, on a service bent
> Of mere humanity, you clomb those heights;   5
> And what a marvellous and heavenly show
> Was suddenly revealed! – the swains moved on,
> And heeded not: you lingered, you perceived
> And felt, deeply as living man could feel.
> There is a luxury in self-dispraise;   10
> And inward self-disparagement affords
> To meditative spleen a grateful feast.
> Trust me, pronouncing on your own desert,
> You judge unthankfully: distempered nerves
> Infect the thoughts: the languor of the frame   15
> Depresses the soul's vigour. |Quit your couch –
> Cleave not so fondly to your moody cell;

> Nor let the hallowed powers, that shed from heaven
> Stillness and rest, with disapproving eye
> Look down upon your taper, through a watch   20
> Of midnight hours, unseasonably twinkling
> In this deep Hollow, like a sullen star
> Dimly reflected in a lonely pool.
> Take courage, and withdraw yourself from ways
> That run not parallel to nature's course.   25
> Rise with the lark! your matins shall obtain
> Grace, be their composition what it may,
> If but with hers performed; climb once again,
> Climb every day, those ramparts; meet the breeze
> Upon their tops, adventurous as a bee   30
> That from your garden thither soars, to feed
> On new-blown heath; let yon commanding rock
> Be your frequented watch-tower; roll the stone
> In thunder down the mountains; with all your might
> Chase the wild goat; and if the bold red deer   35
> Fly to those harbours, driven by hound and horn
> Loud echoing, add your speed to the pursuit;
> So, wearied to your hut shall you return,
> And sink at evening into sound repose.' (IV, 466–504)

The two instances of continuous proportion in this paragraph are each indicated semantically by a shift of verbs to the imperative mood. In the opening twenty-five lines, the phrase 'Quit your couch' places the nine lines that follow it into continuous proportion with the more than fifteen lines preceding it – 25:15::15:9. The phrase 'Rise with the lark' introduces the blank verse sonnet, which becomes the minor section of the continuous proportion that governs the entire paragraph – 39:25::25:14.

One of the principal functions of continuous proportion in this paragraph is to exemplify the scale of being by interrelating settings and by co-ordinating upward with downward directions so that the 'large measures' or symmetries promised at the outset of the *refutatio* may be established successfully. Quite simply, the golden section in the first twenty-five lines juxtaposes the high and low perspectives of mountain and valley. This part of the speech would thus appear to follow closely the sequence of the Solitary's thoughts at the end of Book II when he describes his vision. In the major section of the ratio – the opening fifteen lines – the Wanderer recalls the Solitary's vision of the heavenly city after having 'clomb those heights.' In the minor section of slightly more than nine lines, the Wanderer refers to the Solitary's midnight existence in the 'deep Hollow,' in which the time, as well as the place, contrasts with the mountain daylight of the transcendental vision. With advice that may strike some as being worthy of Ecclesiastes, the Wanderer urges the Solitary to align his life more closely with nature's cycles, apparently finding in the Solitary's personal habits at least one reason for the lassitude, depression, and spiritual torpor that prevent his appreciation of the interconnections between spiritual and mundane activities.

The blank verse sonnet resolves all the contrasts that divide the earlier part of the paragraph. The Wanderer sees the Solitary as a person who lives on horizontal planes – who either experiences sublimity on the mountain or depression in the vale but is unable to discover a way of connecting the high with the low. As a result, the Wanderer prescribes a vertical component, symbolized in the virtually perpendicular flight of the skylark, and shows also how the Solitary's life should follow the course of the sun. In composing the sonnet, Wordsworth has used the octave for descriptions of upward movement and the sestet for those of motion downwards. While exhorting the Solitary to 'climb once again,/Climb every day, those ramparts' as a way of bringing the sublime perspective into closer contact with the familiar life of every day, the Wanderer also recommends the habits of the 'bee/That from your garden thither soars, to feed/On new-blown heath.' If a creature as humble as a bee can range from low to high, surely the Solitary can. The comparison is reminiscent of some lines from 'Nuns fret not,' one of Wordsworth's early sonnets on the sonnet: 'bees that soar for bloom,/High as the highest Peak of Furness-fells,/Will murmur by the hour in foxglove bells' (*PW*, III, 1). The similarity of phrasing is not fortuitous: both descriptions are embodied in sonnet-form, and both attempt to interrelate a range of life within low and high contexts. In the blank verse sonnet, the selection of life portrayed becomes increasingly imposing as one progresses from octave to sestet. Finally, the injunction to follow the course of the sun meets the immediate need of readjusting the Solitary's physical habits to a healthier schedule; the metaphysical dimension draws on the larger context of Book IV. As we saw in the blank verse sonnets from the second and third paragraphs of the book, the sun's course is symbolically parallel to the span of human life, and the sun itself is regent of the godhead. Here, the blank verse sonnet also concerns the span of life, but on the more immediate and specific level of how to make the most of each day and understand that the sun which irradiated a mountain top for the purposes of transcendental insight is the same sun which awakens all life to a round of daily occupations.

Having argued in this part of his *refutatio* for the primacy of the scale of being, the Wanderer continues throughout much of the central portion of Book IV with further examples of how a sensitivity to natural law prepares for the right apprehension of moral law. At the same time, in approaching his eventual goal, which is to counter 'The loss of confidence in social man' (261), the Wanderer is using the scale of being as an argument against solitude and isolation from either man or nature. To the Solitary he says, 'A piteous lot it were to flee from Man –/Yet not rejoice in Nature' (575–6), thus elaborating on a verse paragraph we examined earlier in which the scale of being is the main subject: 'Happy is he who lives to understand,/Not human nature only, but explores/All natures . . .' (IV, 332ff). After asserting that solitude was unknown to the ancients (631–762), he returns to the present and to its rural life as a means of establishing the existence of universal forms of communion which require no special time, place, aptitude, or education. The paragraph on present rural life also provides an arrangement of continuous geometrical proportion different from those examined thus far. Its sixty-eight lines (779–846) divide into three parts, the first and last of which are each twenty-one lines long, contain didactic summaries of the argument, and are to be paired for both content and magnitude. The central twenty-six lines (800–25) concern a specific illustration, a contemporary 'Shepherd-lad' whose imagination is so developed by the natural environment that he 'is not left/With less intelligence for *moral* things/Of gravest import.' The relationship of that central section to the two which flank it is an example of continuous proportion – 26:21+21::21+21:68. In the central section, the 'Shepherd-lad' carves a sundial on the ground and thus regulates his life in accordance with the cycle of light: 'Early he perceives,/Within himself, a measure and a rule,/ Which to the sun of truth he can apply,/That shines for him, and shines for all mankind.' Having learned how to use one kind of objective standard, the boy will be receptive to others, some of a moral nature, and will 'in after-life' find 'Soul-strengthening patience, and sublime content,' a way by which his developing conscience can 'exalt/The forms of Nature, and enlarge her powers.' To augment these claims, the Wanderer, in the ensuing paragraph (847–87), reverts to 'pagan Greece' and to a 'lonely herdsman' – the ancient counterpart of the modern shepherd-lad – who hears his songs sweetened by the sun-god, Apollo: 'Even from the blazing chariot of the sun,/A beardless Youth, who touched a golden lute,/And filled the illumined groves with ravishment' (858–60). From the modern shepherd's sundial to the ancient herdsman's perception of the sun-god, the link between the de-mythologized present and the mythological past is the timeless way in which the forms of nature and the imagination fashion an objective relationship with each other, conform to the scale of being, and assert the principle of community. Wordsworth further strengthens the symbolic force of this argument about objective and universal standards by having the two paragraphs complete another example of continuous proportion – sixty-eight lines on the modern shepherd, forty-one on the ancient herdsman, a total of 109 – 109:68::68:41. In this manner, the world of time and the timeless realm of mythology are brought together in a highly original fulfilment of the function which the poet nearly always strove to have the ratio exemplify.

As is abundantly clear by now, Wordsworth's employment of geometry is intimately connected with his concept of the scale of being: the basic property they have in common is to show how parts build up into wholes in accordance with an objective and orderly standard by which the mind's synthetic powers may be most effectively promoted and measured. Conversely, censure is extended to all things which inhibit the mind's proclivity for growth, abuse its analytical capacities, and lead to a fragmented perception of the world:

> Enquire of ancient Wisdom; go, demand

Of mighty Nature, if 'twas ever meant
That we should pry far off yet be unraised;
That we should pore, and dwindle as we pore,
Viewing all objects unremittingly
In disconnexion dead and spiritless;
And still dividing, and dividing still,
Break down all grandeur, still unsatisfied
With the perverse attempt, while littleness
May yet become more little; waging thus
An impious warfare with the very life
Of our own souls!   (IV, 957-68)

Equally clear is the moral consequence of these elemental attitudes: that one source of evil resides in excessive attachment to the part at the expense of the whole, that magnanimity and humility are virtues nurtured by a sense of the whole, and that evil, because it is generated by limitations, is contained by the good, which places all limitations in a larger context. All these principles are combined in the *peroratio* of Book IV, which summarizes the major arguments on the most generalized and universal level and thereby completes the shape of the entire book as it ranges from the Wanderer's personal background at the beginning to the highly public and didactic tone at the end. The *peroratio* begins with a paragraph of twenty lines that states, in one of Wordsworth's best examples of didactic verse, the primacy of the good in its relationship to evil (here the lighter solid line indicates the golden section of the material up to the heavier solid line, which marks the golden section of the complete paragraph):

'Within the soul a faculty abides,
That with interpositions, which would hide
And darken, so can deal that they become
Contingencies of pomp; and serve to exalt
Her native brightness. As the ample moon,   5
In the deep stillness of a summer even
Rising behind a thick and lofty grove,
Burns, like an unconsuming fire of light,
In the green trees; and, kindling on all sides
Their leafy umbrage, turns the dusky veil   10

>   Into a substance glorious as her own,
>   Yea, with her own incorporated, by power
>   Capacious and serene. Like power abides
>   In man's celestial spirit; virtue thus
>   Sets forth and magnifies herself; thus feeds   15
>   A calm, a beautiful, and silent fire,
>   From the encumbrances of mortal life,
>   From error, disappointment – nay, from guilt;
>   And sometimes, so relenting justice wills,
>   From palpable oppressions of despair.' (1058–77)   20

The main argument of the paragraph is simply that, when attaining its fullest extension, good requires and transforms evil: that light provides a context for darkness. All this is accomplished by the paragraph's three sentences, each of which is in continuous geometrical proportion with the others. The actions of the temporal soul are described in the opening twelve and a half lines – the major section of the ratio for the entire paragraph – and are complemented by the workings of the timeless spirit evoked in the concluding minor section of seven and a half lines – 20:12.5::12.5:7.5. Another example of continuous proportion exists within the first twelve and a half lines, contrasts didactic and descriptive styles, and places the soul in comparison with a double simile: the soul is like 'the ample moon,' which in turn 'burns, like an unconsuming fire of light.' – 4.5:8::8:12.5. The Miltonically 'ample' moon would seem to be at the full, reflecting, for the earthly observer, a maximum of the sun's light. The spiritualized effect of the moonlight on the dark and lofty grove of trees – 'kindling on all sides / Their leafy umbrage' – is attributed to a 'power / Capacious and serene' – perhaps, in the passive construction, another hidden reference to the sun, the only source of light that could incorporate the effects of the moon's light with moonlight itself. In the last seven and a half lines, 'A calm, a beautiful, and silent fire' of the 'celestial spirit' is not specified as being from either the moon or sun probably because it is purely spiritual. Whatever the case, the slight trace of metaphorical language which accompanies the 'celestial spirit' provides one of the most elegant touches of the paragraph. Its 'silent fire' is obviously in parallel with the 'unconsuming fire' of the simile in the major section of the ratio; but, rather than work as a simile within a simile, the 'silent fire' is a direct metaphor of the 'celestial spirit.' In the temporal context, truth evidently is reflected, as is moonlight, and comparisons are approximations, as stated by the double simile; so, in *The Prelude*, Wordsworth and his companions climb Snowdon in order to see the sun rise but have a vision of the moon instead. In the timeless perspective, however, one is at the source of truth, comparisons are direct, and metaphors drawn from objects in time and space may be, as in the present example, excluded as inappropriate. The purpose of continuous geometrical proportion in this paragraph is to unite such distinctions and to show the interdependence of concretions and abstractions and of darkness and light so that the objective and ideal form of the entire paragraph is enabled to express the ascent of soul to spirit along the scale of being.

Between the preceding verse paragraph and the line 'So build we up the Being that we are' (1264), the Wanderer answers a challenge to apply the soul's faculties to daily life. He employs the *peroratio* of Book IV to urge again that the universe be interpreted in accordance with the scale of creation, and to argue that communion 'with the Forms/Of nature' (1208-9) orders the soul (the role of geometrical order in those forms having been stated at the beginning of the book), that such communion provides the best preparation for an appreciation of the forms of human nature, and that all activities, including science, can thereby exercise a power which is no longer 'Chained to its object in brute slavery' (1256) but is free to aid the mind's natural proclivity to apprehend everenlarging relationships and interconnections among all things:

> Whate'er we see,
> Or feel, shall tend to quicken and refine
> The humblest functions of corporeal sense;
> Shall fix, in calmer seats of moral strength,
> Earthly desires; and raise, to loftier heights
> Of divine love, our intellectual soul. (1270-5)

Crowning the argument of the book, each of the phrases and lines just cited is adapted, without much revision, from passages composed in 1797-8. The incorporation of these passages into a fully mature composition, most of which was written after 1806, yields further evidence, as does *Tintern Abbey*, that Wordsworth had formulated his major themes and his geometrically supported transcendentalism by the late 1790s. It is as if, in deciding to conclude Book IV with some of the lines he had written shortly after his careful reconsideration of geometry and the restoration to him of intellectual values, he were paying tribute to his own moment of greatest success in confronting the Solitary within himself.

Biographical speculations aside, it is clear that the fairly abstract principles of Book IV are not confined to the optimum conditions depicted by the Wanderer but extend to the 'Authentic epitaphs' of Books V–VIII. The presence of these principles in the epitaphs helps to account for their distance from the immediacy of grief, for their strangely moving qualities despite low levels of individualized human interest, and for, in sum, their cumulative effect of showing an approach to death that is much the same as the treatment of life and of the forms of nature earlier in the poem. More specifically, the tone of the epitaphs is a consequence of the steadfastness with which the principle of immortality is assumed and of the way in which the synthetic powers of mind required for a proper apprehension of the scale of being are transferred to the social scale represented by those buried in the churchyard. Before attempting the series of epitaphs, the Pastor, at the end of Book V, states the principle of immortality as his thesis – 'That life is love and immortality, / The being one, and one the element' (1002–3):

> Life, I repeat, is energy of love
> Divine or human; exercised in pain,
> In strife, in tribulation; and ordained,
> If so approved and sanctified, to pass,
> Through shades and silent rest, to endless joy. (V, 1012–6)

Evidence of the principle is partly suggested not only by ideals and virtues, the dedication to which does not satisfy or arise from any apparent material conditions, but by an abuse of the same powers:

> For, strength to persevere and to support,
> And energy to conquer and repel –
> These elements of virtue, that declare

The native grandeur of the human soul –
Are oft-times not unprofitably shown
In the perverseness of a selfish course . . . (VI, 663–8)

Accordingly, many epitaphs describe those who, by their fidelity to mistaken goals, unwittingly provide indications of spiritual strength, which, in another context, could testify to the nobility and power of the soul. The reluctance to make too much of such errors is not a result of a partisan's desire to gloss over the misdeeds of the rural populace but reflects, instead, the prevailing character of the epitaphs as studies not so much in psychological or social questions – which are usually confused with ethics – as in ontological values. The counterpart of Wordsworth's principle of immortality is, after all, an ontological principle which states that the existence of immortality requires all things in time to perish but that some things, such as certain moral virtues and mathematics, have an eternal basis and serve as links between temporal and timeless realms. Death itself becomes important chiefly as a means of affirming this principle and of providing an occasion on which the manifestations of the deathless properties associated with being may be contemplated without undue distraction. By means of an ontological principle, then, the epitaphs take death for granted as a necessary support for immortality and thereby attain an attitude of dispassionate tranquillity.

The epitaphs are further distanced from the social and psychological immediacy of life and death by an application of the scale of being to the specific instance of the churchyard and by an equation between scales of humanity and vegetation. The scale of humanity itself in the narrations draws upon a large range of backgrounds, implying thereby that exposure to a wide range of being develops the mind's synthetic powers. In this regard, the portraits of the miner (VI, 212ff), the deaf dalesman (VII, 395ff), and the blind man (VII, 482ff) are especially pertinent for showing the various consequences which attend those who are apparently cut off from a full appreciation of the scale of being. By contrast, the association of people with trees, flowers, and plants seems designed to heighten the sense of community people have with one another and with nature and to turn attention from the individual to the larger pattern in which the individual participates. The oak, the sycamore, the elm, the thistle – to name only a few – all have human counterparts; and from each to each goes the spry and ageless woodcutter, an 'old Man' (VII, 587) yet 'green in age' (VII, 625), the figure of death, of whom it is added that 'like the haughty Spoilers of the world,/This keen Destroyer, in his turn, must fall' (VII, 630-1), bowing to the imperative of the ontological principle. As a means of establishing community between nature and man, then, the equation between trees and people serves a larger purpose, similar to that served by Milton's ontological tree of life in *Paradise Lost* (V, 469ff). The full import of this motif becomes evident at the beginning of Book IX of *The Excursion* in which the Wanderer celebrates the spirit that exists in 'every Form of being' (1), 'subsists/In all things' (4-5), and 'from link to link . . . circulates, the Soul of all the worlds' (14-15). The same principle of a synthesizing vision holds true for the composition of the individual epitaph, the goal of which should be to focus on the totality of a person's being and to include references to the universal aspirations that bind each person to the race. As Wordsworth says in the *Essay Upon Epitaphs*: 'The character of a deceased friend or beloved kinsman is not seen, no – nor ought to be seen, otherwise than as a tree through a tender haze or a luminous mist, that spiritualizes and beautifies it; that takes away, indeed, but only to the end that the parts which are not abstracted may appear more dignified and lovely; may impress and affect the more . . . It suffices, therefore, that the trunk and main branches of the worth of the deceased be boldly and unaffectedly represented. Any further detail, minutely and scrupulously pursued, especially if this be done with laborious and antithetic discriminations, must inevitably frustrate its own purpose . . .' (*PW*, V, 452, 453). In sum, the plants and trees of *The Excursion* constitute a wealth of substantial imagery that enhances the meditative distance of the epitaphs, assists in the implementation of the synthesizing powers required by the scale of being, and helps to suppress dramatic, satirical, and generally psychological implications in favour of ontological significance.

 Most of these characteristics are evident in the following example, which, drawn from Book VI, has the additional interest of showing how geometry is associated with the kind of epitaph Wordsworth took pains to defend. The epitaph in question (VI,

392-521) exemplifies the movement from social to ontological considerations and concerns the mellowing rivalry between a Scotsman and an Englishman, both of whom, because of contrasting political disappointments, have sought refuge and solitude in the country of the lakes. The social backgrounds of these two figures – who are amusingly described as the 'flaming Jacobite/And sullen Hanoverian' (458-9) – and the 'very bickerings' (474) that bind them together 'in constant fellowship' (472) promote an unlikely but increasingly profound sense of mutual respect which runs counter to their individual solitariness and which, in the churchyard, where 'One spirit seldom failed to extend its sway/Over both minds' (480-1), grows into a deeper and more universal communion that rises above 'The field of selfish difference and dispute' (485). The resolution of the epitaph occurs in its last verse paragraph (491-521), a passage divided by golden section into twelve and nineteen lines – 12:19::19:31 – and the last nineteen lines of which, dividing into segments of twelve and seven, are themselves another example of the ratio – 19:12::12:7. The opening twelve lines, the minor section of the entire paragraph, associate the two testy gentlemen with a yew-tree:

> 'There live who yet remember here to have seen
> Their courtly figures, seated on the stump
> Of an old yew, their favourite resting-place.
> But as the remnant of the long-lived tree
> Was disappearing by a swift decay,   5
> They, with joint care, determined to erect,
> Upon its site, a dial, that might stand
> For public use preserved, and thus survive
> As their own private monument: for this
> Was the particular spot, in which they wished   10
> (And Heaven was pleased to accomplish the desire)
> That, undivided, their remains should lie. (491-502)

The yew-tree seems doubly appropriate, not only for its traditional connotations of death and immortality but also for serving as a reminder that such trees provided wood for weapons used in past conflicts between England and Scotland – conflicts, like the old yew itself, 'disappearing by a swift decay' and finding a strange counterpart in the two old gentlemen who have now joined together in a common purpose and destiny. More basic than its role as a witness to the troubled time of human history is the yew-tree's relationship to the sun and to the consequent measurement of the objective time of the natural universe, a function which is continued in the transformation of the organic into the architectural – of yew-tree into sundial – and which may prompt a reflection on the difference between time and its source:

> So, where the mouldered tree had stood, was raised
> Yon structure, framing, with the ascent of steps
> That to the decorated pillar lead,   15
> A work of art more sumptuous than might seem
> To suit this place; yet built in no proud scorn
> Of rustic homeliness; they only aimed
> To ensure for it respectful guardianship.
> Around the margin of the plate, whereon   20
> The shadow falls to note the stealthy hours,
> Winds an inscriptive legend.' - At these words
> Thither we turned; and gathered, as we read,
> The appropriate sense, in Latin numbers couched:
> '*Time flies; it is his melancholy task*   25
> *To bring, and bear away, delusive hopes,*
> *And re-produce the troubles he destroys.*
> *But, while his blindness thus is occupied,*
> *Discerning Mortal! do thou serve the will*
> *Of Time's eternal Master, and that peace,*   30
> *Which the world wants, shall be for thee confirmed!*' (503–21)

The elemental sentiment expressed by the inscription in the final seven lines complements its geometrical design, which is the minor section of the continuous proportion that marks out the nineteen-line passage concerning the sundial itself. Here, as in another passage examined earlier which also refers to a sundial (IV, 800–25), monumental and mathematical expressions combine to show that architecture and geometry not only can reveal an objective standard of time but that time, in its turn, is made to serve their timeless forms. The inscription is at once the most intellectually abstract and the most universal part of the entire epitaph in its embodiment of basic human desires. As the point which is farthest from the immediate circumstances of the two old gentlemen and closest to a pure contemplation of being, the inscription invokes the ontological significance of geometry to complete the shape of the epitaph in its transition from individual to general aspects of life and in its fulfilment of the principles upon which Wordsworth based his ideal for this type of literary endeavour.

In the midst of all these lofty principles and ideals, the protesting Solitary, who is loath to loosen his grip on human misery, may strike some as a warm and welcome figure. Of the epitaph on the two old gentlemen, the Solitary is most struck by the bitter failure of their social and political ambitions and, instead of following the idealism quietly embodied in the conclusion of the epitaph, finds another example of his fatalistic bent and 'Of poor humanity's afflicted will/Struggling in vain with ruthless destiny' (VI, 556-7). Although agreeing with the Pastor and Wanderer that the narratives should not be subject to analytical wit but to a more comprehensive argument – and, in this respect, certain epitaphs, such as that on the bright woman (VI, 675ff) seem designed to prove that even material suited for satire can yield meditative fruit – the Solitary, in this and in all other cases, cannot resist the notion that joy and suffering are ultimately in vain. In his last speech of the poem, he finds an emblem of experience in the dying fire that had been kindled near an island's shoreline:

> The fire, that burned so brightly to our wish,
> Where is it now? – Deserted on the beach –
> Dying, or dead! Nor shall the fanning breeze
> Revive its ashes. What care we for this,
> Whose ends are gained? Behold an emblem here
> Of one day's pleasure, and all mortal joys! (IX, 550-5)

Maintaining his tragic sense to the last, the Solitary is, at best – as numerous readers have noted – only partially restored. Although Wordsworth's characterization of the Solitary is customarily taken as a tribute to the poet's honesty and an admission of his inability to complete the poem, I do not see how he could have written differently: a facile, pat conversion of the Solitary after only a couple of days' acquaintance with the Wanderer would have been untrue both to Wordsworth's respect for human behaviour, as he knew it, and to his entire aesthetic, which requires a gradual progression along a continuum, a meditative, rather than a dramatic, resolution without sharp or antithetical changes. It is probably for this reason that *The Excursion* was not intended to complete more than the first stage of the Solitary's restoration: to another poem, as indicated by the conditional promise of 'future labours' (IX, 796), would be assigned the task of chronicling his further progress. The unexpected form of that future work, however, will be considered at the conclusion of this chapter.

For the present, it is worth noting the larger context for the Solitary's emblem of human life as a fading fire. Throughout the poem, human life has been correlated with the course of the sun, and the fading fire of a magnificent sunset presents itself to the poem's characters after they have returned from the island and climbed a green hill overlooking a valley. The ensuing display by the forms of nature themselves appears to belie the Solitary's melancholic sentiments:

> Soft heath this elevated spot supplied,
> And choice of moss-clad stones, whereon we couched
> Or sate reclined; admiring quietly
> The general aspect of the scene; but each
> Not seldom over anxious to make known   5
> His own discoveries; or to favourite points
> Directing notice, merely from a wish
> To impart a joy, imperfect while unshared.
> That rapturous moment never shall I forget
> When these particular interests were effaced   10
> From every mind! – Already had the sun,
> Sinking with less than ordinary state,
> Attained his western bound; but rays of light –
> Now suddenly diverging from the orb
> Retired behind the mountain-tops or veiled   15
> By the dense air – shot upwards to the crown
> Of the blue firmament – aloft, and wide:
> And multitudes of little floating clouds,
> Through their ethereal texture pierced – ere we,
> Who saw, of change were conscious – had become 20

> Vivid as fire; clouds separately poised, –
> Innumerable multitude of forms
> Scattered through half the circle of the sky;
> And giving back, and shedding each on each,
> With prodigal communion, the bright hues   25
> Which from the unapparent fount of glory
> They had imbibed, and ceased not to receive.
> That which the heavens displayed, the liquid deep
> Repeated; but with unity sublime! (IX, 580–608)

This paragraph, spoken by the Poet/narrator, is divided by a golden section that correlates the lives of all the characters in the poem – and, by implication, human life generally – with the 'multitudes of little floating clouds,' the 'Innumerable multitude of forms,' that become 'Vivid as fire' in the receding sunlight – 10.5:18.5::18.5:29. The comparison between the forms of human and external nature reflects Wordsworth's ability to set the minor and major sections of the continuous proportion in exact parallel with each other, as their sentiments or images move from an external and descriptive pole to one that is internalized and abstract. In the minor section of the ratio, the narrator describes first 'The general aspect of the scene' and the attitudes of his companions. Similarly, a general description of the sunset introduces the major section of the ratio. When the narrator and his companions eventually move from 'particular interests' to a deeper and more synoptic appreciation of 'That rapturous moment,' the influence of the scene upon the mind corresponds to the mirroring of imagery at the conclusion of the major section: 'That which the heavens displayed, the liquid deep/Repeated; but with unity sublime!' In short, as though nature were demonstrating how the mind perceives, the reflections on the lake – which is metaphorically equated with the mind – appear to unify the scene. On another and specifically transcendental level, however, the 'unity sublime' is effected by the geometry of the passage, just as, in the sunset from the Wanderer's blank verse sonnet in Book IV, it was the 'measure' of the soul that saw the elements infused 'With pomp, with glory, with magnificence.'

To this may be added that Wordsworth's treatment of the sunset itself is reminiscent of his procedures in the Snowdon episode from

The Prelude and follows precisely his meditative habit of allowing the abundant details of a scene to be reduced and abstracted into their geometrical composition. The clouds give way to a 'multitude of forms,' and 'the crown/Of the blue firmament' is distilled into 'half the circle of the sky.' Here, as on Snowdon, the translation of images into geometrical forms – of secondary into primary qualities – imparts a psychological sense of elevated austerity to the scene for the purpose of showing a transference of activity from the mutable world to the timeless realm and its geometrical measures. Although neither here nor on Snowdon is the source of light – in keeping with its connotations of transcendence – apprehended directly, the general role of light in the two poems differs markedly. *The Prelude* seems notable for the prominence of its starry skies and moonlit night-scenes, with a major attempt at a sunrise being saved in name, at least, for the last book of the poem. In *The Excursion*, the symbolic sun is sustained throughout as a principal motif in the design of the work, which reveals overarching sunrises and sunsets at the beginnings and ends of books as well as in the development of its central character, the Wanderer, whose career spans twilight at dawn (I, 197ff) to the dusk of the poem's conclusion. Other than this, the final pages of the two poems are remarkably similar, showing, in each case, how private thoughts give way to public participation in the scale of being and how the vision is conducive to a discussion of community, social interdependence, and ethical conduct. In *The Prelude*, the rising scale of perceptions on Snowdon prepares for a twofold tribute to the scale of being. The first, which is general and conventional, ranges from 'rising flowers/And joyous creatures' to 'the Almighty's throne' (1850, XIV, 170–87). The second is specifically adapted to the poem's chief metaphor, which does not follow the course of the sun but of a stream or river as it winds its way 'From the blind cavern whence is faintly heard/Its natal murmur' to the continuation of its progress in 'the sustaining thought' of 'Eternity, and God' (1850, XIV, 194–205). Immediately following these universal and individual tributes, of course, are expressions of the poet's personal gratitude to his friends and of his determination to extend the principles of his work to the entire social fabric. In *The Excursion*, the concluding sunset leads to a less personal but more unified consideration of the ethical implications of his argument.

All those implications, from a belief in a transcendent creator and scale of being to the general moral progress and social responsibility of the race, are touched on in the Pastor's benediction, which begins 'Eternal Spirit! universal God!' (IX, 614ff) – a passage examined in the first chapter of this study – continues with a descent through the scale of creation, and concludes with an ascent back to the 'omniscient Mind, / From whom all gifts descend, all blessings flow!' (754) as the poem attains its most public utterance with an allusion to common prayer. In sum, both Book IX of *The Excursion* and Book XIV of *The Prelude* employ the same conceptual plan in consolidating and concluding their arguments: a vision designed in accordance with continuous geometrical proportion, a consequent celebration of the scale of being, and a practical extension of abstract principles to social and ethical concerns.

The similarity of endings in the two poems perhaps helps to answer questions about the degree to which *The Excursion* is a complete work and about the difficulties Wordsworth encountered in contemplating further additions to *The Recluse*. Obviously, if *The Prelude* does not stand in need of any sequel and is thought to be rounded off satisfactorily, *The Excursion*, which shares the same conclusion, almost as if it were another version of the earlier poem, could be said to have a like merit. At least, this would clearly be the case were it not for the poem's final verse paragraph, in which the Solitary expresses a willingness to moderate his solitude by engaging in further fellowship and in which the poet conditionally promises to chronicle the Solitary's future circumstances. That such a work was never written has been attributed to the failure of *The Excursion* to elicit the kind of critical approval and understanding which Wordsworth cited as a condition preparatory to the undertaking of a sequel. However genuine the small grain of truth in that explanation, the question of what further could be done with the Solitary seems much more obstinate. A sequel ultimately would have shown simply whether the Solitary could or could not embrace the cosmological principles already asserted in the unpublished *Prelude* and again in *The Excursion*. *The Prelude*'s excitement of discovery already having abated somewhat by the time of much of *The Excursion*, a sequel based on the ideas and characters of the latter work might not have appeared particularly interesting. The greatest impediment to the completion of *The Recluse*, then, would seem to be the definitive nature of the accomplishment of *The Prelude* and *The Excursion*. Properly speaking, all the concepts which distinguish Wordsworth's meditative imagination are already definitively embodied in *The Prelude* itself, so that, with the exception of the new material on the 'Authentic epitaphs,' *The Excursion* largely repeats and elaborates the insights of its companion. So long as Wordsworth persisted in composing his major works in a meditative style, the results would be further slight variations of the same theme, which, because of its metaphysical character, could prove rather intractable to presentation in substantially different modes.

It does not seem likely that Wordsworth could have developed the Solitary along fresh lines as a spokesman for an alternative system of idealism or that he could have created a new stylistic mode for a major endeavour, for the poem from the later years which comes closest to the conceptual scope of *The Prelude* and *The Excursion* returns to the themes of its predecessors in a style completely compatible with theirs, despite showing what at first glance is a totally different poetic form. That poem is the undervalued sonnet sequence, *The River Duddon* (1820), in which the two leading metaphors of the long poems in blank verse are combined as parallels to the span of human life: *The Prelude*'s course of a stream from its source to its termination and *The Excursion*'s course of the sun from morning to evening twilight. A further link between *The River Duddon* and *The Excursion* is that, during its progress, the stream evolves from the condition of a Solitary (sonnet XIV) into that of a Wanderer (sonnet XXXIII) – an indication, perhaps, of what would have happened had Wordsworth followed *The Excursion* with a long poem on the Solitary's subsequent life. Finally, *The River Duddon* also has a geometrical frame, in which the traditional and accessible symbolism of the circle is substituted for the more intricate golden sections of the poems in blank verse. Wordsworth's solution to the problem of returning to his cherished great themes may not be especially ambitious, but *The River Duddon* shows that when conceptual changes are not anticipated, retained ideas can pose an inviting challenge and suggest the invigorating prospects of variety by being embodied in a different poetic form. The new work represents the poet's first attempt at a tightly wrought and formal sequence of sonnets; stylistically, however, it has much in common with the long poems, especially with regard to their blank verse sonnets. Wordsworth's decision to touch on the themes of the long poems within the recognizable confines of a sonnet sequence nevertheless resulted in the additional advantage of reaching a wider audience: as he himself noted, it became the most popular of all his poems published in his lifetime (*PW,* III, 505).

Perhaps the greatest value of *The River Duddon* in its role as a successor – however modest – to *The Prelude* and *The Excursion* is the continuing evidence it yields for the view that the psychological and dramatic aspects of Wordsworth's principal poems are always ancillary to an ontological purpose. It seems probable that one of the reasons for the unwarranted neglect of the sonnet sequence is its relative lack of the psychological tensions and ambiguities for which modern literary criticism has been, in large part, devised. In the same way, the ontological power of Wordsworth's greatest poems has also been undervalued. If one adapts Wordsworth's habit of perceiving in geometrical 'frames,' one might think of a horizontal and analytical plane of materialist assumptions in relation to a vertical and synthetic plane of metaphysics and idealism. The metaphysical character of Wordsworth's poetry cannot, of course, be fully appreciated if one's interests are chiefly on the horizontal plane – if one's ultimate purpose is to pursue a union of art and life for social and political reasons, to explore the interrelationships of art and life as evidence for exclusively psychological speculations, or to separate art from life for the sake of a scientific, philosophic, or aesthetic attempt at a clarity of method and a certainty of knowledge that may unwittingly realize the joyless purity of an insubstantial style and of a form without value. All this needs saying because Wordsworth's contributions to the formation of modern consciousness are misappraised so long as their classical and metaphysical basis is not taken into account. In his poetry, the vertical plane of idealism is not only of primary significance but also – in contrast to some visionary artists, who are more mystifying than mystical – effectively intersects the horizontal plane of temporal existence. Conversely, his poetry is about imagination, nature, and psychological growth and development only as they promote his sense of being. For whatever reasons of individual genius and cultural change, Wordsworth may very well be the last great English writer to present a confident and convincing exposition of the scale of being and to unite that cosmology with epistemological and moral correspondences in a manner indebted to the long and diverse tradition of Milton, Newton, Spenser, Dante, Vergil, Plato, Pythagoras, and the writers of the Bible. Of course, an artist of Wordsworth's stature, like any good prophet, looks both before and after; but the ubiquitous presence of an ontological vision in his major poems from *Tintern Abbey* onwards and the relationship of that vision to the transcendental geometry of his artistry establish a universal and comprehensive equivalence between form and value that may serve less to prefigure the wisdom of those who live after him than to remind them of all that has been lost.

CHAPTER FOUR

The Art of Conceptual Form

The purpose of this final chapter is to extend the discussion of Wordsworth's use of the golden section to other aspects of his art. In particular, it is possible to establish correspondences between his employment of geometrical form and the relationships of metre to rhythm and of metrical line-length to phrasing. Allied to these considerations is his attitude towards rhymed verse, in which the type of geometrical form we have been examining is largely absent but in which analogous features of the poetry are found to do the same conceptual work. All these observations rely, of course, on a notion familiar to prosodists – the Platonic or idealist conception of metre – which is expanded to include the correspondences between the small dimensions of linguistic activity within a line of verse and the larger behaviour of a stanza or an entire poem, all of which draw upon the general relationship of what is conceptually fixed to what is, in execution, variable. On that end of the scale which deals with larger questions, for example, Wordsworth's use of the golden section helps to explain his success in designing long poems – a success which is, in no small part, attributable to his mastery of the short poem – the individual stanza and verse paragraph. Just as Milton's blank verse sonnets and *canzoni* are a key to the design of his major works, so Wordsworth's blank verse sonnets and paragraphs in continuous geometrical proportion establish the most critical conjunctions of theme and form in *The Prelude* and *The Excursion*. Besides suggesting that a poet who is incapable of writing a good short poem is most likely also incapable of writing a good long one, the practice of both Milton and Wordsworth reveals something about their general attitudes towards form and about the correspondences that exist within a generically similar frame of cosmological values. Gathering up and elaborating previous assumptions about Wordsworth's employment of form in its various aspects and attempting an analytical treatment of that subject, this final chapter should correct any misleading impression that Wordsworth's artistry is unique in its geometrical concerns. It should suggest, instead, Wordsworth's kinship with a whole strain of poets who are distinguished for their intellectual objectivity and among whom he stands prominently as one who came as close as any to a rigorously logical and comprehensive application of fixed principles to the task of composing philosophical verse.

The first part of this chapter is dedicated to the difficulties and the necessity of associating the proper values with any given form, for it is simply untrue to assert that a form such as metre or the golden section has but one definition which will be observed by all its practitioners. Wordsworth was not the only poet to have employed the golden section, for example, but it would be unwise to assume that the values he conferred upon that geometrical form are the same as those conferred by other poets. The kind of problem which concerns us may be illustrated, first, by George Duckworth's extraordinary book on Vergil in which he proposes that Vergil, like Horace, Lucretius, and Catullus, relied on the golden section for the construction of his poems and that he composed the *Aeneid* on the basis of the golden section in regulating everything from the poem's smallest units to the disposition of entire books:

> If I had listed in the following tables only those ratios ranging from .615 to .621, or even from .610 to .626, Vergil's accuracy in the use of the Golden Section would have seemed little short of miraculous, but our picture of the construction of the individual books would have been lacking in clarity. By extending the range of the ratios .018 in each direction from the exact .618, *i.e.*, from .600 (=3/5 in the Fibonacci series 1, 2, 3, 5, 8, 13 . . .) to .636 (=7/11 in the series 1, 3, 4, 7, 11, 18 . . .), we shall see that Vergil has included every part of every book in amazingly intricate designs, with very short passages combining into ever larger narrative units until we come to the main divisions of

the books and the books as a whole. In the shortest passages
the units are sentences; in the larger passages the major
and minor may be determined by divisions of thought
within speeches or episodes, or by the alternation of
speeches or of speeches and narrative. In the larger proportions, as well as in the main divisions, the major and minor
parts are of course each composed of many shorter passages
in proportion. But in all this development from the shortest
passages to the books as a whole, we have always the ratios
centering about the Golden Section (.618), with a range
from .60 to .636. The dozens and hundreds of passages in
which the proportions occur result in no way from arbitrary
divisions of the text but follow naturally the narrative units
large and small.[46]

If Duckworth is correct – and I have quoted extensively from the passage which most clearly explains the methods and principles that prepare the reader for the lengthy and dizzying array of tables with which the book concludes – then Vergil's use of the golden section greatly contrasts with Wordsworth's highly selective use of the ratio. If one assumes that Vergil apparently did not save the proportion for any special purpose but applied it uniformly to every aspect of his work, it becomes difficult to determine what particular literary function the ratio might have at any given point in the narration or how it might demonstrate a common property in, say, an epic game and the death of Dido. Duckworth nowhere engages in the kind of specific literary analysis which could treat such matters, and the type of argument he pursues may be, to many readers, of much heavenly worth but of no earthly good for a keener appreciation of the poem's language.[47] To think of the golden section only as a principle of construction without specific values imparted to it thus results in a piece of information similar to saying that the *Aeneid* is written in dactylic hexameters: the information begs the important question of value, for it is not unreasonable to suppose that the golden section may have represented something different for the mystical Vergil from what it did for Lucretius, and something different for Lucretius from what it did for Catullus.

As a description of Vergil's method of constructing the *Aeneid*,

Duckworth's analysis also raises an important question of historical bias. His reference to 'the exact .618' betrays the peculiarly modern arithmetical approach to the ratio, which, as I took some pains to indicate in the first chapter of this study, eludes any definition by merely arithmetical exactitude, although the proportion is elegantly simple and exact as a purely geometrical concept. Historically, it is most likely that Vergil, in common with other ancients, tended to think of numbers as geometrical forms and that Duckworth's arithmetical precision in fixing the ratio is consequently a form of conceptual imprecision which unwittingly assumes values inappropriate to Vergil's poem.[48] It is hard to predict whether an analysis of the *Aeneid* conducted along the lines of geometry rather than arithmetic would yield different divisions of the poem, but the attempt might lead to distinctions between less and more significant divisions and might therefore suggest an answer to the question of what Vergil's use of the golden section means above and beyond its architectural utility in joining the mortar, bricks, and walls of a great poem together. In sum, Duckworth's book convincingly shows that the golden section was of paramount importance to Vergil. Now the work begins of figuring out why it was so important to him and what difference it makes to our reading of the poem. Vergil, unlike Wordsworth, may have employed the ratio simply as an aid to composition – as Duckworth implies – or as a mere abstraction that symbolizes the nature of the universe; but one suspects, especially after reading Book VI of the *Aeneid*, that an artist of Vergil's stature was not content to rest with an unexercised virtue and to keep such an abstraction in total isolation from the semantic activity of a text. In this regard, there is recent evidence which suggests that Vergil's use of the golden section is not routine but is, like Wordsworth's, selective and reserved for his most ambitious conceptions.[49]

Although Vergil's use of the proportion is a matter which requires much more examination, the assignation of value to the golden section has been less obscure in recent times. Wordsworth's conception of the ratio, for instance, has almost nothing in common with the prevailing thought of the present century, which brings a materialist position to bear on the interpretation of the proportion. Equiangular spirals, which are based on the golden section, have been associated with many material objects – certain shells, pine cones, sunflowers, and the like – and these scientifically useful discoveries have no doubt contributed to a renewal of interest in the proportion. But they have not touched on any philosophical implications of any consequence other than occasional speculation on the scientific design of nature.[50] In the world of art and architecture, interpretation of the golden section has focused on its aesthetic and psychological effects rather than on its metaphysical possibilities. Psychologists – as could be expected – have tested subjects to ascertain whether circles, squares, and equilateral triangles are more pleasing and beautiful than their counterparts – ellipses, rectangles, and isosceles triangles which have their foci, sides, or angles determined by the golden section. The fitting apotheosis of this line of inquiry would appear to be the dimensions of the modern rectangular plastic credit card. Jay Hambidge was among the first to defend the aesthetic and psychological possibilities of the golden section in contemporary painting, but he also argued that it accounted for the proportions of ancient Greek artifacts and architecture.[51]

Although the argument about the role of the golden section in ancient architecture is not conclusive, the modern architect Le Corbusier has employed a 'modular' system of proportion based on an analysis of the human form as a series of interrelationships in continuous geometrical proportion with one another and has devised architectural structures with correspondences to those proportions. The idea at least has the merit of resulting in buildings which are not designed without reference to their human occupants and also echoes the Renaissance spirit of establishing mathematical correspondences between the human form and its environment.[52] Alongside such a worthy endeavour, the effort of modern street-corner mystics to sell golden section pyramids places the ratio in a comic perspective. These little cones and pyramids, like their great models in Egypt, are usually alleged to harness beneficent cosmic powers – a notion that, on the face of it, is not generically incompatible with Wordsworth's more logically dignified employment of the ratio – but, in keeping a sharp eye on commercial possibilities, the purveyors of these geometrical products urge less than spiritual benefits to the prospective buyer: improvement in the quality of alcoholic beverages, cures for rheumatism, enhancement of sexual performance, and many other advantages for one's enjoyment of the good life. In short, it would seem that the present age brings every sort of interpretation to bear on the golden section except for that which interested Wordsworth.

The preceding collection of heterogeneous opinions of what a form denotes proves nothing, of course, other than the danger of taking anything for granted and of assuming that a form has a basic definition which elicits general agreement. Of greater and much more serious import is what can happen to such a form when it is subjected to highly thoughtful scrutiny within a well-defined tradition. In the history of music, for example, the golden section has – in the composition of fugues – the status of a convention, though the values associated with the geometrical design of fugues have, as the Appendix to this book illustrates, undergone remarkable changes. In English verse, however, Wordsworth may be the only poet to have relied on continuous proportion. It is therefore difficult to speculate on what others might have done had they also employed this type of mathematical composition. As conceptual forms, his geometrical patterns are nevertheless subjected to the same varieties of interpretation as are other such forms, of which metre is perhaps the most basic. A brief look at what has happened to the metrical tradition in English poetry should illustrate the authoritative nature of Wordsworth's assumptions – which are consistent with his attitudes towards geometry – in contrast to subsequent reappraisals of metrical purposes.

As a prelude to a discussion of Wordsworth's metrical standard, it will do well to recall that for at least two hundred years metre has been so effectively beset by various kinds of confusion that the prosodic knowledge required for a sensitive consideration of the older poets is in general now almost non-existent and is rarely discharged properly, if at all, even in the academic treatment of poetry. Increasingly common is the perplexed figure of the professor of literature who, unsure of the scansion of a line of verse, cannot distinguish between rhythm and metre and ends up sincerely doubting that metre has ever existed except as an academic equivalent of the emperor's new clothes. The role of metre and the larger question of prosody, like the study of rhetoric, have, of course, diminished in direct relation to the loss of universal cultural standards and to the rise of psychological aesthetics and new cosmological attitudes. The premium placed on spontaneous expression and the difficulty of coping with authority have spilled over into art and resulted in a general distrust of form in all its tyrannical aspects. As Blake, in his prefatory note to *Jerusalem*, prophetically observes of rhyme and metre: 'Poetry Fetter'd Fetters the Human Race.'[53] Blake, at least, had the excuse of knowing precisely what he was rejecting – and, one might add, the memorable force of this particular outburst may even derive from its resemblance to a line of blank verse in which a trochaic rhythm occupies the first metrical foot. Cosmologically, the association of metre with the music of the spheres and with an orderly universe fares badly in the unwitting subjectivism implied by the phrase 'theory of relativity' and in the births and deaths of the impermanent stars that may leave behind a universe of death swallowed up and lost in the wide womb of uncreated night provided by 'black holes.' But on a less sublime level, the decay of the metrical tradition is attributable mainly to the ineptitude of many of its practitioners, who, especially during the late nineteenth and early twentieth centuries, had no good reason to write in metre and thereby stimulated others to explore more vital, non-metrical alternatives. By the same token, many practitioners of free verse have little idea of why they write as they do, although some recognize that their mode more easily accommodates, as does much prose, the illusion of unself-conscious speech-rhythms and also provides a relatively uncomplicated vehicle for the direct expression of emotional extremes, which, whether chaotically intense, extremely delicate, or merely trivial, would be subdued or ennobled by the tempering effects of metre. Suffering from its negative character of describing only what it is not, the term 'free verse' has, by its pluralistic nature, greatly expanded the quantity of writing which may be called poetry and has, for the most part, substituted various psychologies of the creative process for an artistic standard against which variations may acquire significance. It is perhaps the absence of a twofold approach to form based on principles of fixity and variation that distinguishes any kind of free verse and leaves unexercised the larger complex of faculties required for the appreciation of great metrical poetry.

Oddly enough, verse that is pleased to announce itself as being 'free' from the shackles of metre has rejected a notably flexible tradition: metrical poets have taken widely divergent approaches to the key terms metre, rhythm, and line. Showing his usual good sense in such matters, Paul Fussell, Jr, acknowledges a variety of metrical notions, which range from 'more or less regular poetic rhythm; the measurable rhythmical patterns manifested in verse; or the "ideal" patterns which poetic rhythms approximate.'[54] Moreover, it is clear that the functions of metre can be quite different in dramatic, as contrasted with lyric or with narrative, verse. Despite the various functions and concepts of metre, all good metrical systems contain norms and rules, which, although altering from time to time, provide the basis from which variations can develop. Even in dramatic verse, one cannot but notice that the blank verse line in the late sixteenth century has an exceptionally regular and normative character which asserts and fixes its position as a standard, thereby making possible the ever-increasing variations from it as one approaches and enters the seventeenth century. In lyric poetry, a similar trend extends from Sackville to Milton. The most interesting cases, however, are those in which individual poets exploit all the possibilities available to them. Because Wordsworth is one of the vast majority of English metrical poets who regulate the numbers both of syllables and of accents within a line, it is not necessary to dwell here on purely syllabic verse – which is actually foreign to the basically accentual nature of the English language – or on purely accentual methods of determining a line. It is perhaps sufficient to observe that in each of these instances a principle of variation is possible only between lines, most of which must be set as a norm, and not within the line itself – a disadvantage for those who value precision of utterance on a smaller scale and one that may account, in part, for the relative infrequency of these systems throughout the history of English verse. By comparison, accentual-syllabic lines, such as Wordsworth's, permit a norm and variations for each set of syllables in a metrical foot and thus invite a twofold consideration of their properties.

The dual nature of form which is possible with accentual-syllabic verse is most easily apprehended with the help of a simple distinction in critical terms and by the avoidance of confusion between rhythm and metre. In this regard, I am grateful to adopt Edward Weismiller's eminently sensible insight into the difference between the studies of versification, which refers to rhythm alone, and of prosody, the relationship of rhythm to metre: 'The versification of a line is not its prosody' but is 'the study of rhythm and of the patterning of sound *insofar as these are not metrically determined.*'[55] Unlike what is called 'linguistic prosody' – which usually does not concern metre or prosody at all but is merely a cataloguing of rhythms – the distinction between versification and prosody provides a comprehensive means of distinguishing the actual form of the particular language one hears when reading a poem from the conceptual form of abstract relationships that regulate and run parallel to the language. Thus, as the following lines from the opening paragraph of Dryden's translation of the *Aeneid* demonstrate, the qualities of versification can be quite different from those of prosody: in the first of these lines –

$$\text{/ x / x / x / x}$$
And haughty Juno's unrelenting hate

– one is struck throughout by the procession of falling or trochaic rhythms, but notices how, in the second of the lines –

$$\text{/ x   x / x / x /}$$
His banish'd gods restor'd to rites divine

– the trochaic rhythms yield to rising or iambic rhythms in direct relation to the improvement of Aeneas's fortunes.[56] Dryden's contrasting use of trochaic and iambic rhythms is an exquisite, subtle, and delicate effect of his masterful versification and imparts a distinctive character to each of these lines, which are nevertheless metrically identical. Each line is obviously an example of iambic pentameter – five sets of a metrical foot which calls for an unaccented or weak syllable to be followed by an accented or strong one – so that a textbook example of an actual line would strive to have all its odd-numbered syllables weak and its even-numbered syllables strong. One does not hear the metrical pattern, of course, any more than one can hear a mathematical formula which lies behind the movements of a steam engine. In this respect, S. Jay Keyser has rightly insisted that the 'abstract metrical pattern of a line' or its metre should be distinguished from its prosody or 'the rules which determine when that abstract pattern is suitably filled by an arrangement of linguistic material.'[57] Metre, in sum, is an immutable, given abstract concept which does not change throughout the course of an entire poem unless – as rarely happens – the poem is written in accordance with more than one metre. Versification, by contrast, is the actual sound and rhythm of specific and ever-changing language without reference to metre. Prosody is the comparison of versification's changes in relation to metre's fixity. What one can say of the two lines quoted from Dryden, then, is that their metre is the same, their versification different, and their prosody similar. Both lines show all their odd-numbered syllables to be weak and even-numbered syllables to be strong, although in the case of the first line predominantly trochaic rhythms are fulfilling an iambic metre, and in the concluding part of the second line iambic rhythms correspond exactly to its iambic metre so that the restoration of order and of 'rites divine' in Aeneas's life is matched by language that comes as close as possible to the conceptual form of its metrical idea. Similar refinements of versification occur throughout Wordsworth's poetry, as in the way in which the iambic rhythms of words in 'Our Souls have sight of that immortal sea' precisely follow the formula of iambic pentameter and the way in which the trochaic rhythms of 'And hear the mighty waters rolling evermore' satisfy the requirements of iambic hexameter (*PW*, IV, 284). Such nuances of versification are nevertheless more characteristic of Dryden – and, of course, Pope – than of Wordsworth, who, being less conservative in his handling of a line, concentrates more on large-scale effects which come closer to testing the limits of metrical influence on rhythm.

That poets such as Wordsworth and Dryden composed metrical works for which a distinction between versification and prosody is appropriate may be inferred from the character of their use of substitution rules and of isochronism. With regard to the permissible number of rhythmic variations in a line of iambic pentameter, W.H. Auden has suggested that 'the only rule seems to be an empirical and negative one, namely, that two successive accents cannot be suppressed or displaced without destroying the underlying pattern.'[58] That is to say, from the standpoint of metre, once a line has two adjacent feet – or four syllables in a row – which are rhythmically different from the metrical formula, the integrity of the line is beyond repair. Of course, Auden's generalization does not account for different tastes in substitution rules which range from the conservative practices of the neoclassical poets at one extreme to the daring prosody of radicals like Milton and Yeats at the other. Although Wordsworth's prosody tends towards the daring, his lines are usually not quite so adventurous as Milton's, as the beginning of *Paradise Lost* indicates:

> Of Man's First Disobedience, and the Fruit
> Of that forbidden Tree, whose mortal taste
> Brought Death into the World, and all our woe,
> With loss of *Eden*, till one greater Man
> Restore us, and regain the blissful Seat . . . (*Paradise Lost*, I, 1-5)

Each of these lines has at least one rhythmic substitution against the iambic pentameter frame, although it is clear that the rhythms approximate the metre more closely as one approaches the hopeful sentiment, 'till one greater Man/Restore us, and regain the blissful Seat.' By Auden's criterion of avoiding two successive substitutions, the third line especially presents difficulties: if one reads 'Brought Death into the World' as a spondaic rhythm – two accented syllables – followed by a pyrrhic rhythm – two unaccented syllables – then the appearance of death in the world destroys not only life but also the metrical influence of the line. 'Mere anarchy is loosed upon the world' and upon the metre – another line of which the same judgment could be made. Versification has, unlike metre, an inherently subjective element which eludes all ill-advised attempts at legislation. One need not read the lines by Milton and Yeats in the way suggested, but there is, at least, much dramatic propriety in doing so. Similarly, should one accent the first syllable of 'unrelenting' in the line 'And haughty Juno's unrelenting hate' or emphasize the word 'that' in the line 'Our Souls have sight of that immortal sea'? Such considerations may depend upon nothing more than the mood one is in when reading the lines, although consciousness of the metrical frame may lead to an intelligent decision one way or the other. If one grants the possibility that Milton's prosody may, at times, be calculated to offend metrical integrity, then it is no longer necessary to fuss over the famous case 'Rocks, Caves, Lakes, Fens, Bogs,

Dens, and shades of death' (*Paradise Lost*, II, 621), a line which is clearly unmetrical and decorously so in its description of the dolorous, disordered landscape of Hell. In a similar vein, Raphael's account of how bodily nourishment supports spiritual needs in both men and angels leads to a contrast between rhythms that disregard and affirm a metrical pattern:

> . . . and both contain
> Within them every lower faculty
> Of sense, whereby they hear, see, smell, touch, taste,
> Tasting concoct, digest, assimilate,
> And corporeal to incorporeal turn. (*Paradise Lost*, V, 409-13)

The third line, piling monosyllabic verbs of the senses on top of one another, is full of spondaic rhythms which obliterate any trace of iambic pentameter; metrical influence returns in the fourth line, however, as the senses yield to higher processes. From a metrical point of view, the contrast between sensual and spiritual faculties is brilliantly summarized in the final line, where the word 'corporeal' - accented here, as elsewhere in the poem, on its second syllable - is in opposition to the metrical frame, and the word 'incorporeal' is the agent of metrical restoration. In general - as if there were a scale of creation in Milton's diction - concrete nouns and verbs of the senses weigh down his lines and are furthest from fulfilling an abstract metrical pattern, but, in their ability to draw close to metre, abstract, polysyllabic words are 'more refin'd, more spiritous, and pure' (*PL*, V, 475). In sum, those poets - such as Wordsworth, Milton, and Yeats - who are most liberal in their use of substitution rules also have of necessity a strong concept of metre that results in verse which particularly invites an analysis of actual versus conceptual form.

Poems with marked substitutions of rhythm against metre rarely have a uniform number of accented syllables in each line and are therefore less likely to be in isochronic metre - or the uniform duration of metrical feet - which, if followed carefully, produces another basic metrical form, one with less sense of an abstract pattern. Since the sixteenth century, various poets have attempted to duplicate in English the principles of quantitative prosody which govern most classical verse by means of the notion that a succession of metrical feet should have a uniform flow of equal units or quantities of time. To determine how long it takes to pronounce syllables by noting which vowels are given as short or long or become long by position before two or more consonants is, in Greek and Latin, one thing; but in the heavily accentual character of English and its rather unprincipled orthography, quantitative verse is – as numerous experiments have amply demonstrated – impractical, impossible to sustain, and in conflict with the basic nature of the language. Isochronic prosody is possible, however, not by examining the length of vowels and syllables but by ensuring that equal quantities of accented syllables occur in each line. As nursery rhymes prove – for example, 'One, two, / Buckle my shoe' – it is not the number of syllables but of accents which determines the length of time a line will take to say. A perfectly isochronic set of lines in iambic pentameter would therefore have regular rhythms and show five accents per line:

> The woods decay, the woods decay and fall,
> The vapours weep their burthen to the ground,
> Man comes and tills the field and lies beneath,
> And after many a summer dies the swan.[59]

The opening of Tennyson's 'Tithonus' is strongly isochronic, so much so that most readers pause over the prepositional phrase at the end of the second line and thereby give the line a duration equivalent to its neighbours. Tennyson's blank verse generally tends towards isochronic metre and is probably the only such verse to average almost exactly five accents per line – a number that gives his lines a much slower and heavier movement than blank verse by poets such as Milton and Wordsworth. It is as if Tennyson – and Campion, who also excels in this kind of metre – had perfected an isochronic and therefore a quantitative means of duplicating the principles of classical prosody but in a way appropriate to the nature of English. The physically measurable concept of isochronic metre does not easily admit a distinction between prosody and versification, however, for rhythm and metre are, in this instance, virtually inseparable. Despite the fact that the average line should have five accents, a principle of variation is possible: for those exceptional lines that clearly have fewer accents, Tennyson usually composes complementary ones with more, thereby providing a means of metrical contrast. Unfortunately, if a poet feasts on a steady diet of polysyllabic words and prepositional and other qualifying phrases, the inevitable run of unaccented syllables makes the preservation of an average of five accents per line impossible. For this reason, the blank verse of a Wordsworth or Milton shows an overall average of less than five accents in each line and is lighter and faster in its movement. Although conceptual and not isochronic metre is the basis of their art, such poets can nevertheless be aware of the important subordinate role of isochronism in good versification. In Wordsworth's line 'Surprised by joy – impatient as the Wind' (*PW*, III, 16), it is clear that on either side of the caesura is a phrase with two accents, that each therefore takes about the same amount of time to pronounce, but that in the second phrase, 'impatient as the Wind,' six syllables, rather than four, are crowded around the two accents and thus hurry along in a physical exemplification of the sense of the phrase. However poignant and refined one may deem the effect Wordsworth achieves, what one is assessing concerns the general phenomenon of isochronism, which, being pertinent to the skilful management of rhythms, is an element of versification for any poet. The effect of isochronic rhythm is here accomplished at the expense of isochronic metre, however, and in fulfilment of an abstract metrical pattern, so that, having examined the actual behaviour of language on the surface of the line, one is still left with a consideration of its conceptual dimension. By comparison, in truly isochronic prosody, which attempts to fix a measure of time for all metrical feet, surface and depth are united.

The poets Wordsworth most closely resembles in the use of metre and conceptual form are figures such as Spenser, Milton, Dryden, and Pope. Since Wordsworth's time, Yeats pre-eminently and, on occasion, Eliot have carried on the idealist tradition of metre and form. Of course, Wordsworth's greatest affinities in artistry and technique are with those – Spenser, Milton, and Yeats – who have the strongest Platonic outlook on the entire question of form in art and who also best fit the description in the 1815 Preface of the meditative imagination. Within the complete range of Wordsworth's poetry, moreover, further distinctions are necessary: conceptual form is obviously more highly developed and significant in blank verse, sonnets, and major rhymed poems than in the *Lyrical Ballads* or in light rhymed verses. Although metrical procedures in the lesser works are simple and elementary and, as such, have a limited specific interest within individual poems, the general importance of metre was of concern to Wordsworth from the outset and stands as one of the main themes of his Preface to the *Lyrical Ballads*. The Preface clearly argues – as S.M. Parrish has recently noted by using it as the basis of a collection of fine essays on the *Lyrical Ballads* – that metre is at the heart of the principle of pleasure which verse yields.[60] Wordsworth identifies this pleasure as that 'which the mind derives from the perception of similitude in dissimilitude' (*PW*, II, 400). Amplifying on the poet's observation, it is not difficult to discern that metre's 'strict laws' (*PW*, II, 390) are the source of similitude and that diction, because of its changing rhythms, meanings, and styles, is attended by inherently mutable and subjective considerations which are at once a source of variety and delight but which also frustrate any attempt to impose widely acceptable rules for the sake of regulation or refinement:

> . . . for, as it may be proper to remind the Reader, the distinction of metre is regular and uniform, and not, like that which is produced by what is usually called POETIC DICTION, arbitrary, and subject to infinite caprices upon which no calculation whatever can be made. In the one case, the Reader is utterly at the mercy of the Poet, respecting what imagery or diction he may choose to connect with the passion; whereas, in the other, the metre obeys certain laws, to which the Poet and Reader both willingly submit themselves because they are certain, and because no interference is made by them with the passion, but such as the concurring testimony of ages has shown to heighten and improve the pleasure which co-exists with it. (*PW*, II, 398)

The most effective and reasonable way of preserving a distinction between principles of similitude and dissimilitude – of distinguishing the fixed 'letter of metre' from the more volatile 'spirit of versification' (*PW*, II, 435) – is, in the argument of the Preface, to preclude the subjective, inconsistent, and self-defeating results of imposing rules on the diction of poetry – 'there neither is, nor can be any *essential* difference between the language of prose and metrical composition' (*PW*, II, 392) – and to insist on the clear, objective, and inherent distinction that metre imparts to the definition of poetry – 'the only strict antithesis to Prose is Metre' (*PW*, II, 392n). What is found to be subjective by nature – diction – is left so; what is by definition fixed – metre – becomes the distinguishing element of poetry. By contrast, Coleridge at times seems to treat form and metre as mere ornaments while deeming diction and imagery, if sufficiently highly charged with enough psychological and imaginative significance, to be, by themselves, the chief essentials in the definition, if not of a poem, at least of poetry: In chapter XIV of *Biographia Literaria*, for example, the phrases 'so much for the superficial form' and 'if metre be super-added' prepare for the assertion that 'the writings of Plato, and Bishop Taylor, and the "Theoria Sacra" of Burnet, furnish undeniable proofs that poetry of the highest kind may exist without metre . . .'[61] At the extremes of illustration, to those who are principally concerned with the psychology of the creative process, the philosophical writings of Plato are poetry and a mnemonic jingle is not; to Wordsworth, Plato did not write poetry – a judgment which Plato would, no doubt, be glad to affirm – but a jingle is poetry in which the content is 'trivial' and 'contemptible' (*PW*, II, 403). Although the phrase 'similitude in dissimilitude' sounds, unfortunately, like a Coleridgean 'reconciliation of opposites,' it is not: the Coleridgean definitions of poetry rely heavily on the quality of diction and are, as such, subjective and psychological; the Wordsworthian definition is objectively based on the presence of metre and is therefore – by separating the metrical one from the linguistic many – philosophically old-fashioned but clear. That Coleridgean, rather than Wordsworthian, influences have prevailed is amply demonstrated by the acceptance of free verse as poetry – a phenomenon incapable of justification when measured by Wordsworth's standards. That his standards should not be ignored because of modern practices but should be viewed in a larger context that transcends the past two hundred years is evident from the paramount importance with which he endowed metre in formulating an objective and universal basis of his art in accordance with 'the concurring testimony of ages' – for his analysis of metrical composition is indeed capacious and, in practice, goes far beyond the generalities of his first Preface. Wordsworth's commitment to metrical composition is present in every aspect of his art and, in its all-encompassing nature, distinguishes him from most of the poets in the line with which he is associated. The same principle extends from the smallest to the largest prosodic units: just as the strict and certain laws of metrical feet regulate the actual rhythms and versification of language, so the metrical line-length stands behind the actual phrasing and syntax of entire sentences, which can either correspond to or vary from the given line-length. Finally, in blank verse especially, larger groups of phrases and sentences are governed by the immaterial abstractions of geometry. For this reason, it is appropriate to say that Wordsworth's attitude towards geometry is akin to his use of metre: in both cases, a conceptual form, a principle of fixity, is established against which degrees of variation in actual language may take on significance. To Wordsworth and the older poets, the more uniform and regular actual language becomes, the more closely it approximates the ideal form or conception which lies behind the verse. It seems necessary to recall this commonplace because the most conceptually ambitious moments in much recent verse tend to be those which are most agitated, disoriented, and farthest removed from what is apparently thought of as the placid and rather dull character of regular and rational form. The final verse paragraph of Pope's *Essay on Man I* is as good as any example for the purpose of illustrating that in older poems the points of climax are those which achieve the greatest degree of formal clarity:

> X. Cease then, nor ORDER Imperfection name:
> Our proper bliss depends on what we blame.
> Know thy own point: this kind, this due degree
> Of blindness, weakness, Heav'n bestows on thee.
> Submit. – In this, or any other sphere,
> Secure to be as blest as thou canst bear:
> Safe in the hand of one disposing Pow'r,
> Or in the natal, or the mortal hour.
> All Nature is but Art, unknown to thee;

> All Chance, Direction, which thou canst not see;
> All Discord, Harmony, not understood;
> All partial Evil, universal Good:
> And, spite of Pride, in erring Reason's spite,
> One truth is clear, 'Whatever IS, is RIGHT.'[62]

In the first eight lines, perturbations of rhythm and dislocations of phrasing against metrical line-length – 'this due degree/Of blindness, weakness' – lend prosodic expression to the incomplete harmony between divine wisdom and human interpretations of that wisdom. The rhythms of the three imperative verbs which introduce all phrases in this section succinctly convey the gist of the argument: 'Cease then,' 'Know thy own point,' and 'Submit' not only provide an important gradation of meanings but show the trochaic rhythms of the first two verbs yielding to the iambic rhythm of the third, which thereby achieves perfect congruity with the metrical foot it occupies. In the final six lines, the urgency of imperative verbs is replaced by the more tranquil and authoritative nature of declarative propositions, which are thus higher in the conceptual order and display a much greater uniformity of rhythm, syntax, and even of grammar. The final line, in particular, is notable for the predominantly iambic rhythms of all its words and phrases, their agreement with iambic metre, and for the power – metrically determined – with which Pope charges the simple present tense of the verb 'to be.' Of course, the prosodic effects of the entire passage are so extraordinarily delicate, refined, and skilfully adapted to their sentiment about cosmic order that both prosodic and philosophical aspects of the utterance may seem strange and even amusing to those who are incapable of or unsympathetic to either and who thereby pay an unwitting tribute to the perfection of Pope's achievement.

The profound affinities between the prosodic and intellectual outlooks of Wordsworth and Pope have, of course, been underestimated, partly because of Wordsworth's well-known antipathies to Pope's diction and epitaphs and partly because these two poets so often end up as antagonists in superficial classroom comparisons of Romantic and Augustan themes and attitudes. On the deeper levels, however, they share the same sense of form, as the following passage, selected from the meditation which ensues after the ascent of Snowdon, may help to illustrate:

> There I beheld the emblem of a mind
> That feeds upon infinity, that broods
> Over the dark abyss, intent to hear
> Its voices issuing forth to silent light
> In one continuous stream; a mind sustained
> By recognitions of transcendent power,
> In sense conducting to ideal form,
> In soul of more than mortal privilege. (1850, XIV, 70-7)

Here, as in the previous example from the *Essay on Man*, dislocations of phrasing and disruptions of rhythm – 'that broods/Over the dark abyss' – disappear as the actual form of language attains congruence with the metrical form of foot and line. The force of uniformity is particularly noticeable and thematically appropriate in the line 'In sense conducting to ideal form,' a phrase which has iambic rhythms and is contained by the metrical line-length of iambic pentameter. Utterly characteristic of Wordsworth's procedures, however, is the transition from the process of imaginative apprehension to the metaphysical basis of that apprehension: a searching mind that 'feeds,' 'broods,' and is 'intent to hear' diverges somewhat from perfect metrical form, but when the same mind is 'sustained' by 'transcendent power,' 'ideal form,' and 'more than mortal privilege,' the verse draws close to its conceptual and metrical idea. The single continuous sentence of this passage thus recapitulates in miniature the form of the paragraph on the ascent of Snowdon itself (11–62) – a paragraph which fulfils the idealist interpretation of continuous geometrical proportion and which reveals the upward progress of the mind from psychological to ontological realms and from prosodic, structural, and imagistic variety to a disciplined, metrical, and geometrical ordering of all the elements of poetry. Similar relationships of rhythm to metre, of phrasing to line-length, and of language to geometry are prominent in all the examples discussed throughout this book, providing the essentials of Wordsworth's blank verse style and command of conceptual form from *Tintern Abbey* onwards and taking on especial significance in certain poems for which the quiet subtleties of prosodic principles become virtually indispensable to the effective control of minute gradations in diction. In 'St. Paul's,' for example (*PW*, IV, 374-5), the diction is, as was observed in the Introduction, generally sombre and austere in both the minor and major sections of the continuous geometrical proportion which gives this poem its form. The principal changes throughout the poem are prosodic adjustments which remove enjambed phrases and help the lines approach a metrical uniformity and a tone of certainty that complement the introduction of the main image – the cathedral itself – and suit the increasingly abstract language and concepts of the poem's conclusion. In the same fashion, the diction of the dream-vision of the Arab, stone, and shell falls within a narrow compass of variation, the assessment of which is perfectly clear once one has taken note of the triple golden section that determines the form of the entire passage. As was pointed out in the second chapter, the conceptual centre of the dream-vision is the portion that treats the stone and shell exclusively in their eternal context (1850, V, 98-114). Although most of the dream-vision is heavily enjambed, the lines in the central portion come closest to the metrical chastening by conceptual form so that the apocalyptic message of the stone and shell, which are now two books – 'The one that held acquaintance with the stars' (103) and 'The other that was a god, yea many gods' (106) – does not disturb the dreamer, who, 'Having a perfect faith in all that passed' (114), also participates in the metrically stable versification that befits a calm, immutable standpoint.

    All these observations on Wordsworth's prosody and geometrical art are exemplified – particularly as they apply to poems which have a finely graded and narrow range of linguistic variation – in a verse paragraph from 'Home at Grasmere' that contains perhaps the purest and most joyful tribute the poet ever paid to his home ground:

> Embrace me then, ye Hills, and close me in,
> Now in the clear and open day I feel
> Your guardianship; I take it to my heart;
> 'Tis like the solemn shelter of the night.
> But I would call thee beautiful, for mild   5
> And soft, and gay, and beautiful thou art,
> Dear Valley, having in thy face a smile

> Though peaceful, full of gladness. Thou art pleased,
> Pleased with thy crags, and woody steeps, thy Lake,
> Its one green Island and its winding shores;   10
> The multitude of little rocky hills,
> Thy Church and Cottages of mountain stone
> Clustered like stars some few, but single most,
> And lurking dimly in their shy retreats,
> Or glancing at each other chearful looks,   15
> Like separated stars with clouds between.
> _____
> What want we? have we not perpetual streams,
> Warm woods, and sunny hills, and fresh green fields,
> And mountains not less green, and flocks, and herds,
> And thickets full of songsters, and the voice   20
> Of lordly birds, an unexpected sound
> Heard now and then from morn to latest eve,
> Admonishing the man who walks below
> Of solitude, and silence in the sky?
> These have we, and a thousand nooks of earth   25
> Have also these, but no where else is found,
> No where (or is it fancy?) can be found
> The one sensation that is here; 'tis here,
> Here as it found its way into my heart
> In childhood, here as it abides by day,   30
> By night, here only; or in chosen minds
> That take it with them hence, where'er they go.
> 'Tis, but I cannot name it, 'tis the sense
> Of majesty, and beauty, and repose,
> A blended holiness of earth and sky,   35
> Something that makes this individual Spot,
> This small Abiding-place of many Men,
> A termination, and a last retreat,
> A Centre, come from wheresoe'er you will,
> A Whole without dependence or defect,   40
> Made for itself; and happy in itself,
> Perfect Contentment, Unity entire. (*PW*, V, 317–18)

A golden section divides the first sixteen lines, which are a direct address to the landscape at Grasmere, from the remaining twenty-six lines of meditation – 16:26::26:42. Other than the change in mode of address, there are few linguistic alterations. Images in both the minor and major sections of the ratio include conventional ranges of space and time. In the minor section, the lake, the stones, and – by means of simile – the clouds and stars touch on each of the four elements with the 'open day' and the 'shelter of the night' alluding to the diurnal and nocturnal round. The same images – 'from morn till latest eve' – are recapitulated in the major section, and in both sections the poet says he took the landscape to 'my heart.' Obviously, Wordsworth's usual methods of differentiating linguistic values in a passage which has the form of continuous proportion are not apparent here, and one may well question on what basis, if any, the paragraph is divided. Just as his heart is a core and centre of his sensibility, however, so the landscape in the minor section and the major section's abstractions constitute points around which everything else is gathered concentrically. The images and assertions of enclosure are announced prosodically in phrases which are contained by their metrical line-length: a motif established by the opening line, 'Embrace me then, ye Hills, and close me in.' After a run of largely enjambed phrases, the minor section settles on a description of Grasmere Lake in which 'Its one green Island and its winding shores' become a centre for the surrounding crags, steeps, church, and cottages, all of which are likewise presented in phrases that show the agreement of versification with metrical boundaries. In the same way, the final ten lines of the major section celebrate Grasmere as 'Centre' and are so astonishingly uniform that they probably comprise the most prosodically regular stretch of writing to be found in the whole of Wordsworth's blank verse. As the comparison of the regular lines in the minor and major sections reveals, the basis on which continuous geometrical proportion is accomplished in this paragraph involves a reciprocal relationship between the particulars of the landscape which follow the letter of geometrical perception and their universal significance as an abstraction which is at one with the spirit of geometry. That abstract spirit animates the complete utterance, lends force to the poet's argument on the difference between his chosen place and others of kindred beauty, and justifies the allusion in 'flocks, and herds, / And thickets full of songsters' to Milton's invocation to light (*Paradise Lost*, III, 39–44). This deliberate allusion is an appropriate way of indicating that the imagery of the major section is not the same as that of the opening sixteen lines but is now in another, more abstract, and universal context. In sum, the management of prosodic details is more crucial here than in most of Wordsworth's geometrical paragraphs, but the prosodic subtleties successfully build up and sustain a large and generous tribute and are instrumental in supporting the delicacy of sentiment which distinguishes this paragraph.

The geometry and prosody which distinguish Wordsworth's blank verse are, of course, only indirectly of value in a description of most of his rhymed poetry except in the sense that both his rhymed and unrhymed verse owe more to Italian than to neoclassical models and therefore stem from a tradition in which conceptual form is strongly associated with stanzaic patterns. The affinity between blank and rhymed verse in Wordsworth's poetry is most conspicuous in his use of the unrhymed form of the Italian sonnet at crucial points in the paragraphs of *The Excursion* and *The Prelude*, but the function of rhyme in the rhymed poems themselves often serves a similar architectural purpose which goes beyond the ear's ability to hear the jingling sound of like endings and encourages, instead, the mind's contemplation of a formal pattern that is at one with the idea of a poem. Thus – to take a simple illustration – it is unlikely that the ear perceives how, in the 'Mutability' sonnet (*PW*, III, 401), the fourteenth line, 'Or the unimaginable touch of Time,' rhymes with the first, 'From low to high doth dissolution climb,' although it is indispensable for a full reading of the poem to realize that mutability is contained within the circle of immutable order represented, in part, by the rhymes which enclose the entire sonnet. The logical extreme to which this principle of distant and therefore unheard rhymes can be taken would reveal the achievement of a rhymed form without the actual presence of the rhymes themselves, and this is, of course, precisely what Milton and Wordsworth have done in their blank verse sonnets. The distance between rhymes in the neoclassical couplet is, by comparison, obviously very close, meant to be heard, and thereby weights the end of the English pentameter so that it may approximate the effect of the longer unrhymed Latin hexameters and pentameters on which it is modeled. Despite its audibility, good neoclassical rhyme should not be too obtrusive or call too much attention to itself, for its principal function is to mark syntactical divisions and the primary caesuras in an utterance.[63] In short, neoclassical rhyme is exclusively concerned with the immediate prosodic questions of rhythm and linguistic structure within a line, but Italian rhyming procedures often extend over larger contexts and can turn an investigation of prosody into a consideration of the total form of a poem. As Puttenham remarked in the sixteenth century, 'these wide distances [between rhymes] serve for coupling of staves, or for to declare high and passionate or grave matter, and also for art: Petrarch hath given us examples hereof in his *Canzoni* . . .'[64]

Although Spenser, Milton, and Wordsworth have supplied the finest examples in English of poems indebted to the Italian tradition – just as Dryden and Pope are thought of as the greatest masters of neoclassical rhyme – the same poet could write well in either mode: Dryden's 1687 *Song for St. Cecilia's Day*, for example, is a spectacular illustration of suspended, architecturally significant rhymes – the circular design of the first stanza is carried over into the poem as a whole – and Wordsworth, from *An Evening Walk* to some of the *Inscriptions* and *Evening Voluntaries*, shows first a strict command of the neoclassical couplet and a subsequent assimilation of geometrical techniques developed in the writing of blank verse paragraphs. The prevailing tastes of these poets are what chiefly matter, though, and Wordsworth's ability to achieve conceptual form by means of rhyme may be anticipated with a glance at an illustration from Milton. Puttenham's comment on Petrarch's *canzoni* is apt here, for Milton's 'At a Solemn Musick' is a *canzone*, its lines being divided by rhyme into a *fronte* (1-16), a *sirima* (17-24), and a *commiato* (25-8). The *fronte* is subdivided into two *piedi* (1-8; 9-16), the second of which shows a notable instance of suspended rhyme:

> With Saintly shout, and solemn Jubily,
> Where the bright Seraphim in burning row
> Their loud up-lifted Angel trumpets blow,
> And the Cherubick host in thousand quires
> Touch their immortal Harps of golden wires,
> With those just Spirits that wear victorious Palms,
> Hymns devout and holy Psalms

> Singing everlastingly . . .[65]

A description, in order of rank, of the heavenly populace, these lines are symbolically, if not literally, a high point in the complete stanza and contrast with the prosodic irregularities that occupy the *sirima* (17ff) and its depiction of original sin on earth. As an expression of their state, the heavenly host are enclosed by the rhyming of 'Jubily' with 'everlastingly,' which rhymes are separated by a distance of eight lines or an octave, the interval of unison and a 'perfect Diapason' – as a later phrase in the stanza would have it – that is also enumerated in the eight metrical feet at the conclusion of the *fronte* (15–16). It is unlikely that, being separated by eight lines, these rhymes are meant to be heard: their function is clearly conceptual and represents the unheard music of perfect spiritual harmony. A similar use of rhyme, which comes right out of Milton and the Italian tradition, provides a crowning touch to some triumphant lines from the *Immortality Ode*:

> We will grieve not, rather find
> Strength in what remains behind;
> In the primal sympathy
> Which having been must ever be;
> In the soothing thoughts that spring
> Out of human suffering;
> In the faith that looks through death,
> In years that bring the philosophic mind. (*PW*, IV, 284)

An interval of eight lines separates the rhyming of 'find' with 'mind,' and once again the pattern of rhymes establishes an octave or diapason, which, in this case, expresses the symbolic harmony between time and eternity. Furthermore, Wordsworth has poignantly left the word 'death' – at the end of the seventh line – unrhymed with any other in the set, or, for that matter, with any other in the rest of the poem. The rhyming pattern of these eight lines has the additional virtue of recapitulating the contours of the *Ode*'s argument: couplet follows couplet, as a review of life from primal sympathies to the maturer consideration of 'human suffering' develops; but the thought of 'death' destroys the pattern, only to be transcended by the conceptual and symbolic rhyme of 'philosophic mind' – the meditative imagination – with the first line in the section. The rhymes in this passage thus not only fulfil a traditional motif of cosmological symbolism but also take a form that specifically, appropriately, and succinctly reflects the thought and architecture of the poem's largest movements.

Perhaps artistic refinements are to be expected in Wordsworth's most ambitious rhymed poem, but they also occur regularly in other works, even in the next example, which is one of the most popular and often-memorized in the language:

> I WANDERED lonely as a cloud
> That floats on high o'er vales and hills,
> When all at once I saw a crowd,
> A host, of golden daffodils;
> Beside the lake, beneath the trees,
> Fluttering and dancing in the breeze.
>
> Continuous as the stars that shine
> And twinkle on the milky way,
> They stretched in never-ending line
> Along the margin of a bay:
> Ten thousand saw I at a glance,
> Tossing their heads in sprightly dance.
>
> The waves beside them danced; but they
> Out-did the sparkling waves in glee:
> A poet could not but be gay,
> In such a jocund company:
> I gazed – and gazed – but little thought
> What wealth the show to me had brought:
>
> For oft, when on my couch I lie
> In vacant or in pensive mood,
> They flash upon that inward eye
> Which is the bliss of solitude;
> And then my heart with pleasure fills,
> And dances with the daffodils. (*PW*, II, 216–17)

Interstanzaic rhymes help to clarify why a poem which seems at first to be merely about daffodils actually concerns cosmic rhythms and offers an example of how a dormant imagination may be awakened to embrace, partake of, and create value for the scale of nature – of how, in short, an isolated mind worthy of the Solitary is transformed into one with the Wanderer's synthetic grasp of things. In the two middle stanzas, the sustained rhymes refer, in order, to each of the four main constituents of the lyric: the 'milky way' offers the sublime host of stars and the element of fire; the 'bay' recalls the beautiful pattern of waves and the element of water; 'they' at the end of the first line of the third stanza reinstates the daffodils, which, coming from the earth, are literally humble or on the ground; finally, the poet, who feels 'gay,' has already – 'as a cloud' – associated himself with the air but is now capable of his own vivifying movement of imagination to match the breeze that has animated the entire scene. Ranging across the elements and aesthetic magnitudes from the sublime to the humble, the interlinking rhymes of these two stanzas bring together eight lines at the centre of the poem which provide a graceful and compact summary of the Wordsworthian imagination in full possession of its powers. The first and last stanzas are similarly interlinked. Like the 'never-ending line' (9) of an arc or circle, the rhymes on 'daffodils' at the beginning and end of the poem show it to have a form that is always renewing itself on a level of contemplation which, far removed from the immediate and transitory delights in a physical object, is at one with the imagination's desire for permanence. Accordingly, a quiet but significant shift of emphasis from natural to spiritual activity occurs between the first and last instances of the encircling rhyme: initially separated from the daffodils – a point strengthened by the alternating rhyme of the opening four lines – the poet finally takes them to 'my heart' in the close bond of the poem's concluding couplet, which reveals that the object of perception is now seen exclusively in the light of the subject rather than for its own sake. A related process of development and achievement of form may be observed in 'She was a Phantom of delight/When first she gleamed upon my sight,' an opening couplet which rhymes with the conclusion of the poem – 'And yet a Spirit still, and bright/With something of angelic light' (*PW*, II, 213, 214). In this case, the rhymes at the beginning and end of the poem unite the most spiritual qualities of its subject in a circle of perfection which suggests that the rhyming pattern is representing something akin to a Platonic form. These two lyrics are so different from each other and, in turn, so much smaller in scale than the *Immortality Ode*; yet all three poems are artistically consistent with one another and, as will be argued shortly, are also clearly compatible with the same complex of thought.

Having touched on conceptual form in its manifestations of small effects at the metrical level and on the shorter- and longer-range functions of Wordsworth's type of rhyme, we may readily concede that any concept of form is all the easier to apprehend if it is accompanied by a contingent expression of formlessness; one's sense of rhythmically irregular versification similarly depends on what is fixed and uniform. The great danger for older poetry is that principles of form and unity may be adhered to so strictly and exclusively that their power is lost for want of contrast, just as, conversely, the variety and formlessness of much modern verse sinks into chaos and meaninglessness for lack of an internal standard which could confer value on deviations. Variations without a theme are not really variations but random activity to no apparent purpose and have always been difficult to follow except as illustrations of the law of diminishing returns. The 'concurring testimony of ages' suggests that a work of art is most challenging, gratifying, and natural to the ways of the mind and heart when both Apollo and Dionysus are present to set each other off – with Apollo, in the last analysis, given the nod at least fifty-one per cent of the time.

It is also apparent that Wordsworth carefully implemented this principle of reciprocity on every level of his work. In his rhymed poetry, the principle is most fully elaborated in the *Immortality Ode*: prosody, rhyme, and the shapes and designs of individual stanzas all combine to realize both the disorder and loss expressed in the early parts of the poem and the order and purpose restored at the conclusion. The comprehensive and authoritative stature of Wordsworth's achievement in the ode is reflected by the poem's ability to stand comparison with another work to which it is deeply indebted – Milton's *Lycidas*. The common reliance of these two poems on pastoral motifs and sequences of loss leading to recovery yields more than a general or casual resemblance, for their similarities emerge from a demonstration of the same intimate details of artistic execution. In brief, the form of *Lycidas* reveals that its first ten stanzas are a succession of *canzoni* with the eleventh stanza in *ottava rima* serving as a *commiato* to the whole. Of stanzas one to ten, the first nine are irregular, contain short lines, unrhymed lines, poor divisions between *fronte* and *sirima*, and lament and exemplify the inability of the pastoral tradition to deal satisfactorily with profound loss. In this regard, Milton has risked opening the elegy with a misstep – 'Yet once more, O ye Laurels, and once more' does not rhyme with any other line in its stanza.[66] The purpose of the apparently faulty techniques and faltering thought of these nine stanzas becomes clear in the tenth (165–85), which, in its unvarying line-length, schematically certain internal divisions, and encircling rhymes, is a model *canzone* and a triumph of conceptual form that accompanies the poem's great reversal of perspective: pastoral fiction, which is inadequate in the temporal world, turns out to be divine truth among the 'other groves' and 'other streams' (174) of heaven. The encircling rhymes of the tenth stanza itself not only represent a spiritual perfection of their own but redeem what hitherto appeared to be deficient, for the first line of this stanza – 'Weep no more, woful Shepherds weep no more' – also circles back to the first line of the poem – 'Yet once more, O ye Laurels, and once more' – a line which, in a stanza on the constraints of the temporal world, played out the poet's claim of artistic uncertainty by being unrhymed in its immediate context.[67]

Despite its brevity, this review of only a few aspects of *Lycidas* may be sufficient to suggest how Milton's techniques are similar to Wordsworth's use of formal details in the *Immortality Ode*. In particular, the principles of rhyme and prosody which prepare for the force and impact of uniformity in the transcendental tenth stanza of *Lycidas* extend to the same poetic elements and have a similar conceptual purpose in Wordsworth's poem. From a purely prosodic standpoint, Wordsworth's poem is, like Milton's, notable for the recurrence of its rhymes: every stanza has at least one set of rhymes which is interlinked with at least one other set elsewhere in the poem's eleven stanzas, and approximately half the lines in the last three stanzas, for example, rhyme with their predecessors. One could argue that Wordsworth found the invention of fresh rhyme difficult, but another evaluation is possible: namely, that repeated rhymes build up relationships of both general and specific significance. The most important of the specific instances develops from the transcendental vision at the end of the ninth stanza: 'And see the Children sport upon the shore, / And hear the mighty waters rolling evermore' (*PW*, IV, 284). This set of rhymes takes us back to the first stanza of the ode: 'It is not now as it hath been of yore . . . The things which I have seen I now can see no more' (6,9) – with the Alexandrines at the ends of the first and ninth stanzas adding to the prosodic bond between them. By using this means to bridge the distance between stanza one's theme of time and loss and stanza nine's vision of eternity and restoration, Wordsworth has also employed the same rhymes that perform the same function in Milton's *Lycidas* – 'Yet once more, O ye Laurels, and once more'; 'Weep no more, woful Shepherds weep no more' – a coincidence that sharpens the reliance of these two poems on the same artistic principle of using a particular sound to build up the general form and theme of a work.

Both these poems, in turn, are indebted to Vergil's *Eclogue* IV, from which Wordsworth took the phrase 'paulo majora canamus' as the 1807 epigraph of the ode. The similarities among these three poems not only include the character of their visionary themes, which will be discussed later, but extend even to the minutiae of execution in their common use of conceptual form at the level of prosodic detail. What might be said in brief is that Wordsworth's choices of theme and techniques for the *Immortality Ode* generally associate his work with those of Milton and Vergil and specifically show him moving among the same linguistic particulars and tonalities. The small example of how a sound may be employed – in this case, the syllable *or* – as an essential artistic detail in the thematic development of a work may now be extended to all three poems. As H.G. Edinger has written of *Eclogue* IV:

> It is immediately apparent that this syllable is involved in words that are properly called key words in the poem. *Maiora* announces the higher concern of the poem that segregates it from the surrounding *Eclogues*; it also sets the tone of the poem. *Saeclorum . . . ordo* is a phrase that represents a pair of homodyned *or*'s, in a verse quite central to the poem's theme, the return of the golden age . . . In sum-

mary, the sound *or* in the Fourth Eclogue has been avoided by the poet to such an extent that its few occurrences stand out prominently to color a small number of majestic and important verses, and to underline by emphatic, echoing sound a key train of thought in the poem, *maior, saeclorum, ordo, fatorum, concors, honor, Orpheus*.[68]

In short, it is apparent that the sound *or*, which, by itself, is, like any other noise, inherently meaningless, nevertheless has, in Vergil's poem, a thematically crucial value conferred upon it that resembles the values acquired by the key *or* rhymes of *Lycidas* and the *Immortality Ode*. The similar conceptual function of a specific sound in these poems is symptomatic of their general literary similarities, to which we shall turn in due course, and shows how, to great poets, a formal and artistic principle can possess the force that a major idea has to those whose thought is confined to verbal meaning alone. The fact that the artistic principle in question is even supported, in all three poems, by the same sound – the syllable *or* – may be merely fortuitous but certainly does not detract from the way in which the principle itself is upheld.

The power of sounds, prosody, and other artistic details in the *Immortality Ode* may now be related to the larger consideration of the poem's overall thematic and geometrical plan which also serves to summarize and consolidate the principal arguments of this book. The key to that plan is the recollection of knowledge from the mind's previous existence in an eternal context – an idea that Wordsworth describes in the poem itself and also in his prose notes to the work: '. . . a pre-existent state has entered into the popular creeds of many nations; and, among all persons acquainted with classic literature, is known as an ingredient in Platonic philosophy . . . when I was impelled to write this Poem on the "Immortality of the Soul", I took hold of the notion of pre-existence as having sufficient foundation in humanity for authorizing me to make for my purpose the best use of it I could as a Poet' (*PW*, IV, 464). Despite Wordsworth's life-long insistence on the idea of recollection as the basis of the ode, many readers have pushed the idea aside because, one suspects, they either find it embarrassing or are simply at a loss to know what to do with it. Wordsworth's helpful reference to Plato, however, suggests how he made 'the best use' of the idea in the composition of the ode and thereby imparted to the poem powerfully symbolic properties. Among Plato's various expositions of the concept of recollection, the account in the *Meno* seems particularly worthy of a brief citation, for here the Wordsworthian child has his Platonic counterpart. Before demonstrating that an uneducated child in Meno's retinue of slaves has an innate knowledge of mathematics, Socrates observes: 'Thus the soul, since it is immortal and has been born many times, and has seen all things both here and in the other world, has learned everything that is . . . for seeking and learning are in fact nothing but recollection'; after the demonstration of the child's mathematical capacities, Socrates concludes: 'Either then he has at some time acquired the knowledge which he now has, or he has always possessed it. If he always possessed it, he must always have known; if on the other hand he acquired it at some previous time, it cannot have been in this life, unless somebody has taught him geometry. He will behave in the same way with all geometric knowledge, and every other subject.'[69] Here, as in other arguments for the immortality of the soul, Plato draws on geometry as a mode of knowledge acquired in a previous existence. The historical function of geometry in the philosophical demonstration of the immortality of the soul is also at the heart of Wordworth's ode, which has the additional interest of showing that, among all the kinds of knowledge the child brings from eternity, geometrical thought is of the highest artistic use to the poet.

The geometrical plan of the *Immortality Ode* is based on the same proportion which Wordsworth employs selectively in the greatest passages of his other poems – the golden section, which, as one of the simplest of all ratios, is in its simplicity a considerable aid to composition and which, lying beyond the realm of numerical exactitude, is perfectly suited to the poet's belief in the transcendental value of geometry and also to his assertion of a 'principle of immortality' (*PW,* v, 445). In discussing the symbolic form of the poem, incidentally, I am not in any way disparaging its generic appearance as an 'irregular Pindaric ode.' It is again simply a question of a hierarchy of forms. At a rather low and general level of formal organization, the poem is, of course, an irregular Pindaric, a fact which tells us absolutely nothing about the particular verbal content of the work. At the higher level of symbolic form, the poem's geometrical design has a great deal to do with the theme of recollecting ideas from a prior existence. As a symbolic geometrical form, then, that goes to the heart of Wordsworth's 'principle of immortality,' the ode's last three stanzas, which resolve all the poem's difficulties, are in magnitude to the first eight stanzas, in which the difficulties are stated, as these eight stanzas are to the entire poem. In arithmetical approximations, the last 75 lines in stanzas IX-XI are 0.37 of the 204 lines in the ode, and the first 129 in stanzas I-VIII stand at 0.63 of the whole. The geometrical design of the poem is confirmed by its thematic structure. Stanzas I-VIII, which are the larger part of the ode's golden section, comprise a study of separations – of maturity from childhood and from the natural universe – and are further broken down into passages on the separation of the poet from his own childhood and from nature in stanzas I-IV (1-57) and into an analysis of kindred separations in general humanity in stanzas V-VIII (58-129). The private (I-IV) and public (V-VIII) scope of the mature mind's fragmentation and discontinuity with the past is plainly evident in the poet's loss of childhood powers of vision and in the subjugation of the mind to the mutability of the natural realm (stanza VI) and to the temporal preoccupations of human society; in stanza VII a mocking and satirical tone even emerges towards the adult world's assumption of superiority to that presumably ignorant blank slate, the child as pygmy or miniature adult. The union of private and public viewpoints and the restoration of continuity among poet, childhood, and nature extend throughout stanzas IX-XI and coincide precisely with the poem's division by golden section, as the poet fittingly celebrates the traces of knowledge and feeling that re-establish harmony between maturity and childhood, which, in its turn, is most closely attuned to an eternal origin. In other words, the ode's first eight stanzas discuss the discontinuity between maturity and childhood as tasks for the discursive or analytical intelligence, which 'sees the parts as parts,' just as the final three stanzas give the 'feeling of the whole' which exercises the intuitive or synthetic intelligence in the restoration of continuity and in a demonstration of the power of geometrical thought to provide a philosophically rational sanction for that continuity.

By drawing on the idea of recollection and by imparting a transcendental geometric plan to the ode, stanzas IX–XI recover an immaterial signification for the poem's language and form. The golden section provides a geometrical configuration which, although empirically unattainable by the temporal and numerical sequence of the poem's lines and physical structure, is nevertheless always metaphysically present in those lines, gives purpose to them, and shows them to be participants in a context that transcends their temporal and mutable functions. The idea of recollection, which is the verbal complement to the geometrical form, accomplishes the same service for the poem's language. As the first eight stanzas make clear, the difference between the languages of childhood and of maturity is that the adult's language has been shorn of all immaterial signification and is, to all intents, circumscribed by reference to the mutable and mortal processes of the temporal universe. The disappearance of the metaphysical meaning of language would be of no moment were the mature mind untroubled by the prospect of senseless annihilation or by feelings and convictions of immateriality that no longer have a credible language in which they may be expressed. We have already noted, for example, that the rhyme on 'more' in the Alexandrine at the end of stanza I – 'The things which I have seen I now can see no more' – is indicative of the adult's loss of metaphysical language and his submission to words which reflect only material and temporal conditions. When the same word reappears in a counterbalancing Alexandrine at the end of stanza IX, however – 'And hear the mighty waters rolling evermore' – the rhyme occupies a privileged position in revealing a direct vision of immaterial and transcendental conditions. That this recovery of metaphysical signification for language is rationally – and therefore publicly – credible is underscored by the role of stanza IX in realizing the geometrical form of the poem and by the verbally parallel interlinking of the sea of eternity, the children on the shore, and the adults far inland in a principle of continuity that originates beyond the limits of the material universe. The same reinstatement of immaterial significance in words may also be observed in one of the ode's principal recurring images. To the adult who has yearnings for immortality but a language of mortality, there is no 'glory in the flower,' as there was for the child, but only an enslavement to temporal nature in which even the humble pansy at the end of stanza IV may serve as a reminder of all that has been lost. At the end of the poem, however, even 'the meanest flower that blows' demonstrates, in its growth from an infant bud to an adult blossom, how nature may be rescued from its own processes of mutability and be employed, instead, in the metaphorical representation of the idea of recollection and in the reassertion of a metaphysical dimension in the language of the sense.

When fully understood, the epigraph of the poem – 'The Child is father of the Man' – is a formula for the idea of recollection, a key to the historical role of geometry in the demonstration of that idea, and a convenient summary of how that idea and its geometrical expression impart a philosophical power – which goes far beyond the merely psychological functions of memory – to Wordsworth's principle of continuity between past and present. Stanzas IX–XI share the work of giving detailed expression to the epigraph's principle of continuity by providing a corresponding artistic continuity which becomes the most conspicuous feature of the ode's language. In short, by recollecting and gathering up – in a highly concentrated fashion – many prominent linguistic patterns which were widely scattered and separated throughout the first eight stanzas, the final three stanzas assert a continuity that rescues the value of all that transpired in a temporal context. We have already seen how the final stanzas accomplish their redemptive task by means of an important recurrent rhyme and a floral image. On a larger scale, roughly half of the seventy-five lines in stanzas IX–XI rhyme with lines in stanzas I–VIII. The heavy concentration of interstanzaic rhyming establishes continuity between the temporal and eternal contexts of the poem and shows that the same words – in this case, the rhymes – have both material and immaterial significance, each of which is valid and necessary to the other. In this way, the language of the *Immortality Ode* sharpens a fundamental insight of *Tintern Abbey*: that, for example, the 'something far more deeply interfused' is both 'A motion' and 'a spirit' – both material and immaterial – that it pervades both spirit – 'All thinking things' – and matter – 'all objects of all thought' – and that its identification reflects the character of the context – either temporal or eternal – by which one approaches it. In the great ode, language is itself 'far more deeply interfused': there are not two dictions – one for material and one for immaterial descriptions – but simply one diction with a full range of signification restored to each word. The reappearance of words and phrases from the opening lines of stanza III in the opening lines of stanza X and from the beginning of stanza I in the beginning of stanza XI works to the same purpose, demonstrating that, to Wordsworth, the contexts of time and eternity are not mutually exclusive or antagonistic but are interdependent, as befits both his thematic principle of continuity and his geometrical principle of continuous proportion.

It would not be unreasonable to argue that, because of its profound combination of metaphysical language with geometrical form and its relation to some of the finest short works in the poetic tradition, the *Immortality Ode* is probably Wordsworth's most impressive single passage of poetry. The ode's true companions, as Wordsworth well knew and as we have seen in an earlier examination of small artistic details, are works such as Vergil's *Eclogue* IV and Milton's *Lycidas* and not Coleridge's *Dejection: An Ode*, which is, in this context, out of its element. So, after having made the habitual and unsatisfactory comparison between Coleridge's poem, which concerns one person's genuine loss of poetic power, and Wordsworth's, which reveals that the genuine and universal loss of childhood vision becomes the basis of a transcendent poetic power applicable to all, one returns to the great ode's original epigraph, which is – as was noted earlier – 'paulo majora canamus' – from the opening line of *Eclogue* IV. Wordsworth's sense that his poem shares a higher strain with Vergil's calls attention to the similarity of roles assigned to children in the two works. In the Messianic eclogue, the Vergilian child is a celestial gift that fulfils the pattern of destiny, prepares for the golden age, the transformation of both natural and human worlds, and their consequent harmony with the divine order. The Wordsworthian child, of course, restores a fearful humanity to a sense of eternal origins and destiny, the recognition of which leads to a transformation of the material world by means of a new and higher mode of perception. Vergil asserts that his transcendental theme – the incarnation of a godlike spirit in human form – will help him forge a poetic language which will be able to equal or surpass that of the gods. Wordsworth's language acquires its power of reference to immateriality in direct relation to the appearance of his theme – the entry of the eternal mind into time. Both poems have, furthermore, a mathematical dimension. As I have demonstrated elsewhere, the geometrical form of *Eclogue* IV is, like that of the *Immortality Ode*, based on the golden section and symbolizes a kindred relationship of celestial to temporal orders.[70] In a similar fashion, the conceptual form of *Lycidas* – the sequence of irregularly designed *canzoni* in relation to the ideal example in stanza X of that poem – is reflected in the *Immortality Ode*'s increasingly regular line-lengths and stanzaic symmetries as the poem nears its conclusion. Milton's rescue of the pastoral world, which is a fiction in time but a divine truth in eternity, is parallel to Wordsworth's eventual affirmation of May-Day festivities and to his reappropriation of the natural world as a realm of philosophic value. In both these poems, a private loss provides the occasion for a universal insight and for a prophetic mode of language, which, in all three poems, for that matter, is notable not for its idiosyncratic, but for its public, application. In Milton's poem, the solution to adversities is accomplished 'Through the dear might of him that walk'd the waves' (173), the good shepherd and incarnation through whom the Messianic child in Vergil's poem was endeared to Christian culture and with whom the Wordsworthian child is also compatible. In sum, these three poems are remarkable for the similar ways in which their conceptual forms and universalizing language transform a complex of specific artistic details, individual figures or persons, and pastoral motifs into a perception of general principles that define relationships between transcendental and temporal conditions.

In relation to Wordsworth's own poetry, the *Immortality Ode* shares characteristics of theme and form only with his most ambitious blank verse utterances; in particular, *Tintern Abbey*, the dream-vision in Book V and the ascent of Snowdon in Book XIV of *The Prelude*, and the Wanderer's prayer to the Supreme Being in Book IV of *The Excursion*. All these passages concern the relationship of immaterial to material realities, all have scales of perception or being to support a principle of continuity, and all are geometrically designed in continuous proportion. Among such companions, the great ode is still clearly distinguishable. It is, of course, the only one of these passages which is in rhyme; and its demonstration of geometrical form by means of the golden section is on a more massive scale than any of Wordsworth's other attempts. In addition, its conventional settings and generalized metaphors command a language which is more universal than that of the other major poems – *Tintern Abbey, The Prelude,* and *The Excursion* – in which, by comparison, linguistic textures are largely indebted to a sense of local places, times, and historical particulars. Perhaps more directly than anything else Wordsworth ever wrote, the great ode has the poetic tradition itself as its primary audience – hence, the relatively general, conventional, and timeless quality of its language and the sheer massiveness of its conception and execution. Whatever the case, Wordsworth always held the great ode in special esteem. It stands alone among his classifications and arrangements of his poems and is the work to which he most often alludes in his other verse thereafter – which suggests that the great ode was to its creator something of a testament to the best of his poetic thought and to that which he had identified in the poetic tradition.[71]

What one may learn about conceptual forms, themes, and treatments of the metrical tradition in such shorter works as the *Immortality Ode* and *Lycidas* is therefore pertinent to the identification of passages of central importance in the long poems. Conceptual form in a long poem is, of course, prominent throughout on the metrical level but assumes more ambitious proportions at moments of enlarged vision, the totality of which is best approached on the scale of the individual book. Among the books of *The Prelude* and *Paradise Lost,* the final ones bear a special responsibility in accordance with their valedictory positions. In chapter two, we have seen how Book XIV of *The Prelude* begins with an outstanding example of the golden section – the ascent of Snowdon itself (11–62) – and concludes with a blank verse sonnet (430–43). Wordsworth was to repeat this formal scheme in the last book of *The Excursion,* in which another mountain-view is expressed by means of the golden section (IX, 580–608) and is followed by a blank verse sonnet with geometrically determined internal proportions (614–27). Although these forms appear earlier at crucial points in their respective poems, their conjunction and united force at the conclusions of their works emphasize their especial significance as larger conceptual units which summarize and consolidate the best of their poet's argument. Similarly,

Milton calls upon the blank verse sonnet and *canzone* at the end of *Paradise Lost*. The final paragraph uttered on the top of the Mount of Speculation is a blank verse sonnet (XII, 574-87) and a *canzone* (588-605). The final speech by a character in the poem – Eve's – is a particularly glorious blank verse sonnet (610-23), and it is followed by the last paragraph of the epic which is a schematically regular *canzone* with two *piedi* in the *fronte* (624-32; 632-40) and a prosodically tranquil *sirima* (641-9). Again, these forms occasionally appear in earlier books, but here their extended combinations to the exclusion of virtually everything else lend them a particular force and significance as those vehicles chosen to convey thought of the highest conceptual order of which the poet was capable. The principles of form in the long poems of Milton and Wordsworth are thus, in many respects, simple extensions of the procedures worked out in the best short poems – procedures which impart grandeur to the minor poems, focus to the major works, and conceptual power and consistency to both within the shared values of metrical composition.

The comprehensive and rational artistic vision of a Wordsworth or a Milton is a fairly rare occurrence, of course, but elements of their practices still persist, despite the general loss of the tradition in which they worked. Pre-eminent among Wordsworth's successors is Yeats, who is not usually associated with the older poet but whose art exemplifies the same qualities. In 'Sailing to Byzantium,' for instance, the realms of natural and conceptual pleasures are assigned different prosodic characteristics. The world of generation is presented in enjambed lines, slant rhymes, and rhythmic substitutions against the metrical pattern. The conceptual world of Byzantium is accompanied by rhythms which conform to metre and by phrasing that agrees with the metrical line-length. The two modes are mixed in varying degrees throughout the four *ottava rima* stanzas of the poem, but the reciprocity of disorder and order is masterfully handled to the benefit of both. 'Lapis Lazuli' makes a similar point even more cunningly in its contrast of the modern world with the world of thought represented by the Chinamen on the stone: a person unfamiliar with prosodic conventions will be unable to read the poem correctly and will be thereby included among the hysterical sensibilities of the rootless modern age which Yeats so thoroughly despised. One frequent device is the elision of syllables in response to the requirements of metre: for example, 'It cannot grow by an inch or an ounce' will, to the ignorant, have ten syllables and rhythms which fail to support a metrical basis; in this line, as in many others of the lyric, elision – in this case, of 'by͡ an inch' and of 'or͡ an ounce' – not only restores the line to its metrical foundation, which is usually iambic tetrameter and occasionally iambic pentameter, but is essential to the colloquial style of language which gives so much of this poem's versification its piquancy.[72] Yeats's reliance on metre and rhyme runs against most fashions of modern poetry, but one cannot doubt that his adherence to older ways is well founded in his understanding of the conceptual form that imparts to traditional poetry so much of its precision, elegance, and power. T.S. Eliot's relationship to the same tradition is more tentative. By inclination, he seems to have been a dedicated upholder of the tradition, as the predominantly metrical techniques of the original *Waste Land* – before Pound edited it – testify. His use of free verse seems partly to have arisen out of a sense of moral obligation to contemporary language, and no one has explored the possibilities of this mode more fully or intelligently. The greatest single passage in all his works, though, is probably the 'dead master' section of 'Little Gidding' in the *Four Quartets*. These lines are an adaptation of *terza rima*, with masculine and feminine rhythms used at the ends of lines in place of rhymes. Eliot's handling of rhythm in relation to metre and of phrasing in relation to metrical line-length offers further proof of his command of an all-but-lost tradition, and the visit of the 'dead master' from another world is perfectly suited to the conceptual form of this metrical composition in relation to its actual and mutable language. These lines suggest the instructive implication that Eliot found it necessary – in what is obviously an attempt at a major utterance which can stand comparison with the great examples of the past – to employ the fullness of metrical composition. Whether a similar fullness and authority are possible in a non-metrical mode remains to be seen, but Eliot's artistic struggles argue that a further and deeper communion with the best of the metrical tradition is still indispensable.

Unlike many later poets, whose attitudes towards tradition are highly conspicuous, self-conscious, and often lead to stylization,

Wordsworth developed a relationship to metrical artistry which is so deep and exhaustive that it has largely eluded serious notice. His union of metrical and geometrical principles has gone unrecognized, and, on the thematic level, the nature of his philosophical idealism has been misunderstood or undervalued. Perhaps the omissions and misrepresentations stem from the habit of taking literary history too solemnly and of assuming that Wordsworth is only a Romantic poet – that is to say, a figure who is generally associated with a complex of attitudes that include the breaking down of form, reason, and order in the name of a subjective or personal imperative, the striving for absolutes, the veracity and recognition of which are problematical, and the pre-eminence of the psychological powers and virtues of the imagination. It is manifestly clear, of course, that Wordsworth did not believe poetry fettered would fetter the human race and that his interest in the psychological workings of the imagination was secondary to his assertion of ontological principles which give imagination a role in the scale of being. This is, after all, the point of the contrast between the Solitary and the Wanderer, the purpose of the dream-vision in Book V of *The Prelude*, and the goal which imparts cosmic significance to the ascent of Snowdon. It would appear, in short, that an exclusively psychological assessment of the Wordsworthian imagination is the basis of most misinterpretations of his poetry. Knowledge of the geometrical nature of his art corrects the shortcomings of subjective and psychological approaches and also helps to clarify the most difficult of the fundamental problems in reading this poet's works: the nature of his idealism. There seem to be two principal ways in which a poet can express an idealist viewpoint. One way is to start with the material world, from which the poet tries to escape by leaping, like a pole-vaulter, up into a realm of intelligibles or ideas before a probable fall back to earth. Such would appear to be the effect of much of Shelley's later work, for example, and the idealism in poetry of this type rarely confuses because the yearning for the ideal is so prominent. The other way is to take as one's 'paramount belief' (1850, VI, 132) the point of view of the eternal realm and then apply it to an evaluation of the material world. In this case, idealism is presupposed as a given and not as something towards which to strive. This position, which is Wordsworth's, is also, it could be argued, the more confidently held: priority is assigned to eternal principles, and if the veracity of an experience is to be questioned adversely, it will be that which originates in actuality – 'those obstinate questionings/ Of sense and outward things' (*PW*, IV, 283). Using transcendental values as a point of departure, this type of idealist poet directs most of his energies to the assessment of mutable actuality – a process which can suggest to the unwary that an empirical and materialist sensibility is at work. Some such assumption would seem to be needed to explain the existence of commentaries which express puzzlement over Wordsworth's treatment of nature in the *Immortality Ode* or which deny the poet's transcendentalism in *Tintern Abbey* or *The Prelude* and find, instead, an empirical or pantheistic outlook. In all these poems, needless to say, the mutable world is of value in so far as it helps the mind recollect its transcendent origins – the principal means of recollection being the mind's intuition of a prior state, its intellectual grasp of geometry, and its relation to the external world, the processes of which may be read as analogues of the mind's adaptation to and growth in time and the forms of which recall the geometrical order of the mind. Geometry thus serves as a common link between subject and object, and the fact that Wordsworth was able, moreover, to join his mathematical thought with his metrical practices completes the universal application of this transcendental motif and provides his idealism with an a priori value and an instrument that can quietly and comprehensively exemplify his deepest convictions in his ordering of empirical experience. His radically thorough and geometrical transcendentalism redeems an otherwise pointless world of actuality, establishes a consistent level of thought and artistry from *Tintern Abbey* onwards, and shows him to have more in common with the great meditative and idealist poets of the past to whom he acknowledged his indebtedness than with his contemporaries and successors. His combination of metre, geometry, the forms of nature, and ontological speculation constitutes an art and a body of thought that cannot be comprehended within the limits of a literary period but require the larger context of the best works from Milton to the ancients, whose concepts and principles Wordsworth sought so carefully to extend in his demonstration of the power of the rational imagination.

Appendix

Notes

APPENDIX

Form and Value in Music: Geometry and the Fugue

The use of the golden section in polyphonic music shows Wordsworth's profound kinship with certain artists in another discipline and also suggests, by analogy, how the values associated with a form might vary were that form to be commonly employed in the composition of poetry. Now, almost every commentator on the fugue points out that it is a style of composition, a polyphonic texture, rather than a clearly defined form, such as the sonata-allegro movement from the late eighteenth century onwards. However that may be, it is also true that many composers of fugues from the time preceding J.S. Bach to the present customarily associate the golden section with the regulation of harmonic schemes and musical content in this style of composition. In the present century, composers as diverse as Stravinsky, Bartók, Ravel, Hindemith, Shostakovich, and Carl Nielsen give the appearance of assuming that the use of the golden section in polyphonic music is common knowledge. Most fugues divide into two or three main parts, the interrelationships among which are often geometrically determined. In the double fugue from Stravinsky's *Symphony of Psalms*, for example, there are three main parts: an instrumental fugue of twenty-eight measures followed by a vocal fugue of thirty-two measures and, finally, another section of twenty-eight measures in which the instrumental fugue reappears by itself and then combines with the vocal fugue. In a relationship between human utterance, represented by the vocal fugue, and the divine solicitude symbolized by the instrumental fugue, the proportions of the movement are 32 : 28 + 28 :: 28 + 28 : 88 or 4 : 7 :: 7 : 11. A similar arrangement of the golden section may be found in the ratio of middle to outer sections of Ravel's fugue from *Le Tombeau de Couperin*, although this ingenious composer's most beautiful and successful example of the proportion is present, not in a fugue, but in a waltz, 'The Beauty and the Beast,' from the *Mother Goose Suite* in which the lovely theme of the beauty and the literally sinister and left-handed theme of the beast are presented separately and then combined at a point of golden section five-eighths through the composition. Rather than multiply examples at random, however, it is possible to ascertain the values which certain composers have attributed to the golden section. In pursuing this line of inquiry, we shall find that one composer in particular seems to parallel precisely what Wordsworth had in mind when using the ratio. By maintaining a high level of abstraction, incidentally, the resulting comparison tries to avoid both unwarranted musical obscurities and the usual difficulties attending a discussion of two different arts.

By way of summary, we shall concentrate on three main attitudes towards the golden section in music: the arithmetical, the geometrical, and the merely conventional. The first attitude – the arithmetical – is nicely illustrated by Bartók, whose practices have already been touched on in the first chapter. Bartók has earned the reputation of being one of the finest logicians in the entire history of music, and the thoroughness with which he worked out his ideas is without doubt a main reason for the praise now accorded him. As the Hungarian musicologist Ernö Lendvai has argued, the most profound secret of Bartók's music is that it depends on the tension between two different systems of proportion – the irrational ratio of the golden section versus the rational ratios based on whole numbers – and that the principles of these two systems are extended to such musical details as the shapes of themes and the kinds of harmonies to be used.[73] The golden section is associated with semitones, chromatic harmonies, and themes that spiral and curve around on themselves; simple whole-number ratios are accompanied by linear themes, the generally whole-tone character of modes and of the diatonic scale, and the larger harmonic intervals of the acoustic system. To the listener, the difference between the two systems is likely to be that between themes and harmonies which are hard to remember and are resistant to order – the music governed by the golden section – and those which, based on larger and clearer intervals, conform to simpler, easier, and more memorable patterns. Thus, in the opening movement of *Music for Strings, Percussion, and Celesta*, the main theme or subject is chromatic and is used to build up a fugue in which all the subdivisions, from the smallest to the largest, interlock in accordance with the golden section. In the final movement of the composition, the same theme reappears but is now straightened out with the help of whole-tone intervals and is domesticated in an environment of whole-number proportions and easy, delightful harmonies. A theme which began in a disturbing and restless milieu is transformed to partake of the good humour and joy of the composition's final pages. To Lendvai, the complete process suggests here, as in other works, such as the *Sonata for Two Pianos and Percussion*, an ascent from the infernal realm of the golden section to the paradise symbolized by the acoustic system – from geometrical to arithmetical proportions. In proffering a misleadingly Pythagorean solution, Lendvai is correct in saying that the golden section rests on a geometrical proportion and the acoustic system on arithmetical ratios. Unfortunately, Bartók is not, in Wordsworth's sense, a geometer at all but an arithmetician and a numerologist even in his approach to the golden section. In Bartók's music, the golden section exists only as it comes as close as possible to the cumbersome arithmetical approximations, 0.382 and 0.618. His attitude towards the ratio proves that he was not concerned with its lucidity, elegance, and simplicity as a geometrical concept but, rather, with the vexatious difficulties of representing arithmetically an infinitely non-repeating decimal fraction. His art is not based on geometrical but on arithmetical considerations, and nowhere does he show a geometrical understanding of the golden section: the tension between his two systems does not pit geometry against arithmetic but irrational against rational numbers. Lendvai's recourse to Dante in characterizing the golden section as infernal and the acoustic system as suggestive of paradise seems over-dramatic, for, in a purely ontological sense, Bartók may be indicating a relationship between multeity in the world of nature and the more unified world of the human spirit. Extremely fond of sunflowers, shells, pine cones, and other objects which exemplify the equiangular spiral, Bartók appears to have linked the golden section to scientific evidence about the design of nature and then placed his musical expression of that design philosophically below the more exclusively human discovery and ordering of musical relationships within the acoustic system. In short, his conception of the golden section is neither geometrical nor transcendental; it relies, instead, on a basis of scientific materialism and, as such, is a particularly apt and penetrating expression of the ratio's status in the modern age.

When editing J.S. Bach's *Well-Tempered Clavier*, Bartók – we may safely assume – was aware of and must have been impressed by the older composer's fascinating use of the golden section in a large majority of the fugues and in several of the preludes, especially those which are more solemn, expansive, and fully worked out. Fugues in golden section are the supreme expression of Bach's art, and their frequent appearances in the works for organ, the *Well-Tempered Clavier*, the *Art of Fugue*, the *Mass in B Minor*, and in many other compositions suggest that perhaps no other artist has ever explored the nature of the ratio as variously, profoundly, and consistently as has this composer.[74] Although the full musical meaning of the proportion is revealed only in a close study of harmonic and contrapuntal sequences and inversions, its general significance is abundantly clear as marking that point which divides complex and exploratory techniques from their most elemental, lucid, and ideal arrangements and combinations. The function of the golden section in Bach's fugues is, in other words, to indicate the integration of all musical elements in a condition of complete order and simplicity. The relationship between the two main parts of a Bach fugue might therefore be thought of as a ratio of change to permanence, of variety to order, of becoming to being, and of what is relative, conventional, and variable to what is fixed, symbolic, and absolute. Such contrasts in material which is so logically and rationally interrelated are particularly effective in vocal music, for the semantic value of a text helps to confirm the purely formal meaning of musical sounds. In the first 'Kyrie' of the *Mass in B Minor*, for example, a slow, meditative fugue in five voices begins after a brief four-measure introduction. The one hundred and twenty-two measures of the ensuing fugue divide by continuous geometrical proportion into a major section of seventy-six measures followed by a minor section of forty-six measures – 122 : 76 :: 76 : 46 – so that the final forty-six measures are 0.377 of the entire fugue. The major section of seventy-six measures begins and ends with an instrumental fugue, which is combined with a vocal fugue in its middle portions, and the principal statements of the fugue's subject or theme occur in the less prominent middle voices (tenor, alto, second soprano) and in keys other than the tonic base of b minor. The forty-six measures of the minor section use the same music but in a markedly different and majestic pattern: the voices and instruments are combined at the outset and systematically follow a rising sequence of entries of the fugue subject – beginning with the bass in b minor and ascending to two high soprano entries, the second of which is in b minor – and conclude by descending to a final bass entry in b minor. The total effect of the entire fugue is, in accordance with the text, of a prayer asked in anguish and answered in exalted calm. The suggestion of absolute order in the minor section no doubt owes a great deal to the rising and falling sequences of entries of the fugue subject and to the predominance of entries in the chosen key of b minor, for no matter how human ingenuity may divide a musical scale – by whole tones, semitones, a mixture of the two, or by microtones – what is absolutely true for all systems is that any given root note has a simple multiple which, with the root note, encloses every conceivable scale and thereby encloses all the efforts of human ingenuity by establishing a transcendent and given universal. The opening movement of the *Mass in B Minor*, then, shows the ingenious concept of tonality yielding, at the point of golden section, to the more elemental concept of key itself. The procedure is, on an abstract level, similar to Wordsworth's employment of continuous geometrical proportion in the transition from psychological to ontological values. Bach's music, like Wordsworth's poetry, is most visionary when it is most geometrically elemental. That the golden section in Bach's compositions has a transcendental value may be inferred from the *Mass in B Minor*, the movements of which are largely based on the ratio and the whole of which carries the Latin abbreviation 'S.D.G.' – 'solely to the glory of the Lord.' In this respect, the nineteenth part of the *Mass* contains one of the most astonishing and perfectly realized instances of the golden section in the history of art: a passage of forty-two measures on the phrase 'et expecto resurrectionem mortuorum' (measures 121–62) in which the first twenty-six measures, labelled 'adagio,' are in a slowly moving milieu of shifting chromatic harmonies and yield, at the sign 'vivace ed allegro,' to sixteen measures of music which leaps upward in perfect diapason, octave intervals – 42 : 26 :: 26 : 16. That the composer's attitude towards the ratio is purely geometrical – that is, like Wordsworth's rather than Bartók's – seems clear from a survey of his practices in various works. Bach's calculations of the proportion range arithmetically from 0.36–0.39, with the convenient approximations – three-eights and numbers in the Fibonacci series – supplying the usual limits. The triple fugues from the two books of the *Well-Tempered Clavier* illustrate his habits of calculation, two of the principal ways in which he arranged the golden section in his compositions, and the musical function of the ratio as a barometer of the highest type of order to be found in his works. A triple fugue, as Bach constructs it, has three contrasting themes or subjects which are normally presented separately before being combined and played simultaneously. The perceptive reader will already have anticipated that the point at which the themes combine is of geometrical significance. Resembling the form of the opening 'Kyrie' from the *Mass in B Minor*, the famous triple fugue in c-sharp minor from the first book (1722) of the *Well-Tempered Clavier* (*WTC*, I, 4) has a major section of seventy-two measures followed by a minor section of forty-three measures, so that, working backwards, 43 : 72 :: 72 : 115. The major section is itself a simple binary, the first half of which presents the first fugue and the second half of which adds two more subjects and the combination of all three in a variety of keys, not one of which predominates. In the minor section – the last forty-three measures of the piece – the climax of the fugue is reached as all three subjects are again combined but this time in a series of entries which are restricted to the given key of c-sharp minor and commence with the powerful appearance of the first subject in the deep bass, from which it rises in its subsequent course. The minor section is also a simple binary, and in the second half the first and third subjects are massed in a sequence of overlapping entries (stretto) to bring the composition to its majestic close. In retrospect, the major section of the fugue gives the sense of a search for harmonic and contrapuntal combinations which seem to grow and develop out of one another, and the minor section offers the triumphant discovery of their ideal arrangements in a condition of elemental power and simplicity. The division of an entire fugue into a major section followed by a minor one is common in Bach's works, and further examples of this scheme are readily found in *WTC*, I (2, 6, 9, 11, 13, 17, 22, 23), *WTC*, II (2, 8, 17), and the *Art of Fugue* (I, V).

When composing longer and more complex fugues, Bach tended in his later works to establish three or more principal sections but to place only the last two in golden section with each other or to leave the opening section, which has a predictable character in its fulfilment of several conventions of fugal writing, out of his calculations. By this means, he was also able to heighten the contrast between major and minor sections of the ratio, for the resolution of musical thought in the final section would be juxtaposed only with the harmonic and contrapuntal flux of a middle section and not with the rather conventional formalities of the initial exposition of a subject. The triple fugue in f-sharp minor from the second book (1744) of the *Well-Tempered Clavier* is a case in point (*WTC*, II, 14). Despite showing only seventy measures, it is a lengthy work: its tempo is similar to that of the c-sharp minor triple fugue from the earlier collection, and were its notation given the same time-values as the earlier fugue, it would be one hundred and forty measures long. The f-sharp minor triple fugue falls into three main parts of twenty, thirty-one, and nineteen measures with the middle and final sections constituting a golden section – 19 : 31 :: 31 : 50. Occupied solely by entries of its noble and dignified theme, the first section draws to a formal close, at which point the fugue begins a new career. The middle section of thirty-one measures is a simple binary, in which a second subject of great pathos is presented by itself and later in combination with almost hidden entries of the first subject before giving way in the ensuing half of the binary to the introduction and development of a meandering third subject. The final nineteen measures of the fugue commence with the prominent reappearance of the noble first subject and its combination with both other subjects in the given key of f-sharp minor and in keys symmetrically centred around that given key. The secret of the fugue's powers of resolution thus resides in the first subject – a scheme which is sharpened by the simple binary equivalence between the certainties of the nineteen measures of the minor section of the ratio and the strength and clarity of the fugue's opening twenty measures, in which the first subject is presented by itself. Other examples of golden sections which do not include the opening part of a fugue in the calculation or which develop the proportion only in the final two sections of a work occur in *WTC*, I (8,20), *WTC*, II (3, 4, 5, 9, 13, 18, 19, 20, 21, 22, 23, 24), and in the two triple fugues from the *Art of Fugue* (VIII and XI). Besides the two patterns illustrated in the previous paragraphs, there are, of course, still other arrangements of the ratio, as when a fugue's middle section is in proportion with the combined magnitude of the first and last sections: for example, *WTC*, I, 1; *WTC*, II, 16; and *Art of Fugue*, III.

In leaving Bach's fugues, it remains to be said that the golden section is his favourite but not exclusive means of developing a form for this species of composition – although all examples have a clearly delineated form of some kind – and that there are other patterns which follow from and run parallel to geometrical form. Number symbolism, for example, is a current rage in Bach scholarship, just as it is in the analysis of some Renaissance and Medieval poetry. Although finding numerological significance in the number of notes in a theme or in the total of measures in a composition is, in Bach's case, often justified, numerology here, as in the analysis of poetry, is usually a study of ancillary, ornamental, and subordinate activities, bearing much the same relationship to the concepts of geometrical form that counting the number of stone blocks has to the design of a cathedral after the forms and relationships of masses one to the other have been conceived. In this regard, it may be of interest to observe that Bach's pairings of preludes and fugues often show a shift of proportions from a prelude's common and simple whole-number ratios to the golden section form of a fugue, as the performer advances from a preparatory exercise to a higher level of order. Bach's sense of proportion, which is fundamentally geometrical, is thus the opposite of that found in Bartók, who, as we have seen, would have taken whole numbers to be the goal of a musical journey. What strikes one, ultimately, is that Bach, like Wordsworth, represents the essence of geometrical thought, the sublime and elemental simplicity of which becomes increasingly conspicuous in direct relation to the apparent complexity of a major effort. Hence, the valedictory fugue in b minor at the end of the first book of the *Well-Tempered Clavier* (*WTC*, I, 24) and the *Musical Offering*'s fugue in six voices – thought by many to be the greatest fugue ever composed – are both governed entirely by the placement of a minor before a major section of continuous proportion. The opening twenty-nine measures of the b minor fugue present a chromatic subject, which joins with diatonic counterpoint before yielding eventually to a totally diatonic episode so that an entire range or spectrum of musical possibilities is included. The remaining forty-seven measures of the fugue essentially repeat the process, but with harmonic sequences rearranged and inverted – 29 : 47 : : 47 : 76. The fugue in six voices from the *Musical Offering* contains six entries of its chromatic subject in the opening thirty-nine measures and then six more entries in its final sixty-four measures, but whereas pairs of entries in the minor section move upwards to a key above the given tonal base of c minor, the counterparts in the major section move downwards on their way towards the final re-establishment of the original key and are surrounded by episodes in which fragments of counterpoint from the minor section are inverted in various ways – 39:64::64:103. In each fugue, much of the contrast between the ratio's sections is achieved by the asymmetrical interdependence of inverted harmonic and contrapuntal contexts – a procedure which, like a photograph and its negative, is conceptually similar to Wordsworth's inversion of values placed on abstract and concrete language in 'Yew-Trees.'

All that has been said thus far shows that a critical examination of something even as specific as the golden section can shed light on the quality of an artist's relationship to a form, which, usually involving a relationship to a tradition, also owes a great deal to particular cultural conditions that alter and pass away and thereby render the form peculiar or inappropriate in subsequent circumstances. Although both Bach and Wordsworth left artistic legacies of the highest order, in Wordsworth's case the poet's geometrical sophistication apparently went unnoticed and therefore never became a tradition to be manipulated in various ways by successors. Had his techniques been known, however, it is reasonable to assume that they would have been taken as an end in themselves, divorced from the values that gave rise to them, and have led to the formulation of mere conventions and textbook definitions, which, although always of potential value, have by themselves a way of missing the point of it all. Such, at least, is the fate which usually overtakes other interesting enterprises, be they artistic, religious, or scientific. In the case of the fugue, it is perhaps more accurate to state that the Bachian peak of the tradition has been but partially understood and that what was authentic and appropriate for the baroque era in music has become retrospectively devalued and oversimplified. Not having been widely employed in serious composition for more than two centuries, the fugue has been remembered chiefly by theorists, most of whom think that all proper fugues should conform to certain patterns, the absence of which in the majority of Bach's compositions leads to the conclusion that Bach is a dangerous model to study.[75] Exemplifying various approved rules and taking a routine approach to matters of proportion, the academic and conventional fugue has an imposed form which overlooks the imaginative and logical necessities that yield coherent contrasts between sections in geometrical form, neglects the spirit of speculation that accepts beneficial rules and conventions in order to go beyond them to more fundamental insights into the ways in which the mind invests form with value, and precludes an attempt at the highest sort of decorum: the sense that the total form of a work is perfectly realized from within. Thus, nearly all attempts in the last two centuries to compose fugues of the Bachian variety are notable chiefly as monuments to a careful academicism which sacrifices good geometrical procedures to conventional patterns of musical organization. Even the penetrating and creative analysis of a major composer – in this case, Dmitri Shostakovich, whose attractive and careful *24 Preludes and Fugues* (1951) imitate the *Well-Tempered Clavier* closely while combining his own distinctive lyricism and nineteenth-century tenets on fugue structure with Bach's concepts of geometrical form – may appear to be over-simple and conventional when the use of the golden section is not supported by a sufficiently complex harmony and counterpoint that is capable of simultaneous changes and resolutions and thereby of expressing contrasts between a thorough development and the absolute achievement of the ideal form, contrasts which the works of Bach exemplify time and again. Although not developing a form sufficiently to eliminate the sense that it is merely imposed or embezzled from one's betters, the labours of a keen analytical intelligence can be here, as in the front rank of minor poetry, of considerable value; for, by doing singly, separately, and thus more simply what is more complex, subtle, and perhaps mysterious in the works of the greatest artists, the best partial successes with a form point to the means by which the wider values of a culture, its traditions, a sensibility, and a full command of technique are comprehensively integrated and united. For similar reasons, literary historians have often benefited from an attentive study of Milton's imitators.

Patterns of evidence pertinent to a single geometrical motif are often analogous to what one may find with respect to other manifestations of artistic tradition. In this regard, it is possible for a modern scholar or artist to restore a tradition in ways that will give it as much authenticity, authority, and integrity in the present as it had in the past. One way – that of recreating the original purpose of an old form in a modern idiom – is a stupendous task which exercises the limits of an artist's techniques and philosophical convictions. Another way is to develop a comprehensive new equation between form and value which, although differing greatly from the original purpose of the form, appeals to some of the most significant cultural preoccupations of the artist's own era. In the recent history of music, for example, it seems increasingly apparent that Stravinsky, in his middle and later works, was capable of fulfilling the task of restoring old forms and that Bartók succeeded in creating a justifiable new system of values for old forms. Modern verse in English does not show any wide-ranging reassessment of old forms – although there are outstanding isolated instances such as Yeats's transformation of the *ottava rima* stanza for use in the most ambitious lyric poetry – but a few passages from the works of T.S. Eliot and numerous lyrics by Yeats provide conspicuous examples of how old forms, traditions, and techniques may be kept alive. In comparison with their modern successors, older artists such as Bach and Wordsworth, having the advantage of working within major traditions which were not yet sufficiently contemned or disregarded, were able to synthesize many more elements of their respective arts much more rapidly. For both these figures, the principles behind their employment of the golden section are at one with other features of their artistry – considerations of metre, phrasing, the aesthetics of formal unity, and the purposes of creation – so that from fairly early points in their careers onwards they could face the enormous challenges and gratifications of developing in quality and in quantity a comprehensive vision of virtually all that their arts had to offer.

Notes

1 William Wordsworth, 'St. Paul's,' in *Wordsworth's Poetical Works*, edited by Ernest de Selincourt and Helen Darbishire, rev ed (Oxford 1952-9), IV, 374-5. All subsequent citations of poetry or prose from volumes I-V will be indicated in the text as *PW*.
2 *William Wordsworth: The Prelude - A Parallel Text*, edited by J.C. Maxwell (Harmondsworth 1971), 1850, VI, 135, 137; XI, 330 ff. All subsequent citations of *The Prelude* are from this edition and will be so specified in the text.
3 Otto Skutsch, 'Symmetry and Sense in the Eclogues,' *Harvard Studies in Classical Philology* 73 (1969), 156.
4 See H.C. Robinson, *Henry Crabb Robinson on Writers and Their Work*, edited by Edith J. Morley (London 1938), II, 484.
5 'Milton's Blank Verse Sonnets,' *Milton Studies* V (Pittsburgh 1973), 129-53; 'Sonnet Variations,' *Wordsworth and the Sonnet* (Copenhagen 1973), 174-80.
6 Wordsworth's Shakespearean examples are the early 'Sonnet on Seeing Miss Helen Maria Williams Weep at a Tale of Distress' and the first fourteen lines of 'The Emigrant Mother.'
7 The definitive dismissal of the concept of a *volta*, as imposed on the Petrarchan sonnet, is in John S. Smart's 'Introduction' to *The Sonnets of Milton*, 2nd ed (Oxford 1966), 30-3.
8 Stephen Gill and Jonathan Wordsworth, 'The Two-Part *Prelude* of 1798-99,' *Journal of English and Germanic Philology* 72 (October 1973), 508-9.
9 Rudolf Wittkower, 'The Changing Concept of Proportion,' *Daedalus* 89 (Winter 1960), 204. In this connection, the elegance of the golden section's mathematical and aesthetic properties is the basis of H.E. Huntley's *The Divine Proportion: A Study in Mathematical Beauty* (New York 1970) - an attempt by a mathematician

to show that his subject has a charm equal to that of poetry.
10 S.K. Heninger, Jr, *Touches of Sweet Harmony* (San Marino, California 1974), 258–9.
11 Ibid, 84ff; compare Paul H. Scholfield, *The Theory of Proportion in Architecture* (Cambridge 1958), 37ff and Rudolf Wittkower, *Architectural Principles in the Age of Humanism*, 2nd ed (New York 1965), 159ff. To both Scholfield and Wittkower, the Middle Ages had a truly geometrical approach to proportion, but the Renaissance had an arithmetical penchant which could not deal with incommensurables such as the golden section.
12 Wordsworth, 'A Guide through the District of the Lakes,' *The Prose Works of William Wordsworth*, edited by W.J.B. Owen and J.W. Smyser (Oxford 1974), II, 233.
13 Mary Moorman, *William Wordsworth: The Early Years 1770–1803* (Oxford 1957), I, 97.
14 'The Rydal Mount Library Catalogue,' *Transactions of the Wordsworth Society*, edited by William Knight (Edinburgh 1886), VI, 210.
15 Moorman, 286.
16 B.R. Schneider, Jr, *Wordsworth's Cambridge Education* (Cambridge 1957), 231.
17 A recent assertion, for example, that the earlier Wordsworth is an empiricist is Alan Grob's *The Philosophic Mind* (Columbus 1973), 5–7ff.
18 Edmund Burke, 'A Philosophical Inquiry into the Origin of Our Ideas of the Sublime and the Beautiful,' *The Works of Edmund Burke* (Boston 1899), I, 177 – for example, 'mathematical ideas are not the true measures of beauty.' A good analysis of Burke's views and of those of other eighteenth-century English aestheticians is found in Rudolf Wittkower's *Architectural Principles in the Age of Humanism*, 151ff.
19 As quoted in D.W. Thompson, *On Growth and Form* 2nd ed (Cambridge 1959), II, 766. See also entry under 'Bernoulli' in *Encyclopedia Britannica*, 11th ed (Cambridge 1910), vol III.
20 Euclid, *Elements*, edited by Tacquet (Dublin 1728), 89; as quoted by B.R. Schneider, Jr, 96–7.
21 See Carl B. Boyer, *A History of Mathematics* (New York 1968), 55. Kepler's other great treasure of geometry is, incidentally, the Pythagorean Theorem.
22 The golden section permeates the twelve-sided figure made of regular pentagons. Mark diagonals in the regular pentagon, thereby inscribing a five-pointed star, and the diagonals bisect

each other in extreme and mean ratio; the triangular areas contained by the diagonals and by the sides of the pentagon will also be in continuous proportion.
23 The main articles on 'Yew-Trees' are by Brooks and Warren, *Understanding Poetry*, 3rd ed (New York 1960), 273-9; Michael Riffaterre, 'Interpretation and Descriptive Poetry: A Reading of Wordsworth's "Yew-Trees"', *New Literary History* 4 (1973), 229-56; and Geoffrey Hartman, 'The Use and Abuse of Structural Analysis: Riffaterre's Interpretation of Wordsworth's "Yew-Trees",' *New Literary History* 7 (1975), 165-89. A totally different aspect of 'Yew-Trees' is suggested by my colleague G.H. Durrant, who finds political significance in the work's historical allusions: given the fact that the poem was composed in the years of threatened Napoleonic invasions, contemporary readers might have observed how England – the Lorton Yew – is eventually united with her former enemies to comprise England, Scotland, Wales, and Northern Ireland – the famous four of Borrowdale. In this way, 'Yew-Trees' would be similar to 'View from the Top of Black Comb,' in which the speaker surveys all four countries and rejoices in 'Britain's calm felicity and power' (*PW*, II, 290).
24 M.H. Abrams, 'Structure and Style in the Greater Romantic Lyric,' *From Sensibility to Romanticism*, edited by Frederick W. Hilles and Harold Bloom (New York 1965), 528-30.
25 John Milton, *Paradise Lost*, edited by Merritt Y. Hughes (New York 1962), XII, 576-9. All subsequent citations of *Paradise Lost* are from this text.
26 Maxwell, 'Introduction,' *William Wordsworth: The Prelude*, 18.
27 John Jones, *The Egotistical Sublime* (London 1954), 81.
28 At least, the 'fully developed geometrical procedures' are the case when Wordsworth had differentiated his two long poems and had the plan of the 1805 *Prelude* in mind. The situation is more obscure with regard to a conjectural and early 'two-part' *Prelude*, the content of which antedates passages on his own acknowledged obligations to geometry and the revisions of which doubtlessly were undertaken for more than geometrical reasons. See *The Prelude: 1798-99*, edited by Stephen Parrish (Ithaca 1976).
29 G.H. Durrant, *Wordsworth and the Great System* (Cambridge 1970), 21.
30 On Renaissance poetry and cosmology, the following works and their bibliographies are among those which are useful: Alistair Fowler, *Spenser and the Numbers of Time* (London 1964); Fowler, *Triumphal Forms: Structural Patterns in Elizabethan Poetry* (Cambridge 1970); S.K. Heninger, Jr, *Touches of Sweet Harmony*.

31 Newton's remark is easily found in many encyclopedias and in such popular sources as 'Newton, Huygens,' *Great Books* (Chicago 1952), x, and originates in Brewster's *Memoirs of the Life, Writings and Discoveries of Sir Isaac Newton*, vol II, chapter 27.
32 D.W. Thompson, *On Growth and Form*, II, 766ff.
33 G.H. Hartman, *Wordsworth's Poetry: 1787-1814* (New Haven 1964), 229.
34 Frank McConnell, *The Confessional Imagination: A Reading of Wordsworth's 'Prelude'* (Baltimore 1974), 134.
35 Flemming Olsen, 'Geometry and "Forms" in Wordsworth's *Prelude*,' *Orbis Litterarum* 26 (1971), 41.
36 William Wordsworth, *The Prelude: 1799, 1805, 1850*, edited by Jonathan Wordsworth, M.H. Abrams, and Stephen Gill (New York 1979), 99.
37 Hartman, *Wordsworth's Poetry*, 185.
38 Ibid, 255.
39 Ibid, 293, 295, 312.
40 Wordsworth, 'Letter to Catherine Clarkson, January, 1815,' *Literary Criticism of William Wordsworth*, edited by Paul M. Zall (Lincoln, Nebraska 1966), 132.
41 Ibid, 133.
42 Ibid.
43 See *PW*, V, 423 and 369-72.
44 Hartman, *Wordsworth's Poetry*, 315-16, 317. To give Hartman his due, he eventually discerns in the opening lines of Book IX 'the real Chain of Being' (323) as contradistinguished, one presumes, from the unreal and 'superfluous' scale of being in Book IV – but the distinction seems forced and merely becomes yet another way of avoiding the cosmological mainspring of Wordsworth's poetry.
45 As was the case with one of the three instances of continuous proportion in the dream-vision of the Arab, stone, and shell, so, here, the approximation of the ratio (at slightly more than 0.35 of the paragraph) lies just outside the close range of approximations (0.36-0.39) we have used. For that matter, these two examples are the least accurately calculated of any cited throughout this book. In the present case, the inaccuracy may signify nothing else than the difficulty Wordsworth encountered in co-ordinating all the main geometrical divisions of such a large and complex paragraph. It is possible, though, that a more numerically precise section of twenty-one lines (21:36::36:57) was avoided because the minor section's internal proportions would then constitute one of the simplest and most conspicuous rational fractions – 1:2 –

seven lines followed by the fourteen lines of the blank verse sonnet. Such an internal proportion could lend a false architectural importance to the syntactical parallelism in 'Ah! if the time must come' and 'If the dear faculty of sight should fail' by drawing attention away from the participation of the minor section in the geometrical design of the entirety of the paragraph. That is to say, there could be instances in which, because of strong internal symmetries within a small quantity of verse, a more precise numerical approximation to the golden section might undermine the primacy of continuous geometrical relationships among the larger movements of a passage.

46 George E. Duckworth, *Structural Patterns and Proportions in Vergil's Aeneid: A Study in Mathematical Composition* (Ann Arbor 1962), 47.

47 The relationship of value to form is becoming increasingly important in discussions of proportion, symmetry, and numerology; a brief summary of some recent thoughts on that relationship and on its use in critical analysis may be found in *PMLA* 92 (1977), 126-9.

48 Further comments on Duckworth's method appear in Janet P. Bews, '*Aeneid* I and .618,' *Phoenix* 24 (1970), 130-43. For a companion to Duckworth's approach, see Edwin L. Brown's detailed treatment of the golden section in *Numeri Vergiliani: Studies in Eclogues and Georgics (Collection Latomus)* 63 (1963), 64ff.

49 See my 'Virgil, Wordsworth, and the Power of Sound,' *Mosaic* 13 (Fall 1979), 92-109.

50 D.W. Thompson, *On Growth and Form*, again deserves to be cited for containing the pioneering and yet most comprehensive attempt to use mathematics in the description of common objects.

51 Jay Hambidge, *Dynamic Symmetry: The Greek Vase* (New Haven 1920); and *The Elements of Dynamic Symmetry* (New Haven 1926).

52 Rudolf Wittkower, *Architectural Principles in the Age of Humanism*, is still probably the best account of the interrelationships among mathematics, architecture, and the human form. Further thoughts on the kind of geometrical system Le Corbusier developed may be found in *Module, Proportion, Symmetry, Rhythm*, edited by Gyorgy Kepes (New York 1966).

53 William Blake, *Jerusalem*, in *The Poetry and Prose of William Blake*, edited by David V. Erdman (New York 1965), 144.

54 Paul Fussell, Jr, 'Meter,' *Encyclopedia of Poetry and Poetics*, edited by Alex Preminger (Princeton 1965), 496.

55 Edward R. Weismiller, 'Studies of Verse Form in the Minor English Poems,' *A Variorum Commentary on the Poems of John Milton*,

edited by A.S.P. Woodhouse and Douglas Bush, II, iii (New York 1972), 1007-8.
56 *Virgil's 'Aeneid,'* translated by John Dryden (New York 1968), 9.
57 S. Jay Keyser, 'The Linguistic Basis of English Prosody,' *Modern Studies in English*, edited by David A. Reibel and Sanford A. Schane (Englewood Cliffs 1969), 379.
58 W.H. Auden, 'Introduction,' *Medieval and Renaissance Poets*, edited by W.H. Auden and Norman Holmes Pearson (New York 1950), xxi.
59 Alfred Tennyson, 'Tithonus,' in *The Poems of Tennyson*, edited by Christopher Ricks (London 1969), 1114.
60 Stephen Maxfield Parrish, *The Art of the Lyrical Ballads* (Cambridge, Mass. 1973), 21-2.
61 S.T. Coleridge, chapter XIV, *Biographia Literaria*, edited by J. Shawcross (Oxford 1907), 9-12. Chapter XVIII is also interesting throughout, for it provides a sustained defence of imaginative diction while attacking the functions of metre as Wordsworth describes them.
62 Alexander Pope, *An Essay on Man I*, in *The Poems of Alexander Pope*, vol III: i, edited by Maynard Mack (New Haven 1950), 49-51.
63 See William Bowman Piper, *The Heroic Couplet* (Cleveland 1969), for a discussion of rhyme and syntax in the neoclassical couplet and its variants.
64 George Puttenham, *The Art of English Poesie*, edited by Gladys Doidge Willcock and Alice Walker (Cambridge 1936), 86-7.
65 John Milton, 'At a Solemn Musick,' in *The Student's Milton*, edited by Frank Allen Patterson (New York 1930), 19.
66 John Milton, *Lycidas*, in *The Student's Milton*, edited by Frank Allen Patterson (New York 1930), 40.
67 In 'Milton's 'Destin'd Urn': The Art of *Lycidas*,' *PMLA* 84 (1969), 60-70, J.A. Wittreich, Jr, demonstrates how the continuous rhyming of the poem shows it to be a madrigal, which is similar to the *canzone*. Wittreich's splendid article, however, is devoted more to classification than to the critical evaluation of disordered and ordered form which occupies the present argument and which is, in many respects, more clearly foreshadowed by Ants Oras in 'Milton's Early Rhyme Schemes and the Structure of *Lycidas*,' *MP* 52 (1954), 20.
68 H.G. Edinger, 'Paulo Maiora Canamus,' *Vergilius* 14 (1968), 31.
69 *Meno*, translated by W.K.C. Guthrie, *The Collected Dialogues of Plato*, edited by Edith Hamilton and Huntingdon Cairns (New York 1961), 364d, 370e.

70 A fairly thorough consideration of the geometrical designs and patterns of sound in *Eclogue* IV and the *Immortality Ode* may be found in my 'Virgil, Wordsworth, and the Power of Sound.'
71 The thematic importance of the *Immortality Ode* in Wordsworth's career is not confined to *The Prelude* and *The Excursion* but is alluded to more succinctly in rhymed poems from the later stages of his career, appearing most notably in the ode *Composed upon an Evening of Extraordinary Splendour and Beauty* (1817), in *The River Duddon* (1820), near the end of the *Ecclesiastical Sonnets* (1822), and in the ode *On the Power of Sound* (1828). The 1828 ode is of particular interest, if only because Wordsworth attached such significance to a work that is not of the highest poetic quality: 'I cannot call to mind a reason why you should not think some passages in it equal to anything I have produced; when first printed in "Yarrow Revisited" I placed it at the end of the Volume, and in the last ed. of my Poems, at the close of the Poems of the Imagination, indicating thereby my own opinion of it' (*PW,* II, 526). As was true of the *Immortality Ode*, that *On the Power of Sound* also had as its working epigraph 'paulo majora canamus.' A brief review of the later ode may indicate why the poet held it in such high esteem.

The ode *On the Power of Sound* is probably the best representative from Wordsworth's later years of the philosophical themes that had occupied him since *Tintern Abbey.* The fourteen stanzas of the ode examine the nature of sound by systematically ascending a scale from physical noises and their psychological effect to their metaphysical basis. The poet's use of the metrical principle to exemplify his rational idealism is perhaps most clearly evident in stanza twelve, which was developed from some lines that gave rise to the poem and which is described in the 'Argument' as treating of 'the Pythagorean theory of numbers and music, with their supposed power over the motions of the universe':

By one pervading spirit
Of tones and numbers all things are controlled,
As sages taught, where faith was found to merit
Initiation in that mystery old.
The heavens, whose aspect makes our minds as still   5
As they themselves appear to be,
Innumerable voices fill
With everlasting harmony;
The towering headlands, crowned with mist,

>   Their feet among the billows, know   10
>   That Ocean is a mighty harmonist;
>   Thy pinions, universal Air,
>   Ever waving to and fro,
>   Are delegates of harmony, and bear
>   Strains that support the Seasons in their round;   15
>   Stern Winter loves a dirge-like sound.
>   (*PW*, II, 329)

Perhaps the first thing that strikes one about this stanza, whose formal plan is repeated throughout the ode, is the irregular, presumably rhapsodic, character of line-lengths and literary style. Not only are line-lengths unusually variable, but they may have extra syllables (as in 1 and 3) or suffer initial truncation (13). Beneath the apparent confusion on the surface, however, Wordsworth has established a simple metrical design of great clarity and simplicity: the rhyming pattern – ababcdcd efegfghh – divides the stanza into two main parts, two eight-line sections, each of which contains precisely thirty-five metrical feet. A simple, abstract metrical order thus governs the apparent linguistic freedom of the stanza in a way that befits its Pythagorean subject. Further indications of the skill with which Wordsworth organized the stanza may be found by noting that the celestial manifestations of the 'one pervading spirit' are presented in the first eight lines, whereas terrestrial aspects of harmony occupy the latter half. As is so often the case when Wordsworth makes a major statement, the four elements are touched on in a synopsis of the cosmos: the element of fire is suggested by 'the heavens' in the first half of the stanza, and air, water, and earth provide principal images in the second half. The seasons, of course, are also subjected to harmonizing strains of sound so that Wordsworth, at the end of the poem, can proclaim the power of eternal harmony over the music of time. In sum, as this stanza illustrates, the ode *On the Power of Sound* reiterates the main concern of Wordsworth's philosophical verse – the scale of perceptions that moves from psychological to transcendental conditions – and becomes another way of demonstrating the intellectual consistency of his work from the late 1790s onwards. Unfortunately, most of the other stanzas in this late ode are substantially less interesting – especially those which catalogue physical and psychological qualities of sound – and ensure that the poem as a whole will continue to be largely unregarded. On the basis of poetic quality, the treatment of

sound and harmony is far more successful in the finest masterpiece of Wordsworth's later years – the 'Mutability' sonnet.
72 W.B. Yeats, 'Lapis Lazuli,' in *The Collected Poems of W.B. Yeats* New York 1965), 292.
73 Ernö Lendvai, *Bela Bartók: An Analysis of His Music* (London 1971), 74–6. An even more extreme and concentrated argument by the same author appears in 'Duality and Synthesis in the Music of Bela Bartók,' *Module, Proportion, Symmetry, Rhythm*, edited by Gyorgy Kepes, 174–93.
74 On the use of the golden section by Bach and other composers, see Augusta Rubin, *J.S. Bach: The Modern Composer* (Boston 1976), and J.A. Rothwell's dissertation, *The Phi Factor: Mathematical Proportions in Musical Forms* (The University of Missouri 1977).
75 For an incisive and entertaining account of the theorists' difficulties with Bach, see Donald Francis Tovey's 'Preface' and 'General Instructions' to *J.S. Bach: Forty-Eight Preludes and Fugues*, edited by Donald Francis Tovey (London 1924), vol I, 7–20.

Index

Abrams, M.H. 60,109
Auden, W.H. 184-5

Bach, J.S. 49, 50, 219, 221-8
Bartók, Bela 43, 219-21, 223, 227
Bernoulli, Jacob 49
Blake, William 15, 181
Burke, Edmund 48

Campion, Thomas 187
Catullus 176-7
Chaucer, Geoffrey 84
Coleridge, S.T. 15, 60, 104, 110, 112, 120, 123, 190, 210

Dante 33, 174
Descartes 46, 48
Dryden, John 183-4, 198
Duckworth, George 176-8
Durrant, G.H. 81, 231n

Edinger, H.G. 204-5
Eliot, T.S. 188, 214, 228
Euclid 5, 40, 45, 46, 50, 88, 92
Euler, Leonhard 49

form, metrical
- blank verse sonnet: defined 33-4; illustrated 34-5, 72-3, 74, 120, 146, 149, 155
- continuous geometrical proportion: defined 11, 41-5; illustrated 6-7, 34-5, 37, 53, 59-60, 77-8, 83, 87-8, 89, 91-2, 100-4, 107, 109, 110, 113-15, 130-1, 138-40, 143, 152, 154-5, 157-8, 159-60, 165-6, 168-9, 194-5, 207
- simple binary: defined 26-31; illustrated 6-7, 29, 53, 60-1, 76, 77-8, 80, 88, 89, 91, 107-8, 110, 133-4, 139-40, 143, 149, 153
forms of nature, in relation to geometrical forms 14, 19, 51-2, 62, 64-5, 69-70, 77-8, 81, 84, 102, 108-9, 111-12, 118, 119, 158, 161-2, 216
four elements, as symbol of the universe 63, 74, 147-8, 196, 201, 236n
Freud 48
Fussell, Jr, Paul 182

Galileo 84
geometry and poetry, equivalence of 39, 48, 76-7, 80-5, 86-93, 121
golden section: *see* form, metrical: continuous geometrical proportion
Gray, Thomas 58

Hambidge, Jay 179
Hartman, Geoffrey H. 94, 116, 118, 123, 145, 232n
Hindemith, Paul 219
Horace 27, 38, 86, 176

isochronism 186-8

Jones, John 78
Jung, Carl 48

Kant 48
Keats, John 15
Kepler, Johannes 50
Keyser, S. Jay 183

Le Corbusier 179
Lendvai, Ernö 220-1
Lucretius 176-7

Maxwell, J.C. 70, 109
McConnell, Frank 94-5
metrical principle 4, 9-10, 23-4, 191-7, 235n
Milton, John 15, 17, 19, 27, 32, 33, 35, 39, 70, 75-7, 78, 93, 119-21, 127, 146, 151, 174, 175, 182, 185-6, 187, 188, 197, 198, 211, 212, 213, 216, 227; 'At a Solemn Musick' 198-9; *Lycidas* 202-5, 210, 211, 212; *Paradise Lost* 27, 32, 45, 63, 106, 119-20, 164, 185, 186, 196, 212-13; *Paradise Regained* 27, 125
Moorman, Mary 46

Newton, Isaac 46, 49-51, 67, 81, 90, 107, 174
Nielsen, Carl 219

Olsen, Flemming 98
ontological principle 21, 93, 124-5, 145, 162-3, 167, 173-4, 206-7, 216

Parrish, S.M. 189
Petrarch 33
Plato 3, 48, 174, 190, 205-6
Pope, Alexander 27, 184, 188, 191-2, 198; *Essay on Man I* 191-3
'principle of immortality': *see* ontological principle
Puttenham, George 198

Ravel, Maurice 219

Sackville, Thomas 182
scale of being or creation 35, 37, 41, 45-6, 67, 78, 95, 109, 124, 134, 142-7, 152, 154-8, 162, 163, 170-1, 174, 211, 232n
scale of perceptions 7-9, 12, 14, 107-9, 113-17, 142-4, 170, 193, 211, 236n
Schneider, Jr, B.R. 47
Shakespeare 32, 93
Shelley, Percy Bysshe 15, 215
Shostakovich, Dmitri 219, 227
Skutsch, Otto 24-5
Spenser, Edmund 174, 188, 198
Stravinsky, Igor 219, 227
Swift, Jonathan 49

Taylor, William 46
Tennyson, Alfred 15, 187-8
Thomson, James 27

Vergil 24, 38, 54, 56, 174, 176-8, 204-5, 210-11
Voltaire 49, 77

Weismiller, Edward 182-3
Wittkower, Rudolf 41
Wordsworth, William: 'Composed by the Side of Grasmere Lake' 117; *Composed Upon an*

Evening of Extraordinary Splendour and Beauty 235n; *Ecclesiastical Sonnets* 235n; *Elegiac Stanzas Suggested by a Picture of Peele Castle* 58; 'Essay, Supplementary to the Preface' of 1815 144; *Essay Upon Epitaphs* 164

- *The Excursion* 5, 19, 20, 21, 26, 34, 36, 38, 39, 41, 51, 57, 59, 61, 63, 65, 70-9, 109, 113, 115, 121, 123-73, 175, 197, 211; Wanderer's address to the Supreme Being 95, 137-51, 211
- 'Home at Grasmere' 21, 194-7; 'I wandered lonely as a cloud' 200-1; *Immortality Ode* 14, 19, 21, 59, 142, 199, 202-13, 216, 235n; 'London, 1802' 75; 'Mutability' 85, 197, 237n; 'Nuns fret not at their convent's narrow room' 156; 'Ode to Duty' 140; *On the Power of Sound* 235n-7n; 'The Pedlar' 70, 71, 79, 134; Preface to *Lyrical Ballads* 24, 132, 189-90
- *The Prelude* 5, 7, 12, 13, 14, 19, 20, 21, 26, 28-31, 39, 40, 45, 47, 48, 51, 59, 61, 65, 67-70, 79-121, 124-6, 127, 129, 141, 170-3, 175, 197, 212, 216; Bk V dream-vision 14, 85-96, 104, 105, 119, 138, 142, 145, 194, 211, 215, 232n; Druids and Sarum's Plain 102-5, 116-17; Snowdon episode 14, 20, 46, 74, 96, 98, 112-21, 152, 161, 170, 193, 211, 212, 215
- 'Prelude, Prefixed to the Volume Entitled "Poems Chiefly of Early and Late Years"' 24-5, 28; *The Recluse* 171-2; *Resolution and Independence* 17, 58; *The River Duddon* 172-3, 235n; 'The Ruined Cottage' 71, 134; 'St. Paul's' 6-14, 16-17, 51, 63, 194; 'She was a Phantom of delight' 201; 'Surprised by joy - impatient as the Wind' 188; 'The world is too much with us' 34, 117; *Tintern Abbey* 14, 19, 28, 46, 47, 52, 57-65, 69, 70, 95, 124, 125, 136, 174, 193, 209, 211, 212, 216; 'With Ships the sea was sprinkled' 17; 'Yew-Trees' 19, 52-7, 226

Wren, Christopher 12-13, 92

Yeats, William Butler 185, 186, 188, 213-14, 227-8
Young, Edward 27

This book

was designed by

ANTJE LINGNER

and was printed by

University of

Toronto

Press

OHIO UNIV... LIBRARY

Please return t... s soon as you
have finished v...
fine it must be
...ed below